IMAGES
of America

PORTSMOUTH CEMETERIES

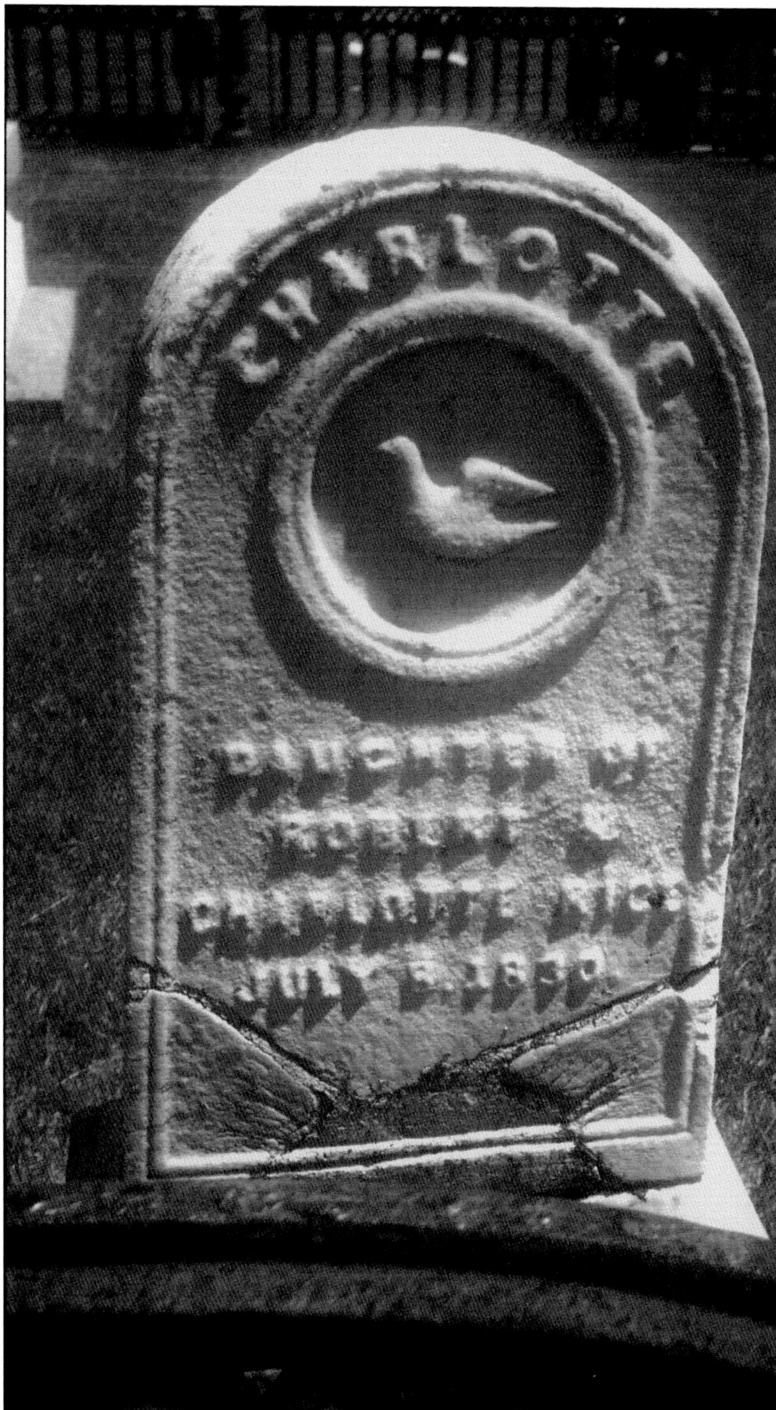

CHARLOTTE RICE, 1830, PROPRIETOR'S CEMETERY. Charlotte is buried in the Rice family plot, along with her sisters Lucretia and Anna. The dove on her marble gravestone is symbolic of many ideas often expressed for those that have died young, including resurrection and rebirth, the Holy Spirit, and love and purity.

IMAGES
of America

PORTSMOUTH CEMETERIES

Glenn A. Knoblock

ARCADIA
PUBLISHING

ISBN 978-0-7385-3761-0

Published by Arcadia Publishing
Charleston, South Carolina

Printed in the United States of America

Library of Congress Catalog Card Number: 2004115478

For all general information, contact Arcadia Publishing:
Telephone 843-853-2070
Fax 843-853-0044
E-mail sales@arcadiapublishing.com
For customer service and orders:
Toll-free 1-888-313-2665

Visit us on the Internet at www.arcadiapublishing.com

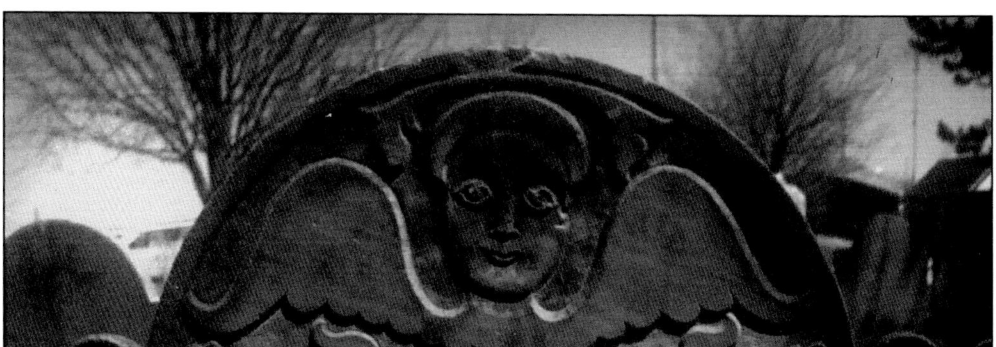

This book is dedicated to my daughter Anna, a wide-eyed angel who is the apple of her parents' eyes.

Contents

Acknowledgments

In returning to this, a favorite area of study, I have many people to thank. First and foremost among them is my wife, Terry. For many years now, she has both tolerated and encouraged my wanderings and studies in local cemeteries and has been my biggest supporter.

In the area of gravestone and cemetery studies, I wish to thank the following individuals: Louise Tallman for her expertise regarding Portsmouth's family cemeteries; James Blachowicz for important information on the Treats, Noah Smith, and their Newburyport connection, as well as gravestone carvers; Ralph Tucker for providing background on John Marble and his early carving career; Valerie Cunningham for help regarding Portsmouth's African American community; Rabbi David Mark, Irwin Bierhans, and Richard Grossman for helping with Temple Israel Cemetery and supplying a better understanding of Jewish burial customs. I also wish to thank the ever helpful staff at the Portsmouth Public Library, especially Suzanne Loder, as well as Gail Pare and Barbara Myers of the Newington Historical Society.

I wish to collectively thank my fellow members of the Mayor's Blue Ribbon Cemetery Committee of Portsmouth. Together, we have done an excellent job in restoring and raising public awareness about the city's oldest public burying grounds and will, I hope, continue to do so for years to come.

For photographs of many other early gravestones in Portsmouth, especially those in Point of Graves and North Cemeteries, consult my previous work, *Historic Burial Grounds of the New Hampshire Seacoast*, published in 1999 by Arcadia. I have used several of the photographs from that work in this book, but not nearly all.

For information on those buried in all of Portsmouth's cemeteries, visit the history room at the Portsmouth Public Library and consult the bound lists for each public site, compiled by Louise Tallman and others, and Tallman's manuscript entitled *Family Graveyards of Portsmouth*. For genealogical information throughout this work, I have relied heavily on the two volumes of *Rambles About Portsmouth*, by Charles Brewster; *The Genealogical Dictionary of Maine and New Hampshire*, by Noyes, Libby, and Davis; *In Female Worth and Elegance*, by Labranche and Conant; and the several excellent works by Raymond Brighton and Richard Winslow published by the Portsmouth Marine Society.

All photographs in this book are by the author unless otherwise noted.

Introduction

The old city of Portsmouth has a wealth of preserved history, perhaps more than any other in the state. One unique way of experiencing this history, oft forgotten, is by visiting one of the city's historical cemeteries. A walk among the gravestones provides a tangible link to the past, and one that is immediately accessible to all.

The oldest cemeteries that remain in Portsmouth today were formally designated, beginning in 1671, as "burial" or "burying" grounds. They retained this designation until after 1835, when the term "cemetery," a Greek word for "sleeping chamber," came into vogue. Prior to 1671, the town's dead were usually buried in private family plots in graves that were often either unmarked, or marked with pieces of natural stone with no identifying name, depending on the wealth of the family. The earliest dated grave marker in Portsmouth, however, is the table stone for Hannah Cutt, the wife of John Cutt, president of New Hampshire's Provincial Court in 1680. She died in 1674 and was laid to rest in the Cutt-Penhallow family plot on what would later become Green Street. As the town increased in population, land for formal burial grounds was purchased and open for use by many inhabitants. Despite this, the custom of private burials on family land continued on a regular basis well into the 20th century.

The oldest cemeteries in town are found in well-populated areas that were close to the early neighborhoods established at Strawberry Banke and, later, Christian Shore. Later cemeteries were established outside the center of town for a variety of reasons, including health and sanitation concerns and the availability of open land. With the advent of the rural cemetery movement, started in the United States in 1831 with the founding of Mount Auburn Cemetery in Boston, large, parklike spaces became the most desirable areas for new cemeteries. Portsmouth's Proprietor's and Harmony Grove Cemeteries are local examples of this new concept that emphasized monumental burial markers and individual plots separated by decorative ironwork fencing, all surrounded by a landscaped terrain.

The most interesting features in any cemetery, of course, are the markers themselves. Depending on the time period, these can be found in four distinct forms: gravestones, table stones, monuments, and tombs and mausoleums. Gravestones, used since early Colonial times, were made in a variety of forms. Most were professionally crafted by stonecutters who, until 1800, came from either Boston or the Merrimack Valley region of northeastern Massachusetts. As far as is known, Portsmouth did not have a resident stonecutter who specialized in gravestones prior to 1801. Gravestones were almost always supplied in pairs—the headstone and footstone. The headstone, the larger of the two, bore all the carved information about the deceased. It was placed at the head of the burial site while the footstone, usually much smaller in size with little or no decoration beyond, perhaps, the initials of the deceased, was placed at the foot of the grave. Together, the two stones marked the grave's boundary. These smaller footstones have often been misplaced or moved over the years in older cemeteries so that they no longer correspond with the headstone, leaving the mistaken impression that they mark additional gravesites for children, due to their small size. Early gravestones were usually made of durable slate, while those from the Merrimack Valley were often made of an inferior brown sandstone. Early in the

19th century, marble made its first appearance in Portsmouth and seems to have come from Middlebury, Vermont. Later stones are found made of white limestone and eventually, by the second half of the 19th century, granite came to be the dominant material.

Table stones were a more expensive type of grave marker used only by the town's elite. Made of large, heavy slabs of stone measuring about six feet long by three feet wide, table stones were usually cut from slate, sandstone, or marble and engraved, either directly on top or on a marble inset, with information about the deceased. They lie flat, either directly on the ground or on a supporting base, usually bear extensive inscriptions, and are sometimes adorned with a family coat of arms. The base they rest on might be a simple brick platform, or one of a more elaborate nature with pillars.

The introduction of monumental gravestones closely coincides with the appearance of both the rural cemetery movement and the Victorian era and denotes those markers that in both size and form are sculptured works with a classical appearance. Common among them are lofty columns, obelisks, or square bases often topped by funerary urns.

Above-ground burials, another indicator of wealth, are also found in Portsmouth cemeteries. In their earliest form, these tombs were made of brick and earth, often with a granite-framed entryway and an iron or marble door. Inside the tomb were built-in shelves where wood coffins containing the remains of the deceased, often identified with brass nameplates, were placed. These above-ground tombs evolved over the years into the mausoleums that we know today, imposing structures made of polished marble and granite.

While the majority of New Hampshire's population, including that of Portsmouth, over the years has been less ethnically diverse than many other regions in the country, different cultures have still been an important part of the historical landscape. The African American and Jewish communities have had a presence stretching well into the past. Both have played an important part in developing the community that is Portsmouth today, and their cultures, too, can be discovered through visits to local cemeteries.

One

Gravestone Art and Symbolism

More than anything else, perhaps, it is the art of the gravestone that captures the imagination. What do all the images carved upon them, some frightful, some tender, and others enigmatic, really signify?

The earliest gravestones were carved with stark images of death: winged skulls, hourglasses, drapery suggestive of the communal burial shroud, and tools of the gravedigger like the pickax and shovel. All of these were carved by stonecutters from the Boston area. The Calvinistic doctrine predominant in Massachusetts and New Hampshire preached, among other ideas, that the fate of everyone's soul, children included, was predestined and that nothing could be done to change one's path either to Heaven or Hell. All that *was* certain was the uncertainty of one's fate after death, and death itself. Such ideas were a part of everyday life in New England, enforced by fiery preaching of ministers on the Sabbath. These sermons, with their stark visions of Hell, were augmented by the images found in local graveyards. Few individuals could read the Bible at this time, but all could understand the pictures carved in stone.

By the early 1730s, the zeal for such fiery thought had dimmed, and the portrayal of winged skulls, while still dominant, was now rather bland and no longer carried much meaning. When a religious revival, the Great Awakening, hit New England in 1740, a new kind of religious thought and fervor—one offering hope and joy—emerged. At this time, gravestone symbolism began to change. The use of the winged skull was soon eclipsed in favor of images that portrayed ideas of redemption and salvation. Popular were faces, often with wings, that have been variously called cherubs, angels, and soul effigies. These faces were carved in many different forms, both female and male. The expressions on their faces vary from the happy and quirky, the sad or foreboding, to the downright enigmatic. Gravestones with these faces convey a dual message. While the angelic figure represents the possibility of salvation, the face's expression reveals the hope, doubt, and a fear of the unknown associated with death.

Further changes in gravestone-carving traditions would evolve quickly as our country grew. The first and most enduring change was the use of the weeping willow tree and funeral urn. These symbols came from abroad, influenced by the Greek Revival in Europe and the discoveries made by the French in Egypt. Their use, often flanked by obelisks and architectural columns, became all the rage by 1790 and soon became a standard lasting nearly a century.

Other factors also influenced gravestone carving. Americans are a social people, and the symbols of various societies like the Masons and Odd Fellows are often portrayed on area gravestones, as are those representing a man's occupation or military service. Another influence came with the reign of Queen Victoria in England from 1839 to 1901, the sentimentality of which encouraged the use of such images as the lamb, the dove, and flowers.

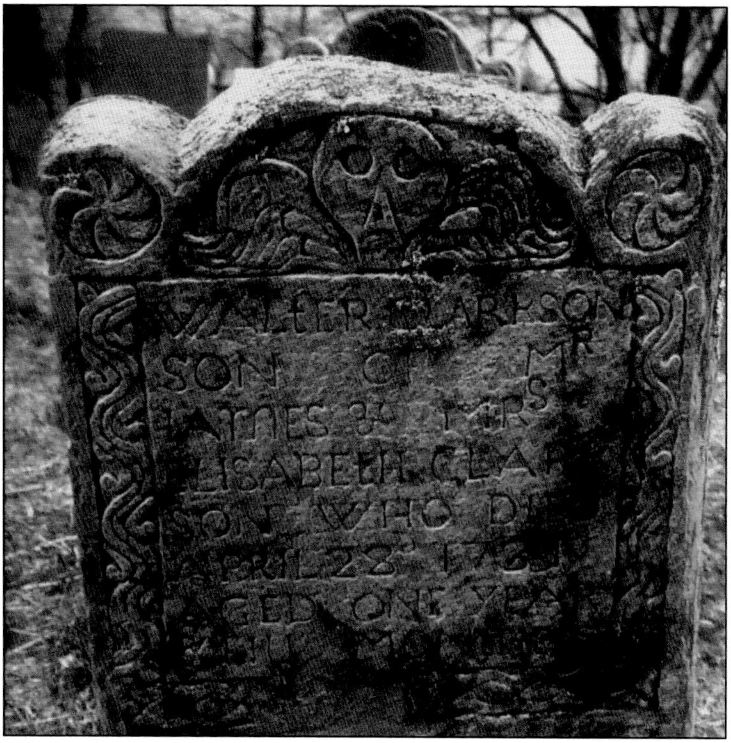

WALTER CLARKSON, 1739, COTTON CEMETERY. This winged-skull design was carved by Robert Mullicken Jr. in the Merrimack Valley style. For a child, the dour imagery is startling but representative of a time (1735–1740) when hundreds of children died in New Hampshire due to the effects of the Throat Distemper epidemic.

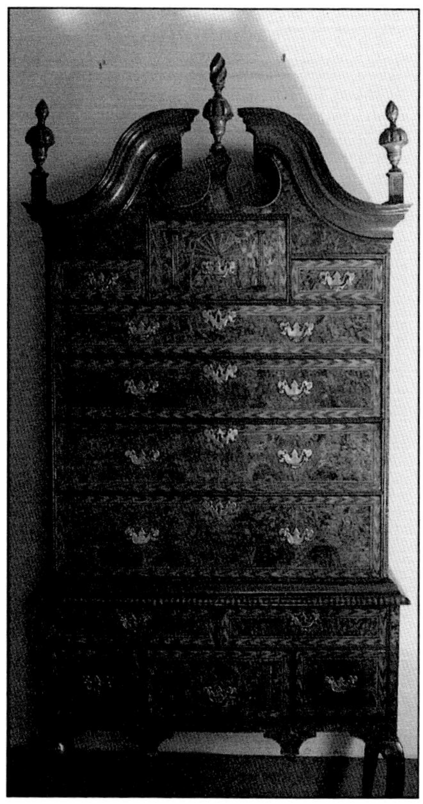

SHERBURNE HIGH CHEST, 1733, WARNER HOUSE. Gravestone carving sometimes influenced, and was influenced by, the motifs used in other crafts and trades. This elaborate chest of drawers, with its unique designs, was crafted by an unknown Portsmouth furniture maker. (With permission of the Warner House Association.)

SARAH LOUD, 1738, POINT OF GRAVES. This unique gravestone for the wife of John Loud, a cordwainer of Portsmouth, was cut by an amateur, possibly Loud himself. The carvings bear a strong resemblance to those found on the Sherburne high chest. Whether Loud saw this piece of furniture while it was being crafted and later copied its motif for his wife's stone is unknown, but an intriguing possibility.

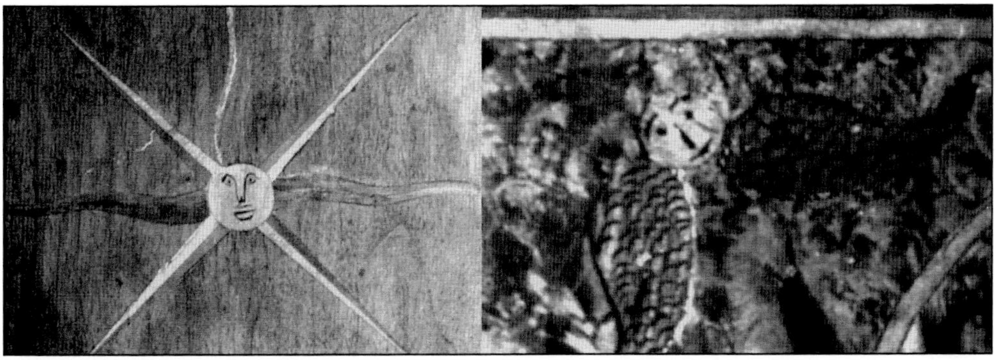

SHERBURNE HIGH CHEST DETAILS, 1733, WARNER HOUSE. The motifs found on this chest are repeated on gravestones found in Portsmouth dating from 1738 to 1812. While it is unlikely that it was the direct inspiration for all such gravestones, it clearly demonstrates that some images portrayed on gravestones were also used as decorative devices in the homes of Portsmouth's upper class. (With permission of the Warner House Association.)

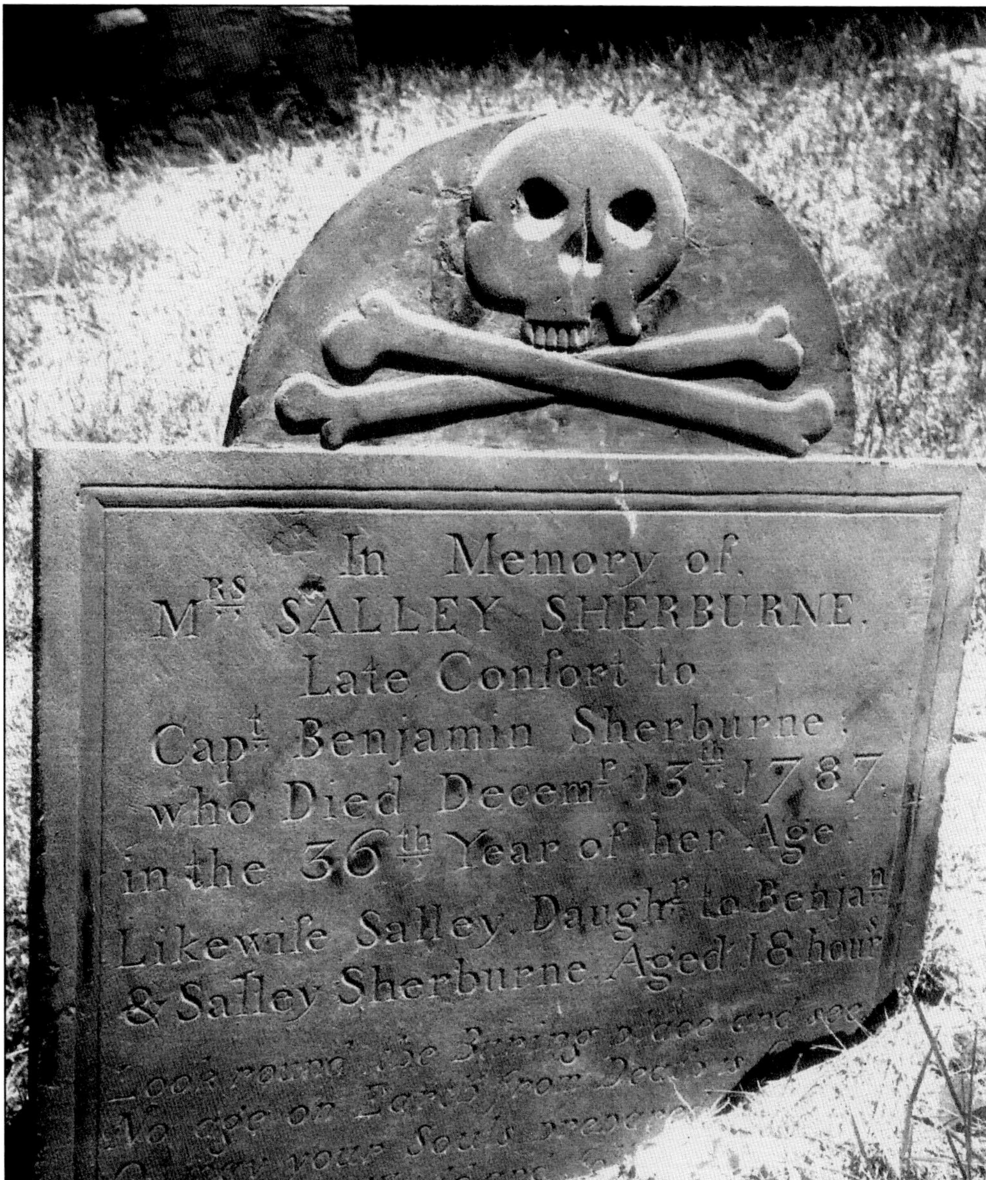

SALLEY SHERBURNE AND DAUGHTER, 1787, COTTON CEMETERY. The stark imagery of death on this gravestone, possibly the work of Boston stonecutter John Homer, is unusual for this date, but very understandable. Not only did Capt. Benjamin Sherburne lose his wife during childbirth, but his infant daughter also died just 18 hours later. Though death during childbirth before the advent of modern medicine was all too common, this did not make its acceptance by loved ones any easier. The sadness and despair felt by Sherburne is evident in the epitaph carved at the bottom of this stone, which reads in part, "Look round the Buring [Burying] place and see, No age on Earth from Death is free."

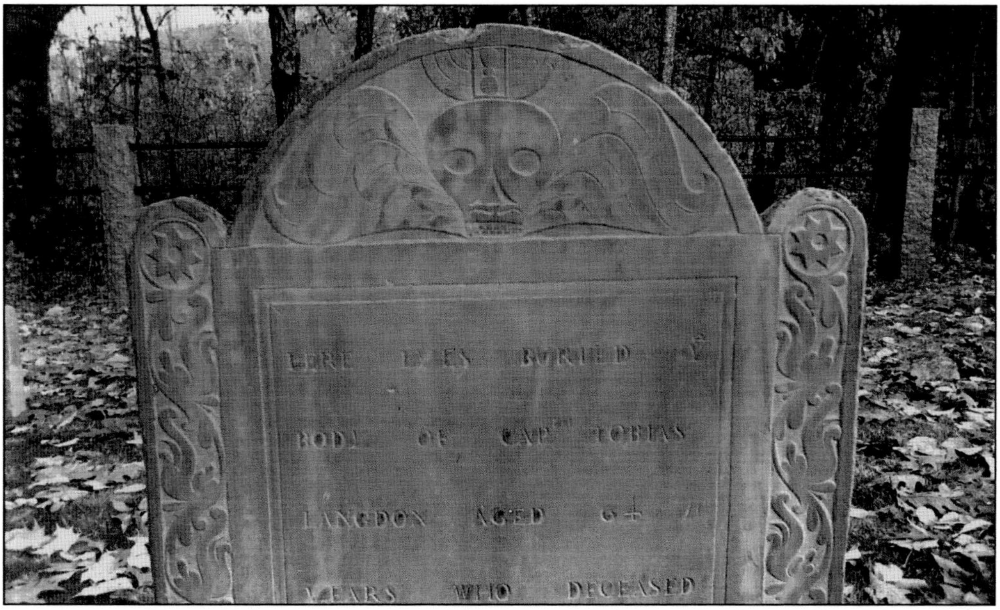

TOBIAS LANGDON, 1725, LANGDON FAMILY PLOT. The death's-head and hourglass design on this Portsmouth wheelwright's gravestone was carved by James Foster of Dorchester, Massachusetts. While such symbols illustrate the idea of man's mortality and short time on earth, the floral motif on the side borders and starred finials is more hopeful, signifying the rewards of the afterlife and divine guidance.

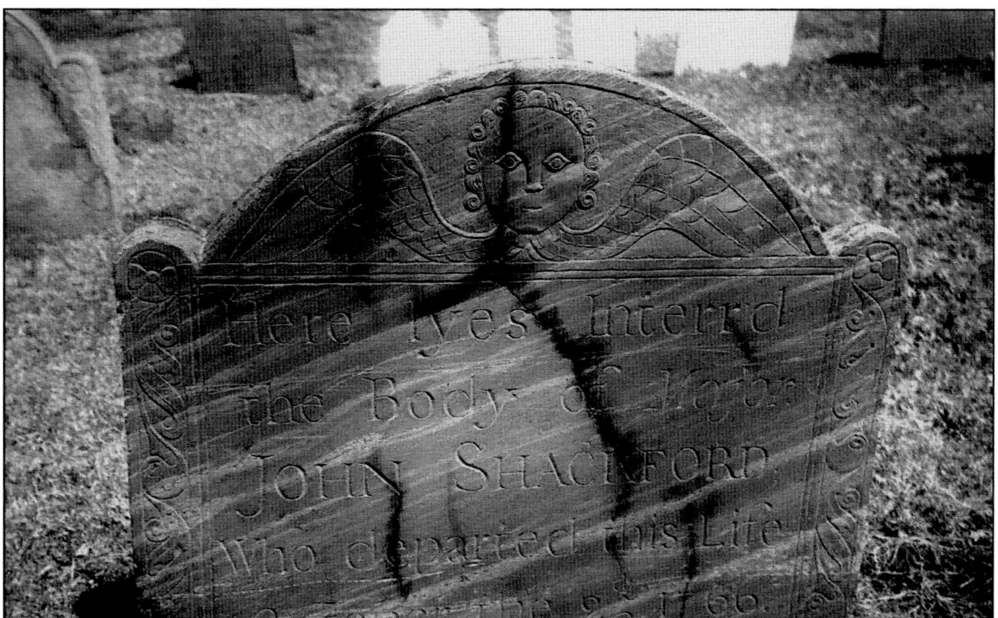

MAJ. JOHN SHACKFORD, 1766, NORTH CEMETERY. This stone is typical of those carved by the Lamson family of Charlestown, Massachusetts. The well-executed and finely detailed female angel has wide eyes and a non-committal facial expression, neither smiling nor frowning. Like his namesake father, Shackford was a blockmaker and wharf owner in maritime Portsmouth.

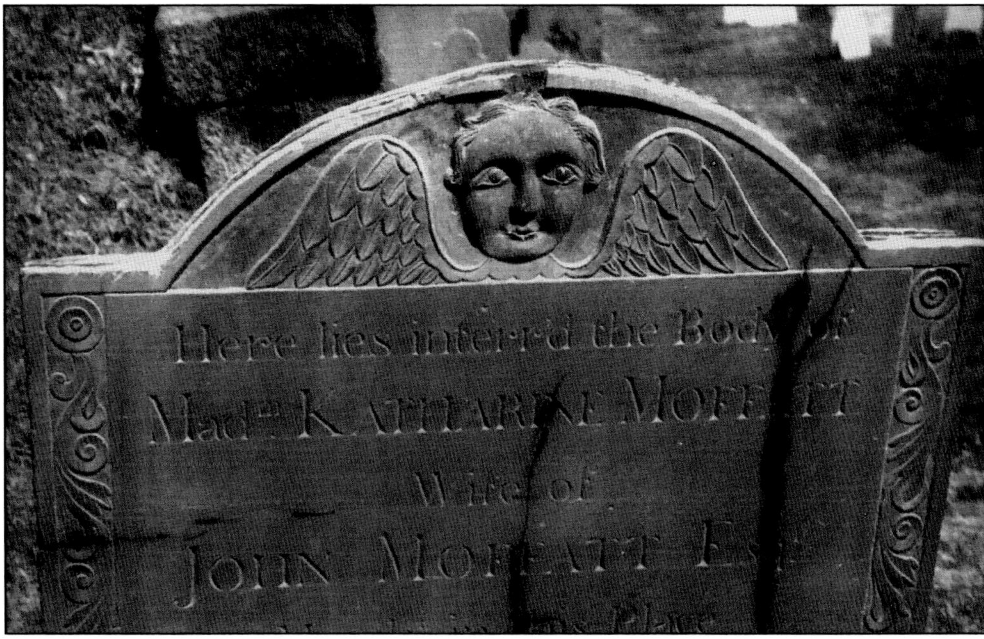

KATHARINE MOFFATT, 1769, NORTH CEMETERY. "Madame" Moffatt was the wife of Portsmouth merchant John Moffatt. Her namesake daughter would later marry Capt. William Whipple and reside in the family house on Market Street. The gender of the angel portrayed here, with its rather quirky expression, is undetermined.

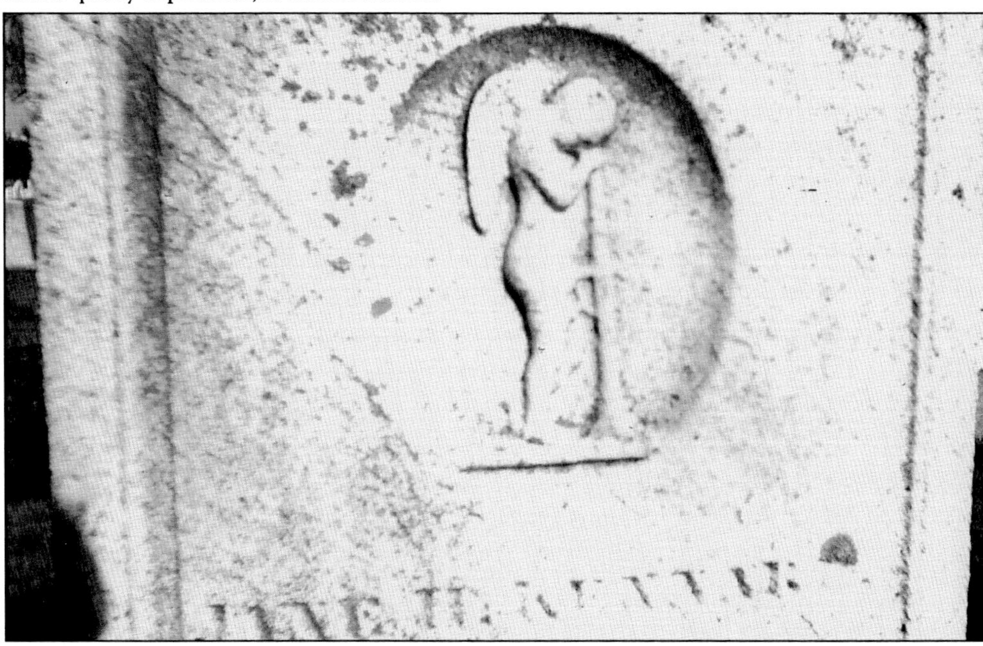

JANE KENNARD, 1832, HARMONY GROVE CEMETERY. Later gravestone portrayals of angels often show them in full form. The angel here may represent the Archangel Gabriel, who is weeping over the trumpet he has just used to call the deceased to her maker. Biblical tradition variably describes Gabriel as an angel of mercy, incarnation, judgment, and consolation, making his appearance on gravestones very appropriate.

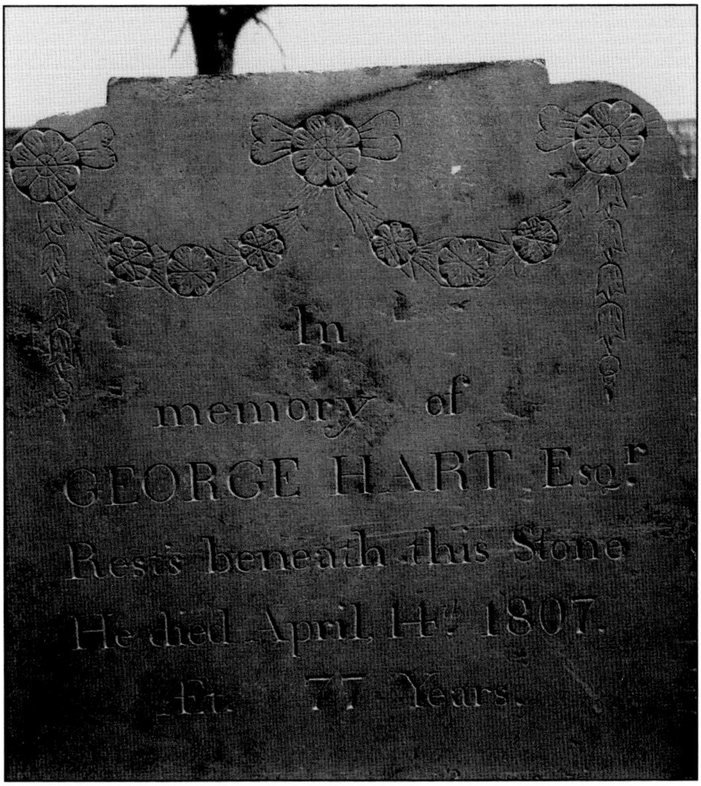

George Hart, 1807, North Cemetery. With the decline of religious influences in New Hampshire, images of a secular nature began to appear on gravestones, such as this one with a simple floral garland, probably carved by local stonecutter Samuel Treat. Hart, one of the 12 sons of Col. John Hart, practiced the trade of blacksmithing. His father owned the land that would later become North Cemetery.

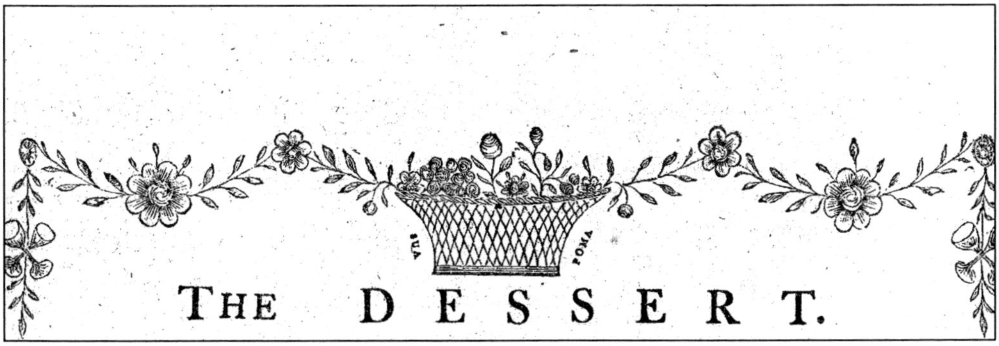

A Newspaper Illustration, 1798. As the nation grew in size, the number of books and newspapers available to the general public proliferated rapidly. Any town of size soon founded its own publisher. The illustrations that appeared within them, such as this from Walpole's *The Farmer's Weekly Museum: New Hampshire and Vermont Journal* (dated March 6, 1798) provided yet another source of design inspiration for local stonecutters.

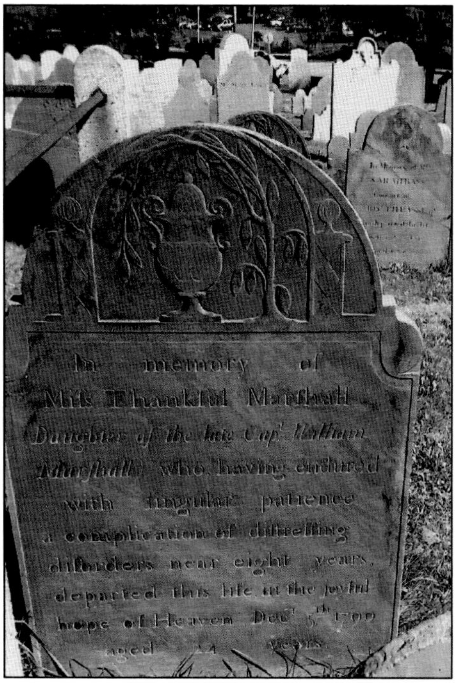

THANKFUL MARSHALL, 1790, NORTH CEMETERY. Gravestones with the urn-and-willow design began to make their appearance in the 1770s and, by 1790, were predominant. This stone for the daughter of Capt. William Marshall combines a number of elements, including the urn and weeping willow tree, as well as the architecturally influenced diamond columns on each side.

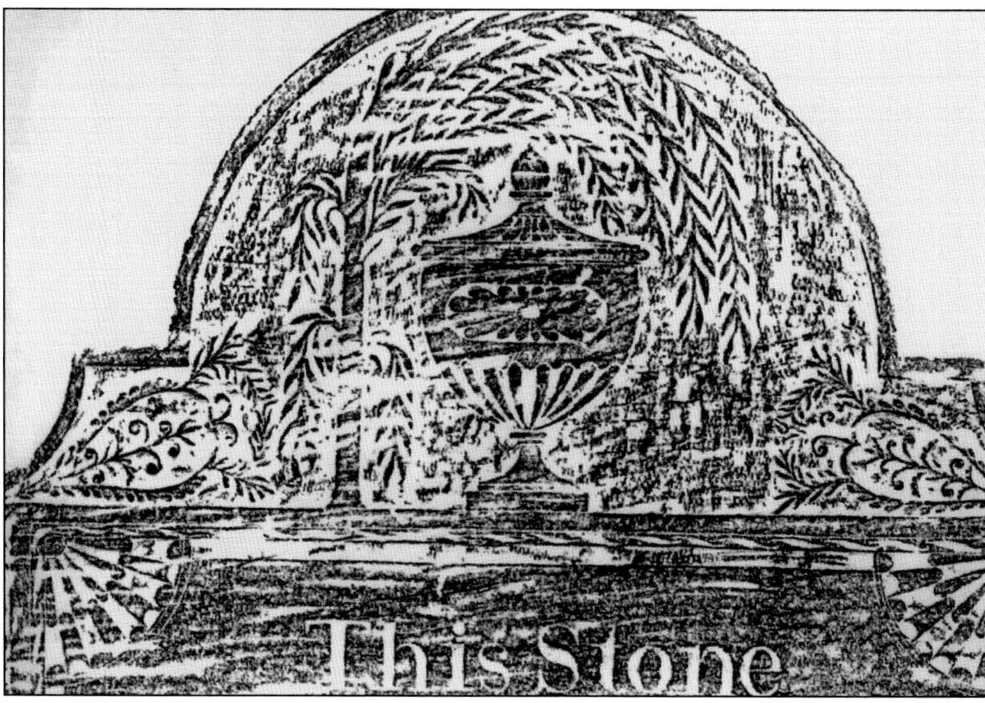

WILLIAM HART, 1812, NORTH CEMETERY. This rubbing portrays the tympanum of the gravestone for William Hart, "late a Mathematical Instrument Maker of this Town." This urn and willow gravestone was likely carved by Samuel Treat. This unusual design is distinguished by finely carved heart and floral patterns in the corners and side borders. The son of Colonel Hart, William died from "inflammation of the urethra" on January 18.

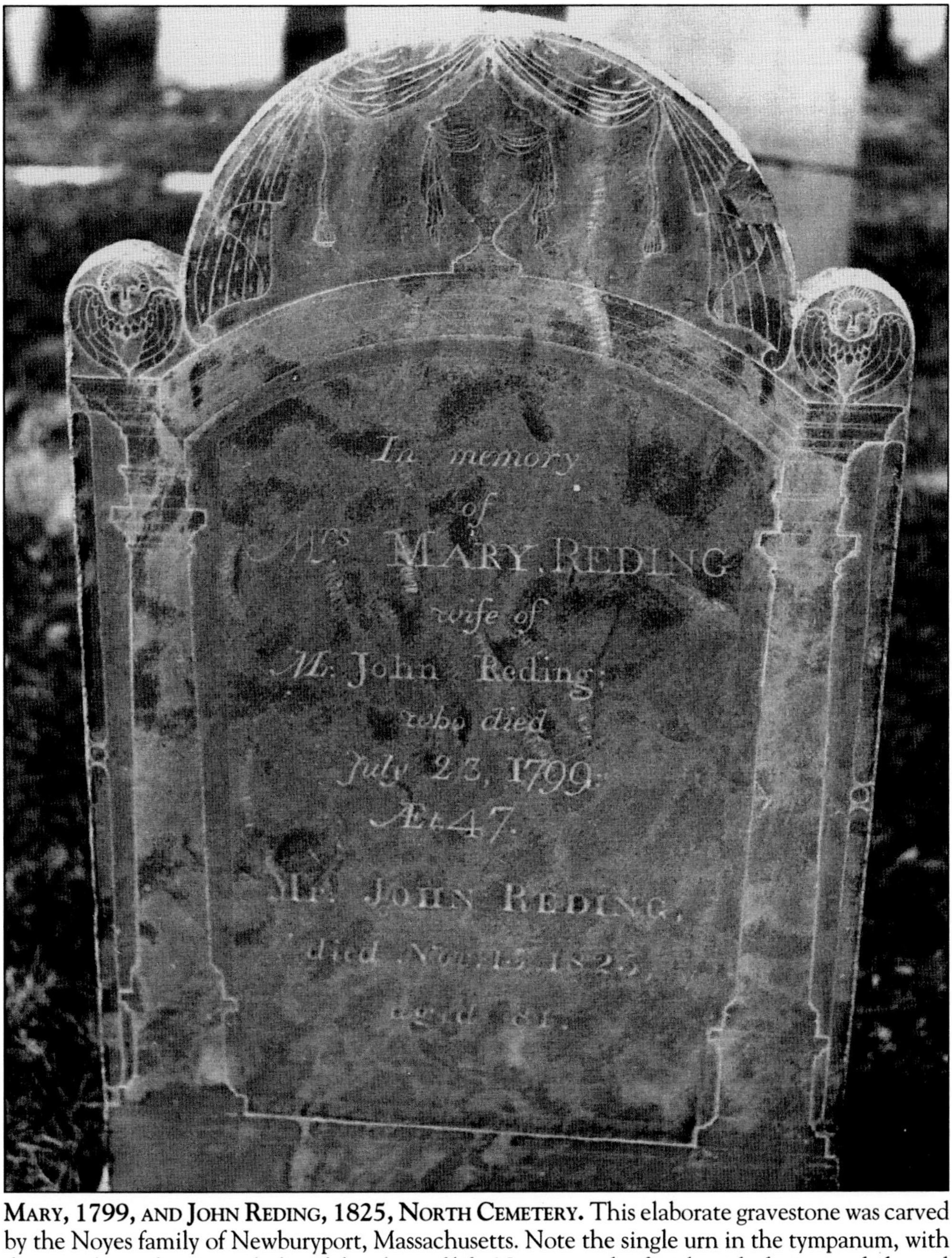

MARY, 1799, AND JOHN REDING, 1825, NORTH CEMETERY. This elaborate gravestone was carved by the Noyes family of Newburyport, Massachusetts. Note the single urn in the tympanum, with drapery above that is symbolic of the close of life. Note, too, the finials with their rounded angel figures and the side borders depicting monumental columns, all carved in the best urban tradition. Interestingly, this stone was crafted around 1799 and may have been brought to Portsmouth in a ship owned by John Reding. The lower inscription for John Reding was added to the stone in 1825 by local carver Samuel Treat. Whether Reding's heirs did this at his request, or to save the expense of an additional gravestone, is unknown. John Reding was involved in Portsmouth maritime affairs and, as a young man around the time of the Revolution, was employed at a local ropewalk.

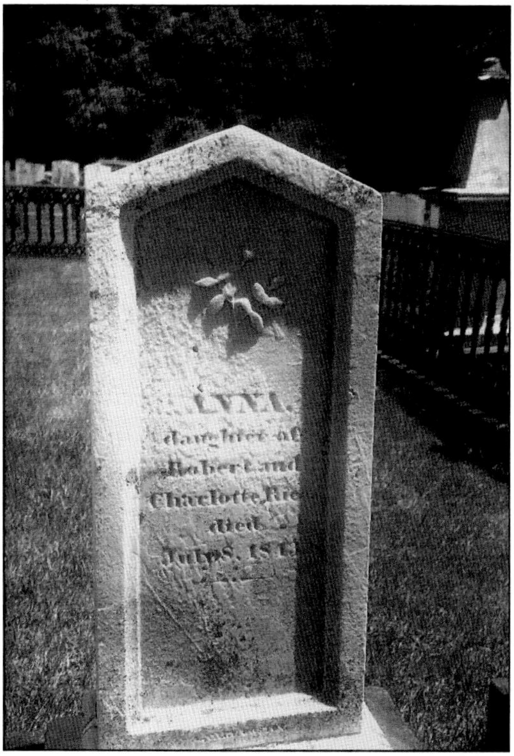

ANNA RICE, 1813, PROPRIETOR'S CEMETERY. With the advent of the Victorian era, floral motifs in gravestone carving became very popular. Here, the rose is symbolic of purity and love. Though back-dated to 1813, this marble stone, likely carved by the Treat family, was not crafted until the 1830s or later, as Proprietor's Cemetery was not established until 1831.

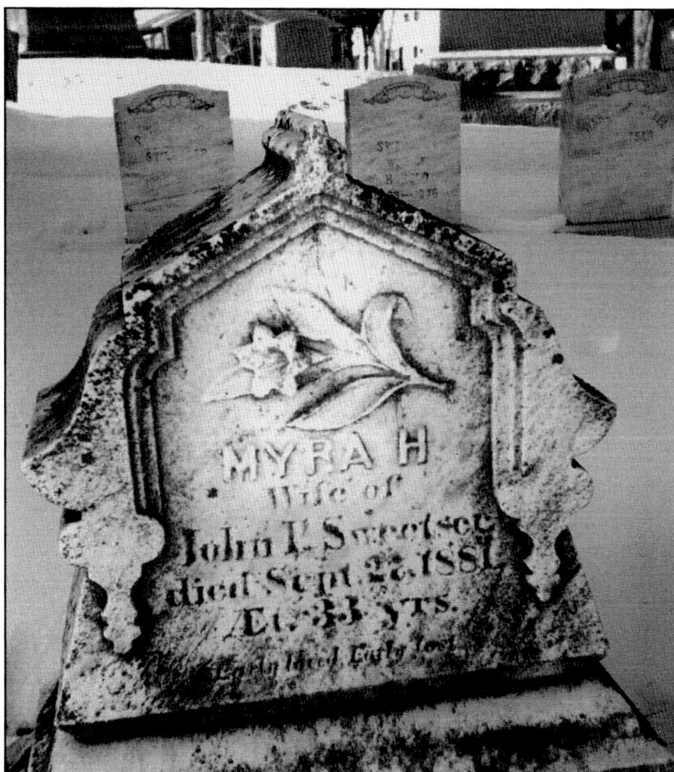

MYRA SWEETSER, 1881, HARMONY GROVE CEMETERY. This simple gravestone was likely crafted by third-generation stonecutter John Treat of Portsmouth. The Lilly of the Valley flower depicted here is a distinctly Catholic symbol of rebirth and the Virgin Mary and is augmented by the cross at the point of the stone. Note that this young wife, who died at age 33, was "Early loved, Early lost."

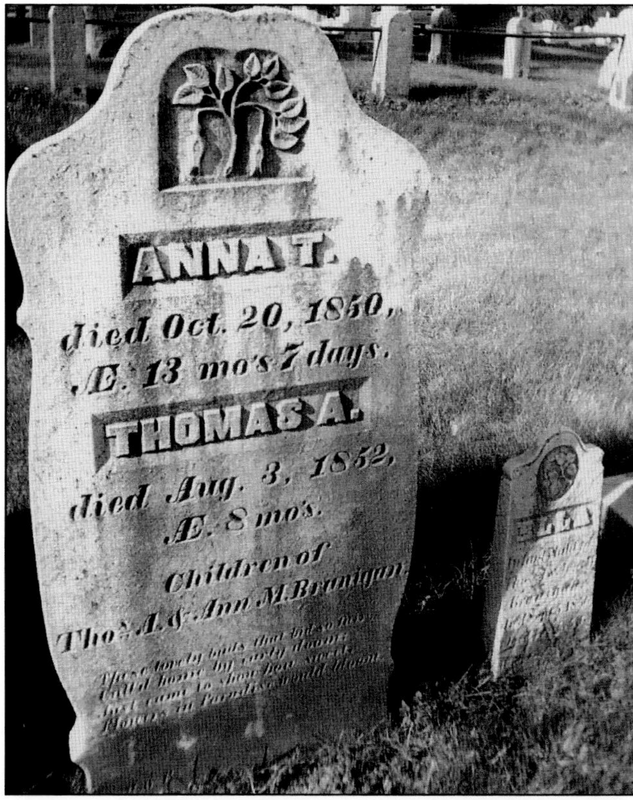

ANNA, 1850, AND THOMAS BRANNIGAN, 1852, AND ELLA BRANNIGAN, 1856, HARMONY GROVE CEMETERY. The broken roses on these gravestones are symbolic of love, purity, and a life cut short. The epitaph at the bottom of the larger stone, indicative of the great anguish suffered by their parents, reads, "Those lovely buds that bid so fair, Call'd home by early doom; first came to show how sweet, Flowers in Paradise would bloom."

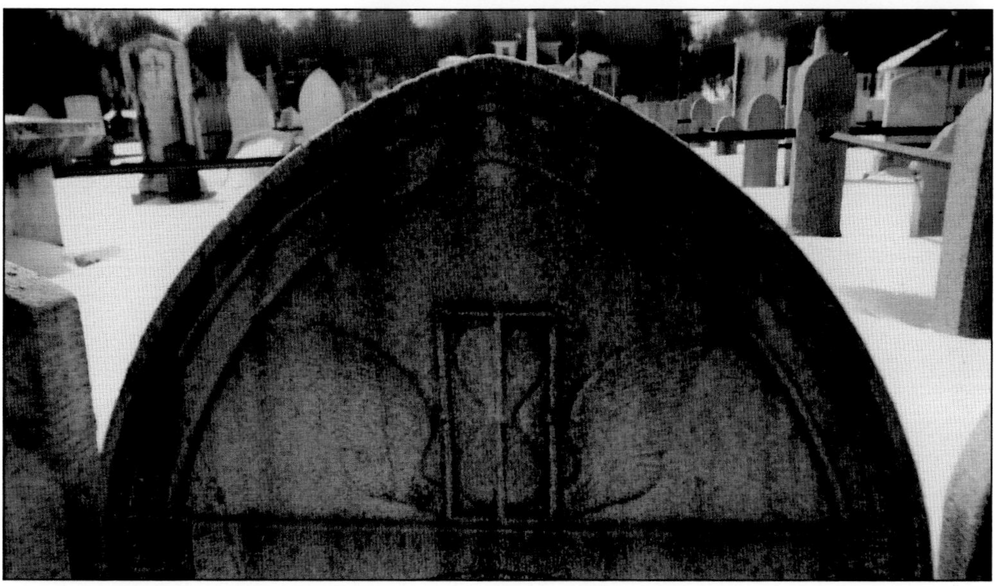

ELIZABETH ADAMS, 1845, PROPRIETOR'S CEMETERY. This Gothic-arch stone has a winged hourglass that is unusual for both its large size and its use at this late date. The hourglass was used on New England gravestones from the earliest days, often in conjunction with a death's head, and signifies that man's time on earth is but fleeting. Elizabeth's husband, John, has an identical gravestone.

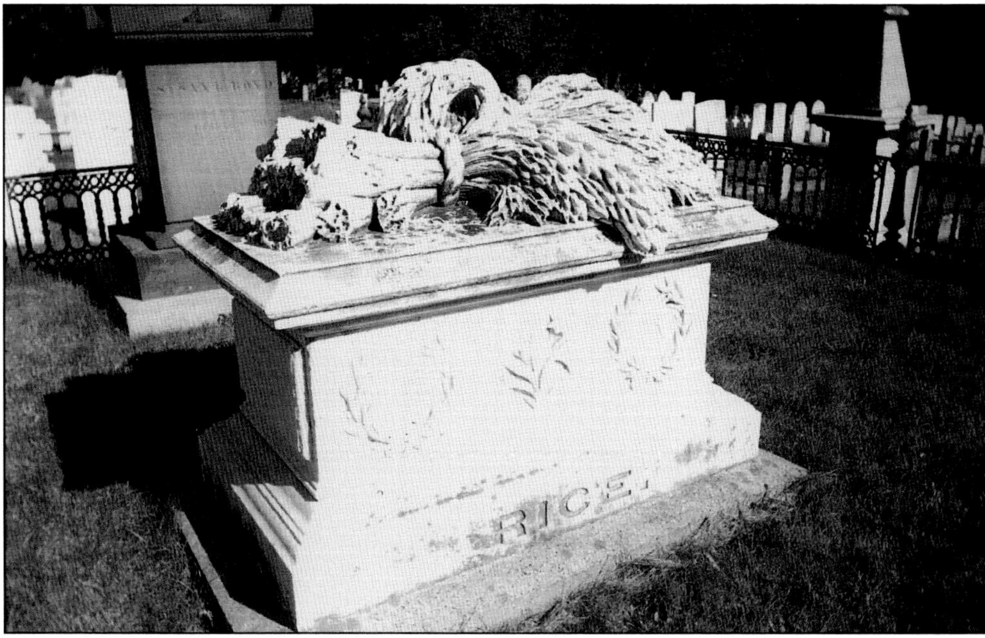

THE RICE FAMILY TOMB, PROPRIETOR'S CEMETERY. This elaborate marble tomb is the centerpiece in the Rice family plot. The large sheaf of wheat depicted on the top is symbolic of a long and fruitful life and is indicative of the life led by Portsmouth merchant Robert Rice. He was "dangerously attacked" by the yellow fever epidemic that hit Portsmouth in 1798, but he survived.

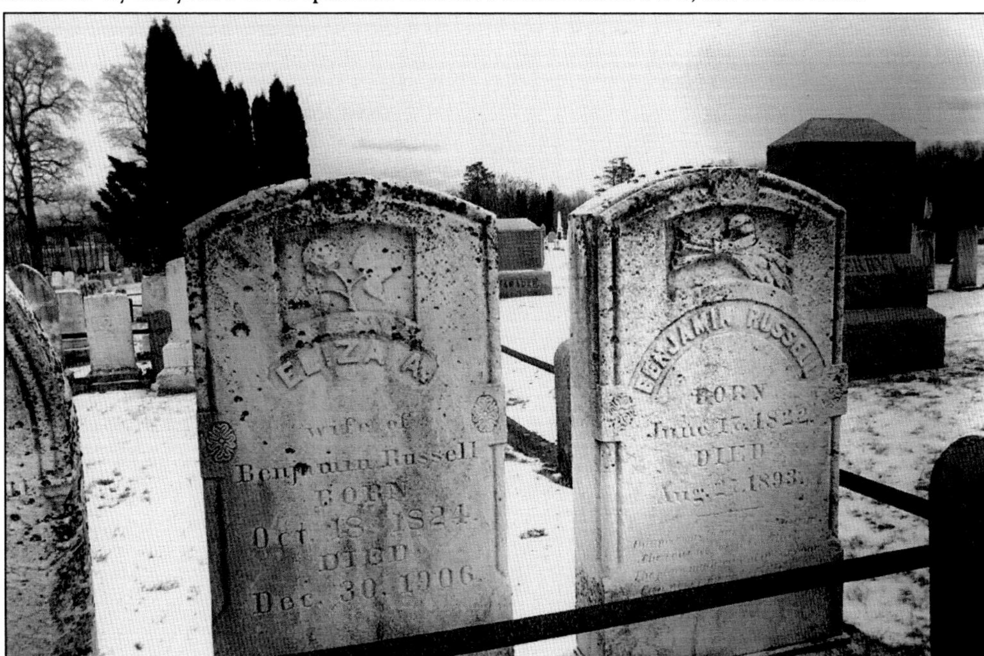

BENJAMIN, 1893, AND ELIZA RUSSELL, 1906, HARMONY GROVE CEMETERY. Benjamin's stone uses a sheaf of wheat as a different symbol. Note that a portion of the sheaf is broken, signifying not the loss of a young and fruitful life, but the end of a happy marriage. Eliza's stone depicts a rose in full bloom, an emblem of love and purity.

GEORGE GAINES BREWSTER, 1872, HARMONY GROVE CEMETERY, SOUTH STREET. This style of gravestone, with its Gothic arch and finger pointing skyward, was very popular and symbolic of heavenly reward. It was also a motif that was sometimes used, albeit in larger form, on New England church steeples. George Brewster supplied Charles Brewster with many anecdotes for his *Rambles About Portsmouth*.

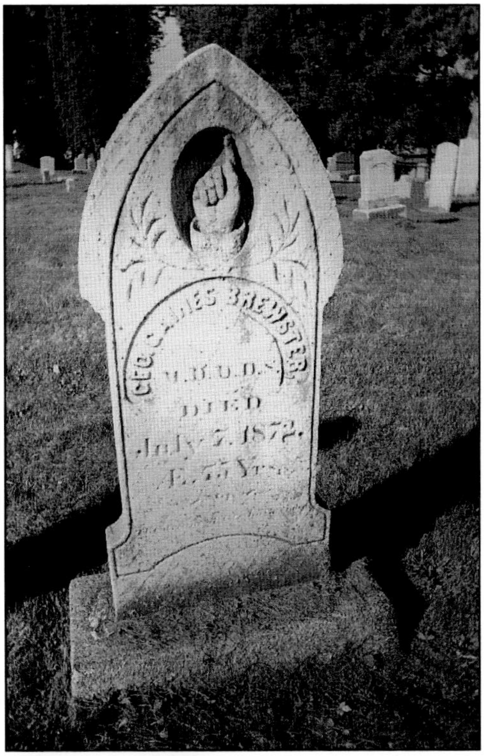

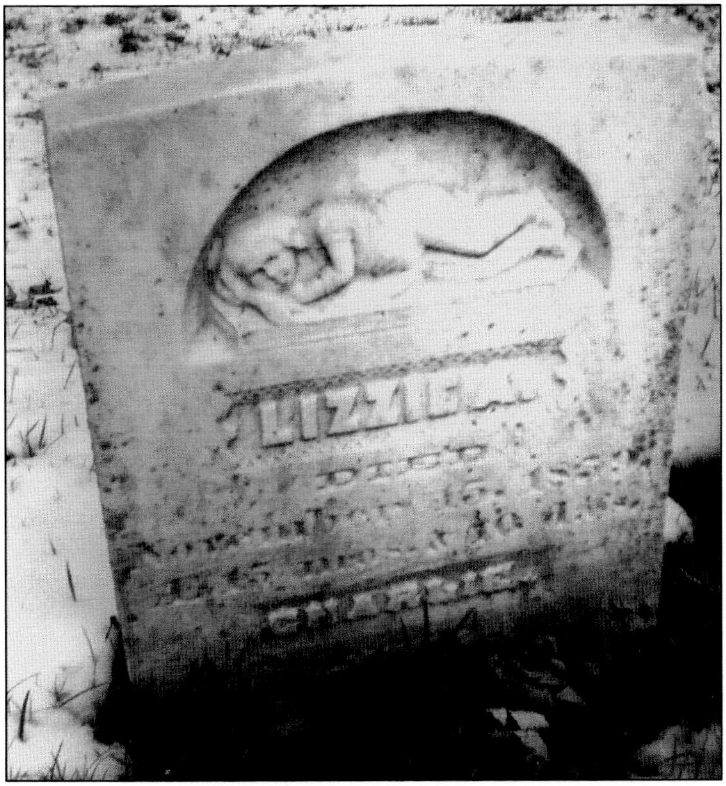

LIZZIE, 1858, AND CHARLIE LEAVITT, 1860, NORTH CEMETERY. The sleeping child on this marble gravestone is a symbol of innocence and is usually only found on those for children. Both Lizzie, aged 15 months, and Charlie died young, and the image is a comforting reminder of them at eternal rest in heaven.

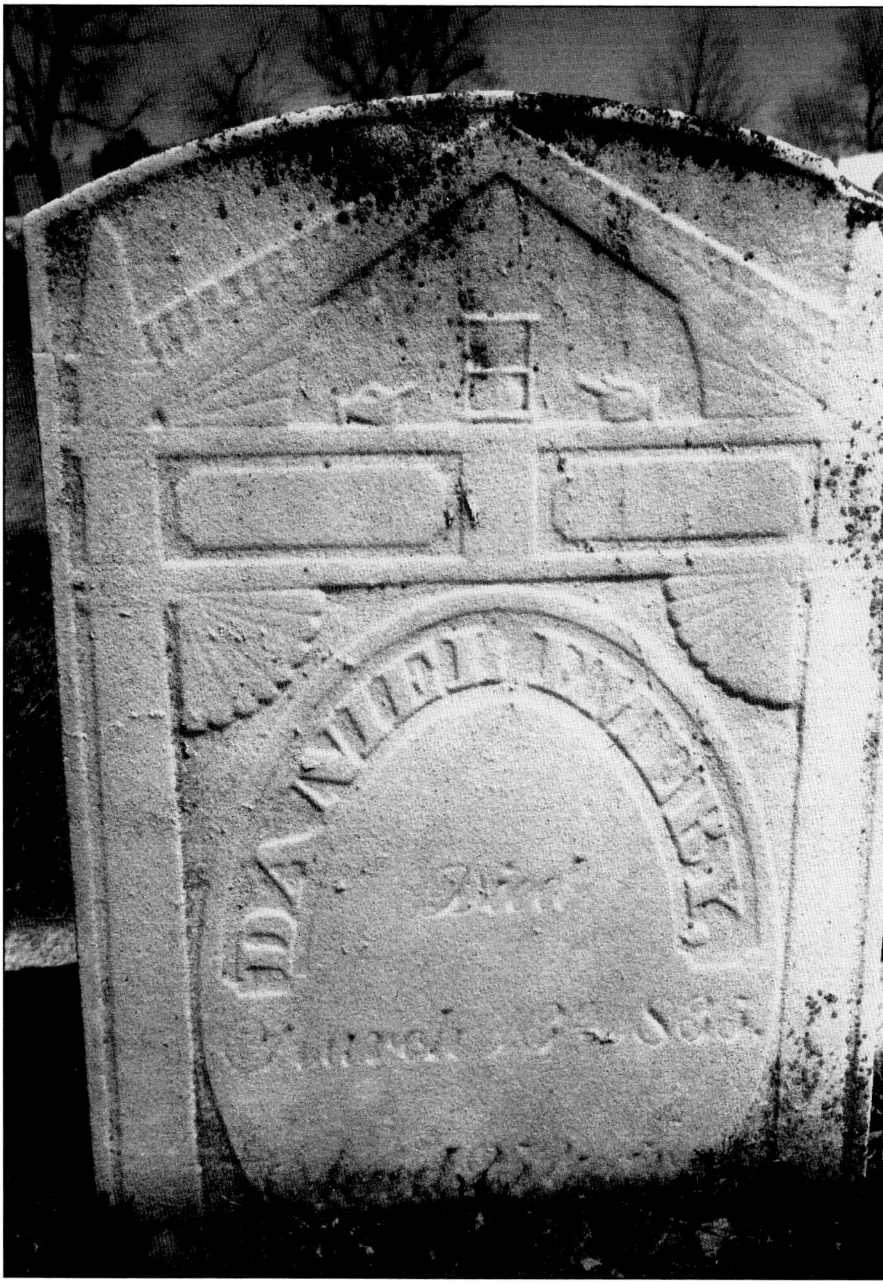

DANIEL EMERY, 1835, NORTH CEMETERY. Many gravestones from the first half of the 19th century combine modern design motifs with older symbols that had already been in use for more than 150 years. Such is the case for the gravestone of Daniel Emery, who died at the age of 25. The hourglass, symbolic of man's short time on earth, was certainly used here because Emery died in the prime of his life. It is a motif that in earlier times often appeared in unison with a death's head. The hands pointing at the hourglass for emphasis are a new addition, as is the overall architectural theme of this stone carved in marble. Note the side columns, each topped off with an obelisk, as well as the peaked roof over the hourglass. The lettering, carved on the oval-shaped inset in both block and elegant cursive text, adds to the overall effect.

LUCRETIA RICE, 1835, PROPRIETOR'S CEMETERY. This marble stone was created for one of Robert and Charlotte Rice's three daughters buried in the family plot. The lamb, symbolic of innocence and resurrection, became quite popular at this time and is still in use today on the graves of children.

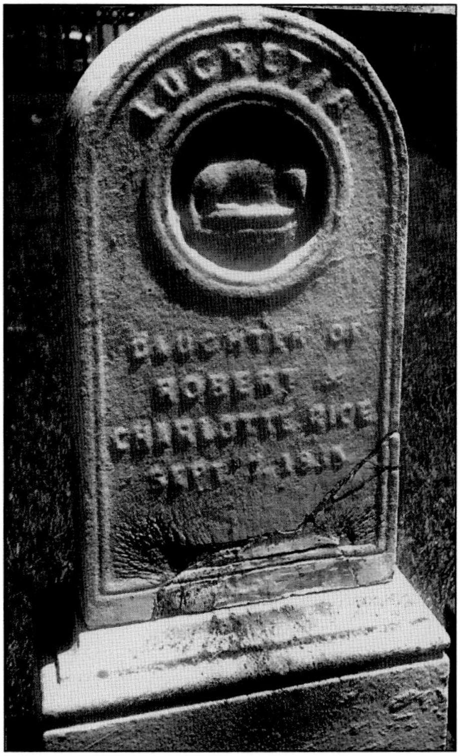

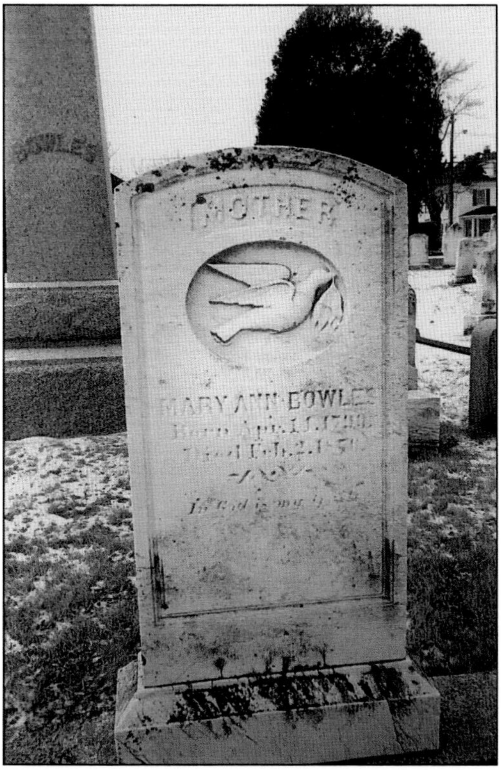

MARY ANN BOWLES, 1856, HARMONY GROVE CEMETERY. A dove is in flight on this graceful stone. The dove itself is symbolic of love, purity, and the Holy Spirit, while its flight skyward, with a wilted flower in its beak representing the deceased, signifies heavenly reward and resurrection.

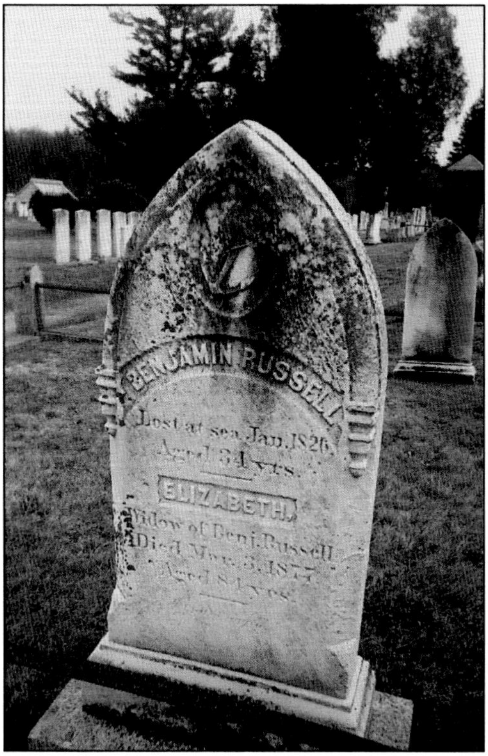

BENJAMIN, 1826, AND ELIZABETH RUSSELL, 1877, HARMONY GROVE CEMETERY. The portrayal of an anchor on a gravestone can have a dual meaning. Not only is the anchor a Christian symbol of hope, but it also usually denotes that the deceased was a sailor. When the words "lost at sea" are added, as is the case here, we know that both meanings were probably intended.

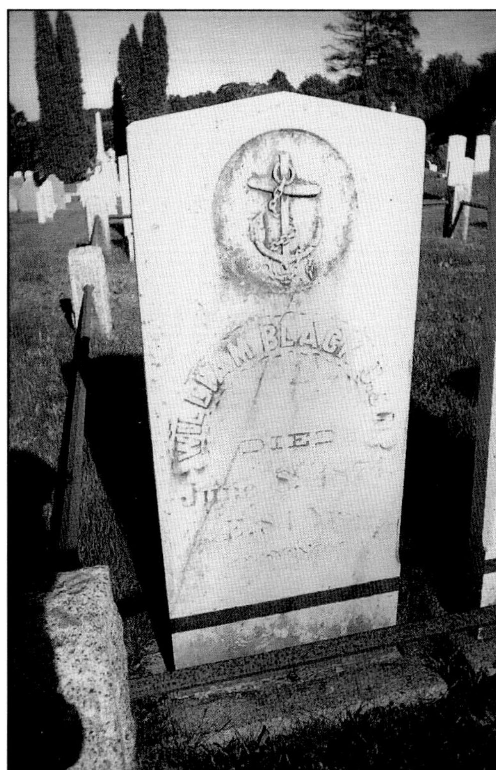

WILLIAM BLACK, 1874, HARMONY GROVE CEMETERY. The anchor on this stone leaves no doubt as to its meaning. Note the initials "U.S.N." carved after Black's name, indicating that he had served in the U.S. Navy. Given his old age, one wonders what wars Black may have served in, perhaps the War of 1812.

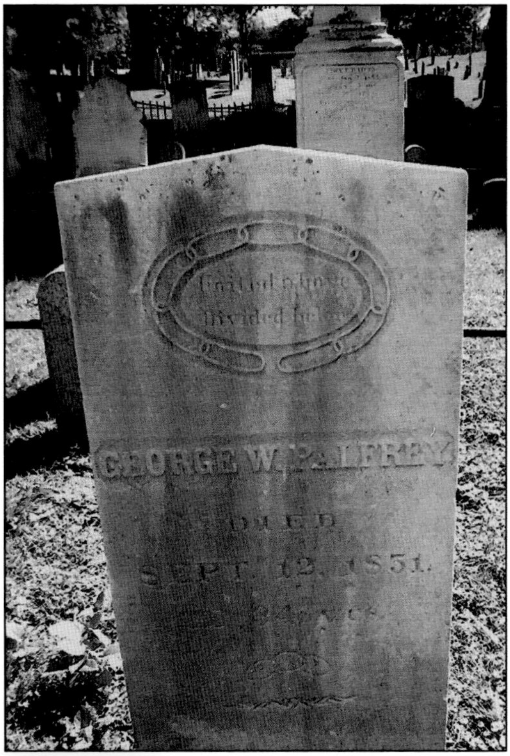

George Palfrey, 1851, Union Cemetery. Like many gravestone motifs, the linked chain can have a number of meanings. Not only is it symbolic of faith and the Holy Trinity, especially when three links are used, but it is often a symbol of the deceased's membership in the Odd Fellows. Note the words within the circular chain at the top, which read, "United above, Divided below."

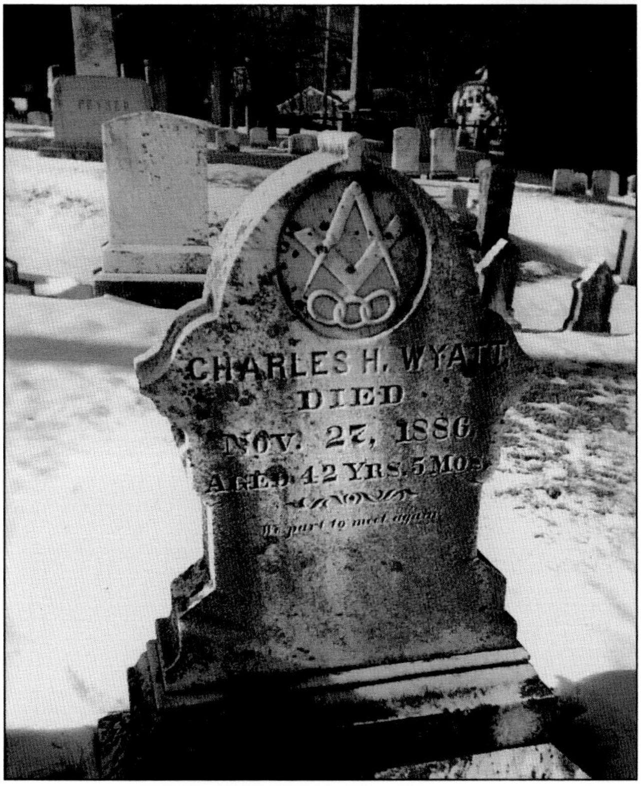

Charles Wyatt, 1886, Harmony Grove Cemetery. Probably the most common societal emblem found on area gravestones is that of the Masons. Their compass and set square motif is symbolic of uprightness and good moral judgment. Note that this stone also has the three-link chain device below the Masonic emblem, likely signifying that Wyatt was also a member of the Odd Fellows.

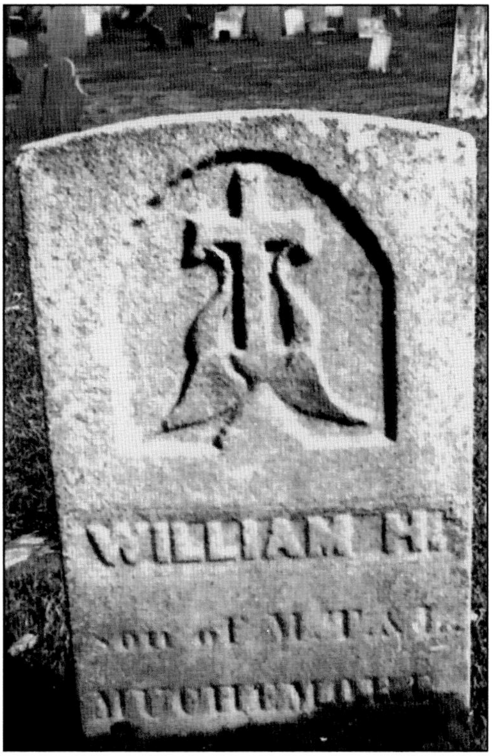

WILLIAM MUCHEMORE, 1852, NORTH CEMETERY. Carved of limestone, this gravestone signifies that the deceased was Catholic. The design shown here was rarely used in Portsmouth at the time. The triangle that serves as the base of the cross is symbolic of the Holy Trinity, while the flaming hearts on either side of the cross denote religious fervor.

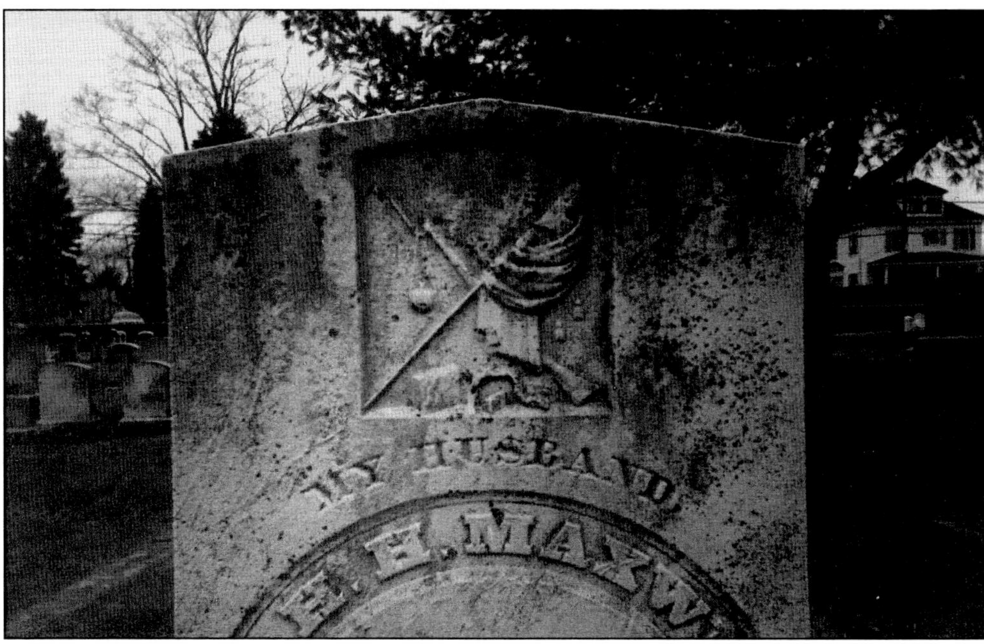

WILLIAM MAXWELL, 1865, HARMONY GROVE CEMETERY. The era of the Civil War brought a new design element. Patriotic in nature, gravestones such as this denoted a man's military service in the bloodiest conflict the nation had ever experienced. Note the crossed musket with bayonet and furled battle flag. Hanging off the end of the musket is a soldier's canteen, while below is his cartridge box and ammunition belt.

Catherine McCarthy Murphy, St. Mary's Cemetery. The influx of Irish immigrants to the New Hampshire seacoast in the late 19th century is evident throughout St. Mary's Cemetery. The letters "IHS," often carved next to the cross on Catholic gravestones, has a dual meaning. Not only do they signify the words "In His Service," but they are also the ancient initials, Greek in origin, for the name Jesus Christ.

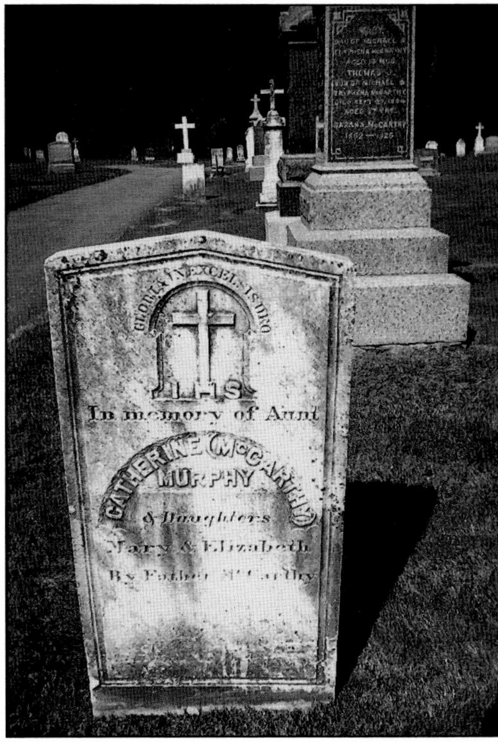

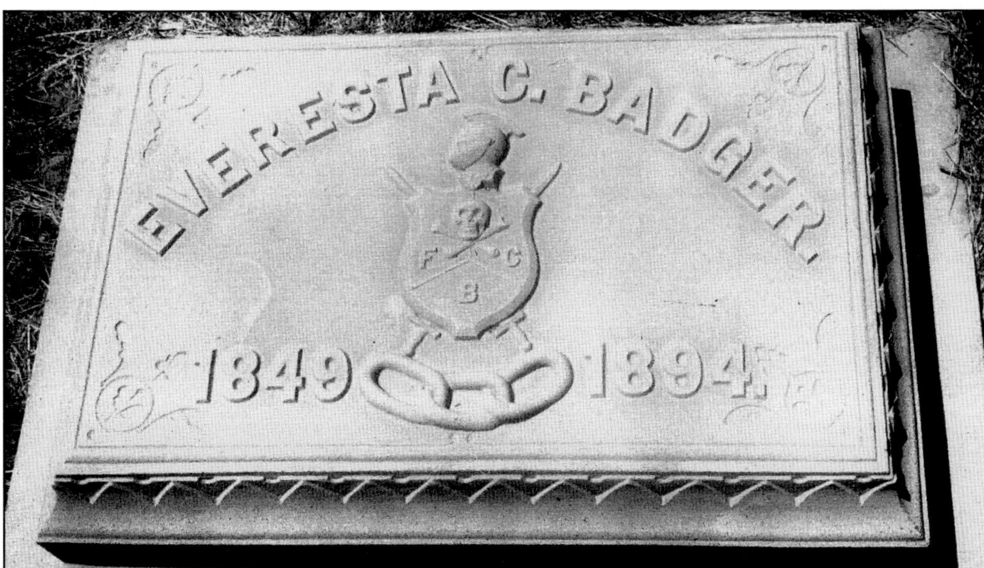

Everesta Badger, 1894, Proprietor's Cemetery. By the late 19th century, gravestone carving had started to become plain, often with little or no ornamentation. The design of this stone, with what appears to be a family coat of arms and the three-link chain of the Odd Fellows, is a throwback to earlier times. Note the skull and crossbones on the family crest and the floral motif in each corner.

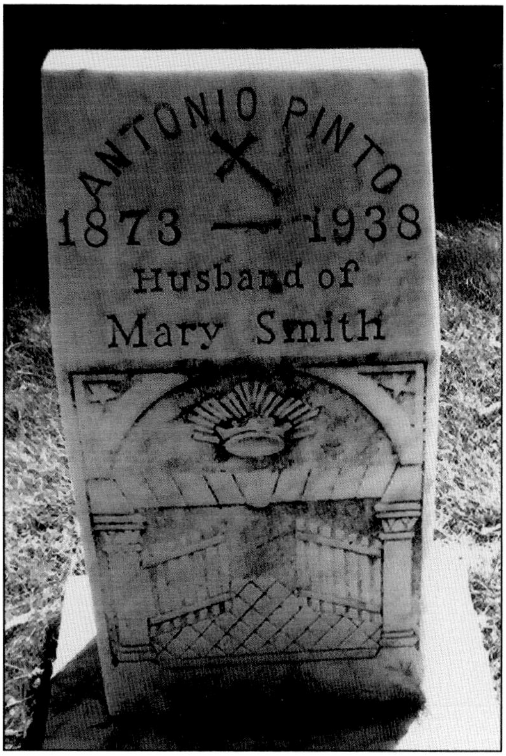

Antonio Pinto, 1938, Calvary Cemetery. This gravestone is more elaborate than most carved during this time. Made of marble, it has three major symbols: the shining crown in the center, signifying the glory of life after death; the stars in each corner above the arch, meaning divine guidance; and the open gates, signifying the deceased's entrance into heaven.

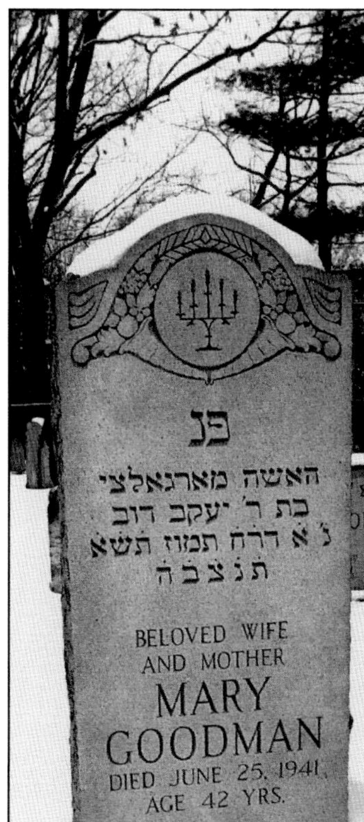

Mary Goodman, 1941, Beth Israel Cemetery. Jewish gravestones are most interesting and appealing. This stone depicts horns of plenty encircling a menorah. The menorah is often, but not exclusively, used on the graves of Jewish women, as it is they who usually attend to the blessings and lighting of the menorah. The writing in Hebrew at the top usually gives the deceased's Hebrew name, father's name, and date of death.

Two

Point of Graves, Pleasant Street, and St. John's Cemeteries

Point of Graves Cemetery was formally established in 1671, when the half-acre parcel of land was deeded to the town by Capt. John Pickering. Pickering retained the right to graze his cattle within Point of Graves, so stones dating before 1682 are missing, and many others after this time have been knocked askew and damaged. Point of Graves is aptly named, because at one time it sat almost directly on a point of land that looked out over the Piscataqua River. Standing as a silent sentinel surrounded by the masts of the many sailing vessels that crowded the nearby wharves, Point of Graves was even more picturesque then than it is now. With a burying ground so close by, one wonders if sailors on their departure gave a passing thought about their own mortality. Point of Graves is most notable for the gravestone styles found here, mostly carved by the finest stonecutters of eastern Massachusetts. Here, the winged-skull design can be found in all its glory.

Pleasant Street Cemetery, the third oldest of the city's Colonial-era public burying grounds, was deeded to Portsmouth in 1754. Situated on a spot of land once called Pickering's Neck, it too was carved out of the original land holdings of John Pickering. This cemetery was once called South Burying Ground due to its location and because it served the communicants of South Church. Many of those notable in the mercantile and maritime trades are buried here, including members of the Manning, Wendell, and Salter families. A must-see is the stone for Mary Manning. Now restored, it bears an image of a skeletal grim reaper, rare in New Hampshire.

St. John's Churchyard is one of the most unusual cemeteries in New Hampshire. Its establishment dates to 1732, when Portsmouth's original Anglican church, Queen's Chapel, was built. Queen's Chapel burned down on December 24, 1806, and was replaced by St. John's soon after. Burials on this hillside site are of three types: above-ground tombs, most notably that of the Wentworth family; regular below-ground sites marked by gravestones; and burial vaults further underground. The doors to these vaults can be seen from street level and are an intriguing sight. The underground activity in this area below the churchyard is interesting. In later years, an underground passageway connected the basement of St. John's with the nearby Portsmouth Brewery, and the space underneath the church was used to store casks of ale. Some of the individuals interred in these underground vaults are remembered not with gravestones above ground but with memorial plaques on the wall inside St. John's Church. This is a longstanding tradition in the Anglican Church, not unlike those in London's famous Westminster Cathedral.

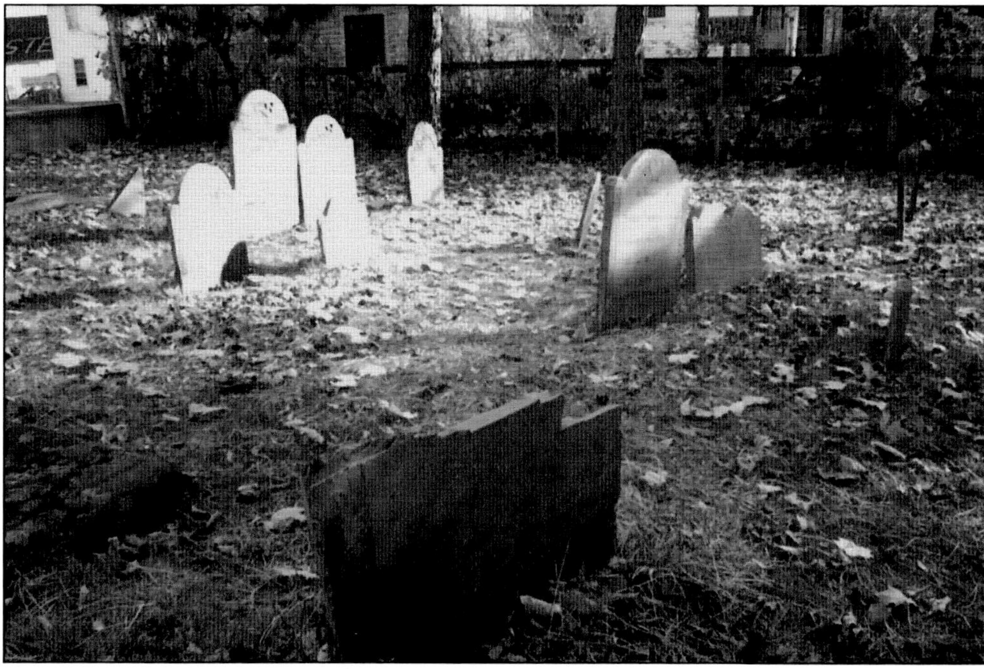

Point of Graves Cemetery. This cemetery was formally established in 1671 but had been in use as a burial place many years before. Broken stones such as the one shown were perhaps damaged by the cows allowed to graze here.

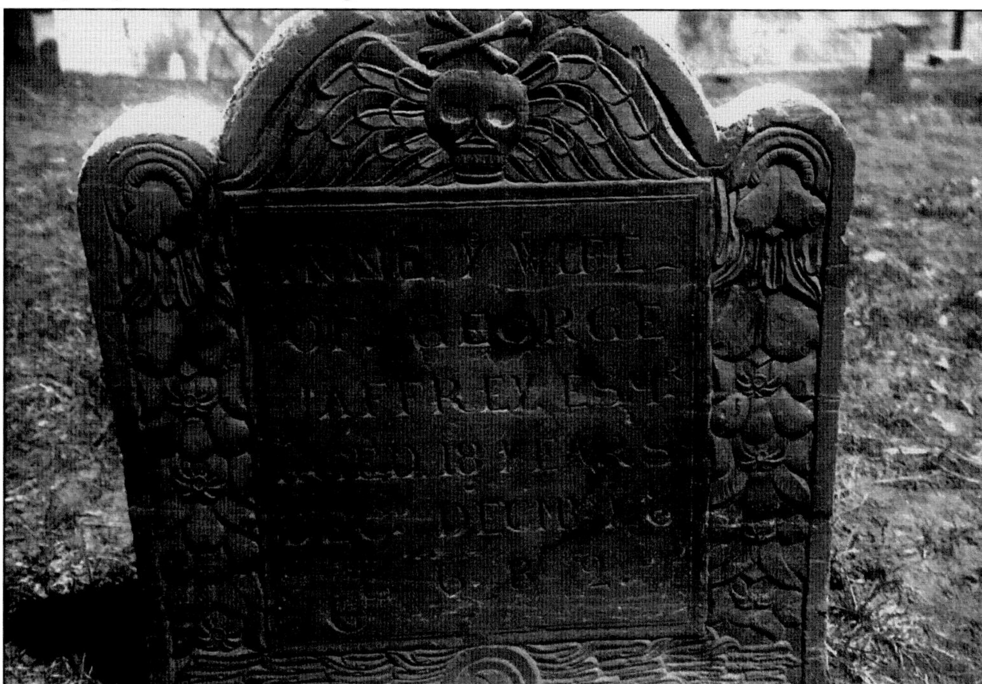

Anne Jaffrey, 1682, Point of Graves. Anne was the young wife of a Scottish merchant who owned land on Star Island at the Isles of Shoals and sold his wares to local fisherman. She died after the birth of their son, George Jr., on Great Island just two weeks before.

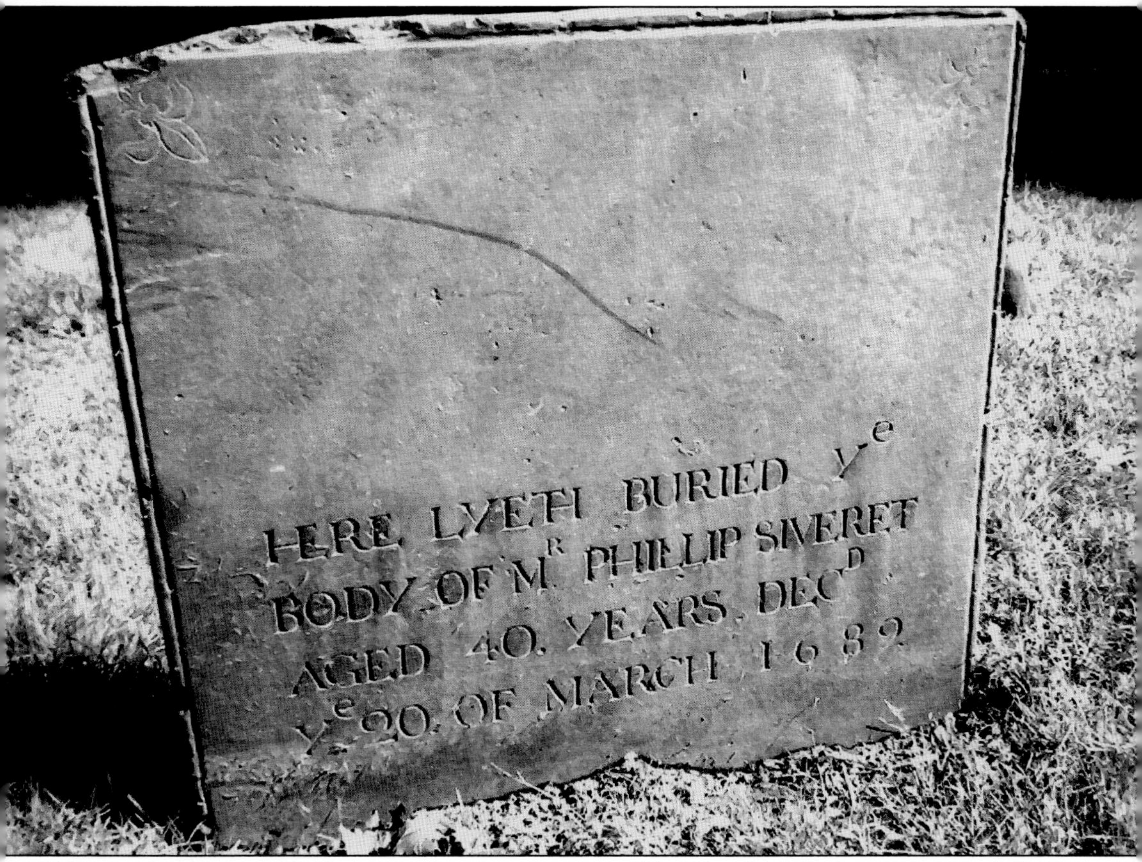

PHILLIP SIVERET, 1689, POINT OF GRAVES. A native of the Isle of Jersey, Siveret was settled in Portsmouth by 1671. He was owner and commander of the ship *Joanna*, named after his wife, whom he married in 1680. Upon his death, Siveret left the ketches *America* and *Prosperous* to his wife, as well as at least one slave woman. When his widow died less than two years later from smallpox on January 10, 1691, she left her "Negro woman Elisabeth" to her sister Margaret, stating that she would serve for 20 years and then be freed. This gravestone is unusual and may in fact be the remains of a table stone that once lay flat on the ground. Note that the only ornamentation is the fleur-de-lis in the upper corners. The lower portion of the stone might have had the coat of arms of the Siveret family and matching fleur-de-lis in the corners. It is likely that the table stone was broken, the remaining piece later set in an upright position.

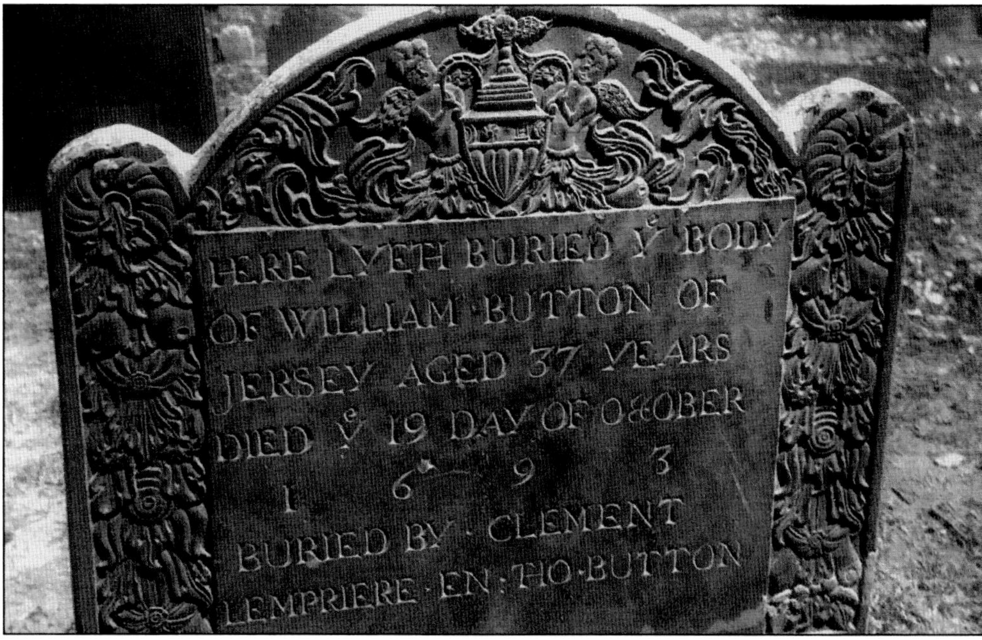

William Button, 1693, Point of Graves. This gravestone for a wealthy merchant who fell overboard and drowned from his own ship, the *Lyon*, is one of the most unusual in all of New Hampshire. It was carved by the stonecutter known only by the initials "J. N.," thought to have been the Boston silversmith John Noyes. Its intricate carvings are certainly the work of a highly skilled artisan.

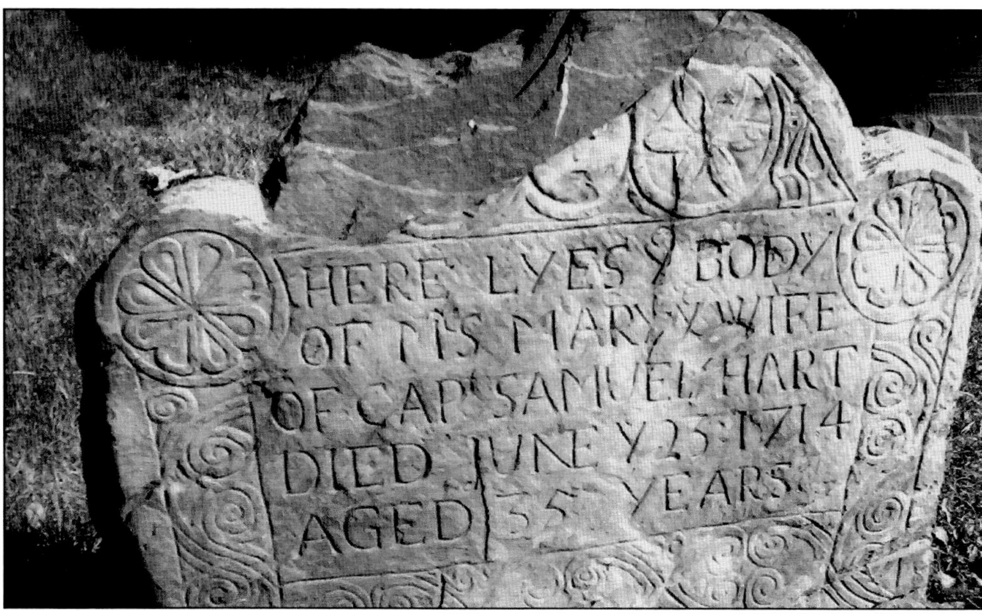

Mary Hart, 1714, Point of Graves. This worn stone is the work of Merrimack Valley carver John Hartshorne. The round face in the center is flanked by acanthus leaves, which are in turn flanked by small birds with upturned beaks. Note the heart-shaped scrollwork on the lower border. Mary was the daughter of innkeeper Robert Evans of Dover, while her blacksmith husband originally hailed from Ipswich, Massachusetts.

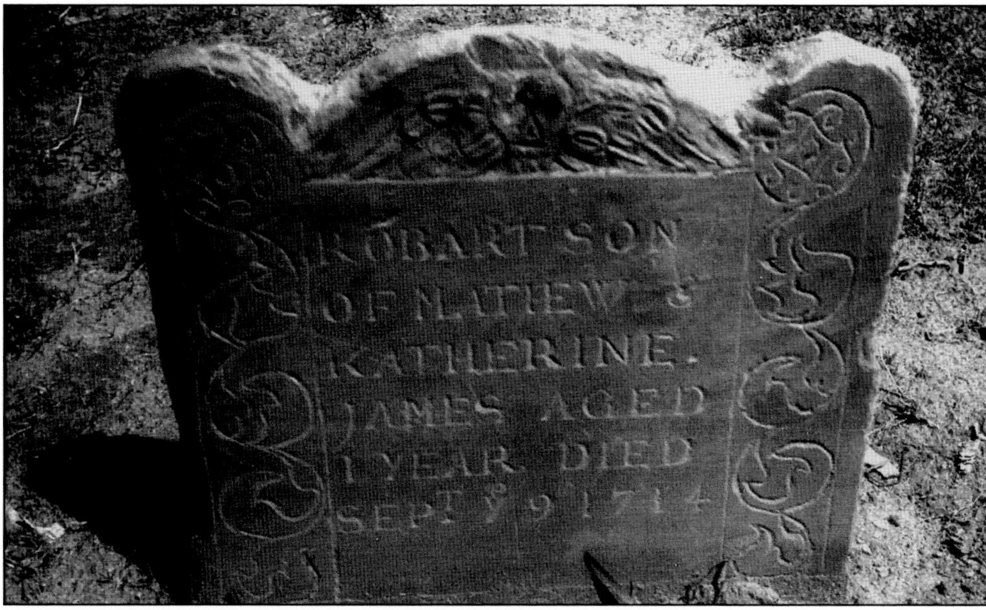

Robert James, 1714, Point of Graves. Matthew and Katherine James were married in Portsmouth on November 20, 1712, and later lived in Somersworth. While little is known about Matthew James, his wife was the daughter of carpenter and ferryman Elisha Clark. This stone for Robert, likely their first child, was carved by James Foster I of Dorchester, Massachusetts. The lightbulb-shaped skull and finely etched borders are characteristic of his work.

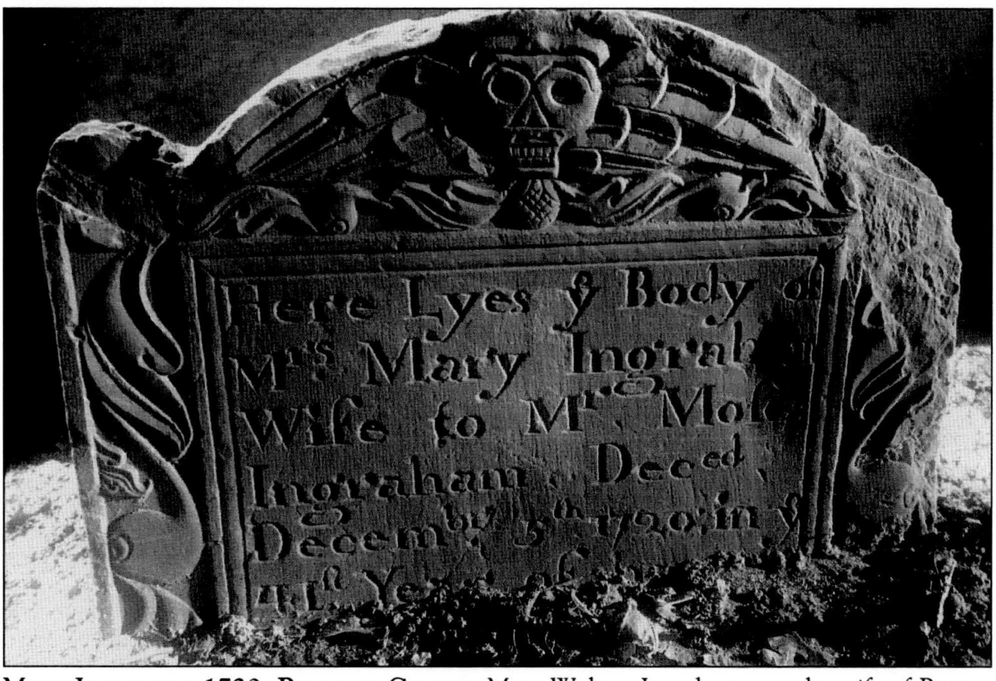

Mary Ingraham, 1720, Point of Graves. Mary Walton Ingraham was the wife of Boston native Moses Ingraham, who practiced the trade of a tailor. They were married in Boston on July 25, 1706. This stone was carved by the young stonecutter Caleb Lamson, the son of professional carver Joseph Lamson of Charlestown, Massachusetts, and bears his initials.

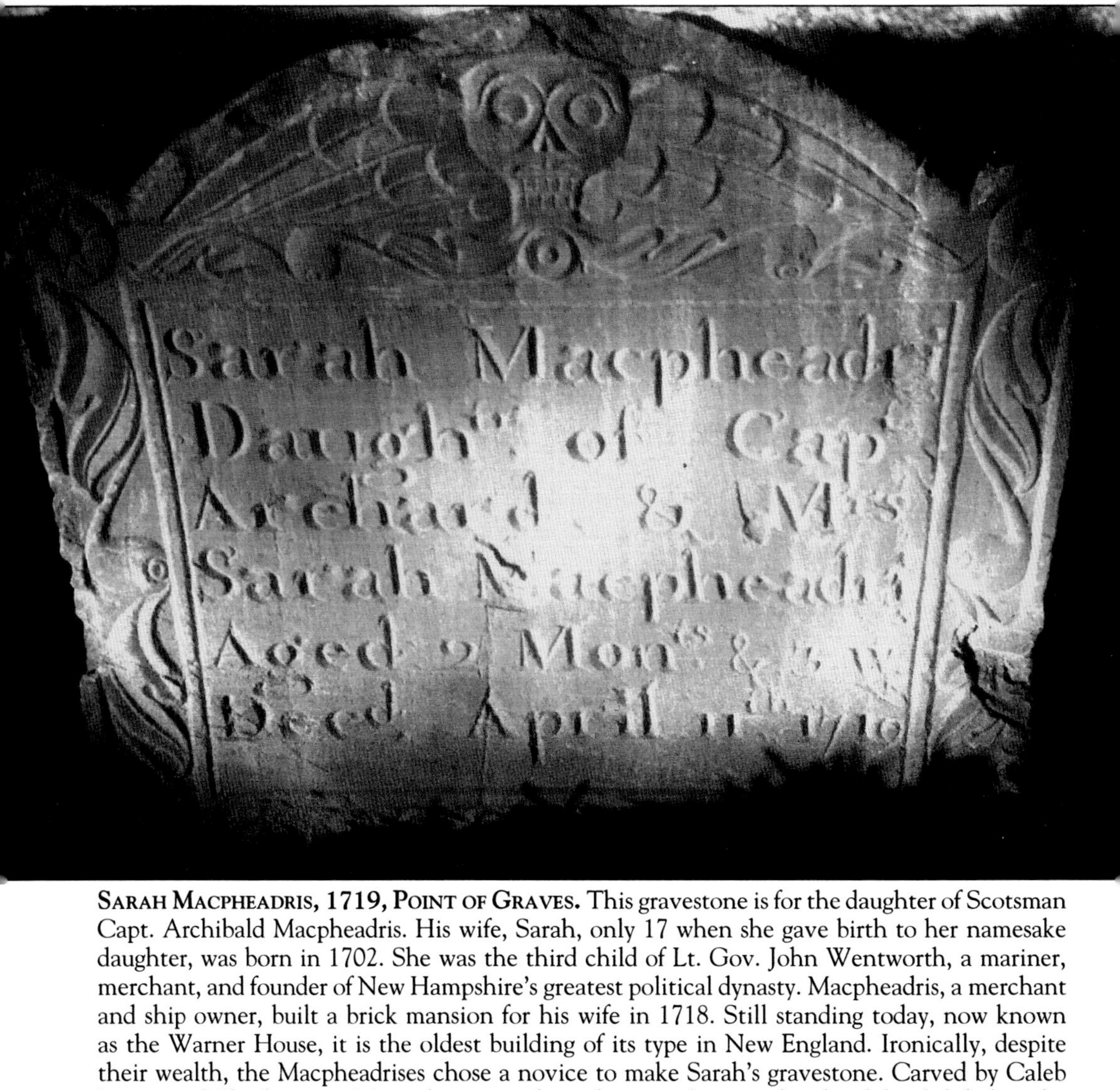

SARAH MACPHEADRIS, 1719, POINT OF GRAVES. This gravestone is for the daughter of Scotsman Capt. Archibald Macpheadris. His wife, Sarah, only 17 when she gave birth to her namesake daughter, was born in 1702. She was the third child of Lt. Gov. John Wentworth, a mariner, merchant, and founder of New Hampshire's greatest political dynasty. Macpheadris, a merchant and ship owner, built a brick mansion for his wife in 1718. Still standing today, now known as the Warner House, it is the oldest building of its type in New England. Ironically, despite their wealth, the Macpheadrises chose a novice to make Sarah's gravestone. Carved by Caleb Lamson of Charlestown, Massachusetts, it bears his initials on each side of the disk below the skull's jaw. This is one of seven Lamson-initialed stones found in Point of Graves. All date from his earliest time as a carver; his still uneven skills are easily visible in the crowded wording on the right side of Sarah's gravestone.

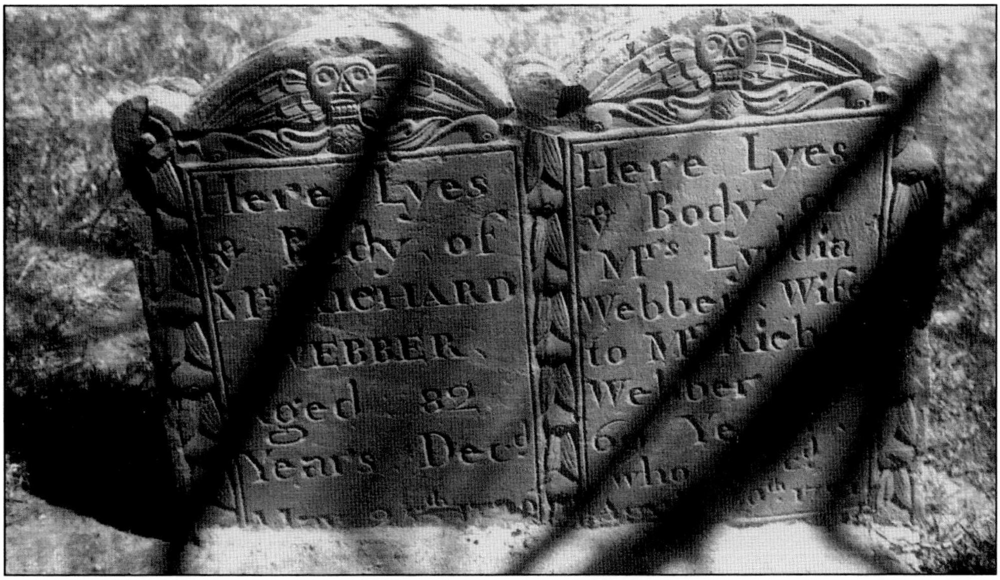

Richard and Lydia Webber, 1720–1721, Point of Graves. Carved and initialed by Caleb Lamson, this dual gravestone marks the resting place of a Portsmouth couple. Richard Webber, a tailor and butcher, came to the Isle of Shoals around 1669. He was married to Lydia Green by 1674, and their life together was very interesting. She was a tavern operator in 1678, while he was arrested for assaulting Sarah Reed in 1684.

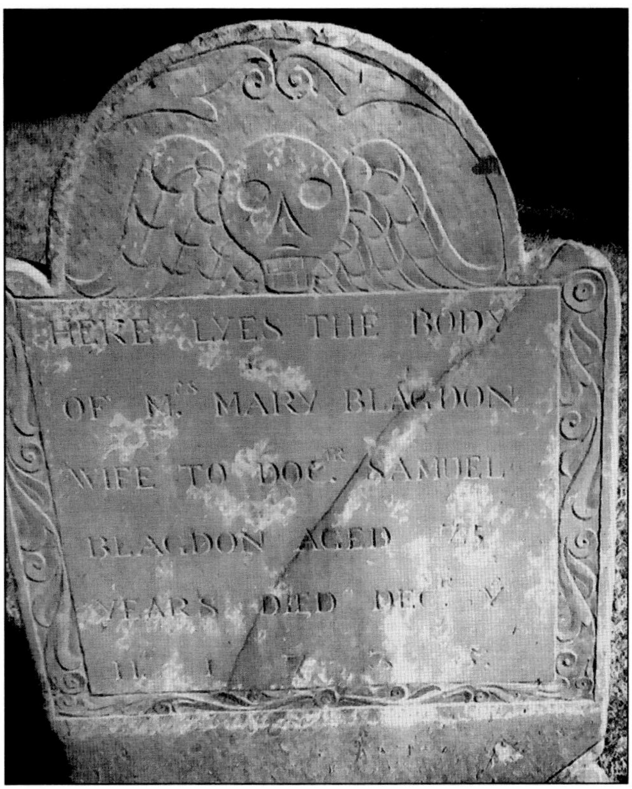

Mary Blagdon, 1735, Point of Graves. Mary Seward Hull was married to Dr. Samuel Blagdon by 1688. Blagdon was a surgeon in Portsmouth for a time before the couple moved to Boston. He had died by 1713, and Mary lived the remainder of her life in Portsmouth with her daughter Hannah. Her gravestone was likely carved by James Foster II of Dorchester, Massachusetts.

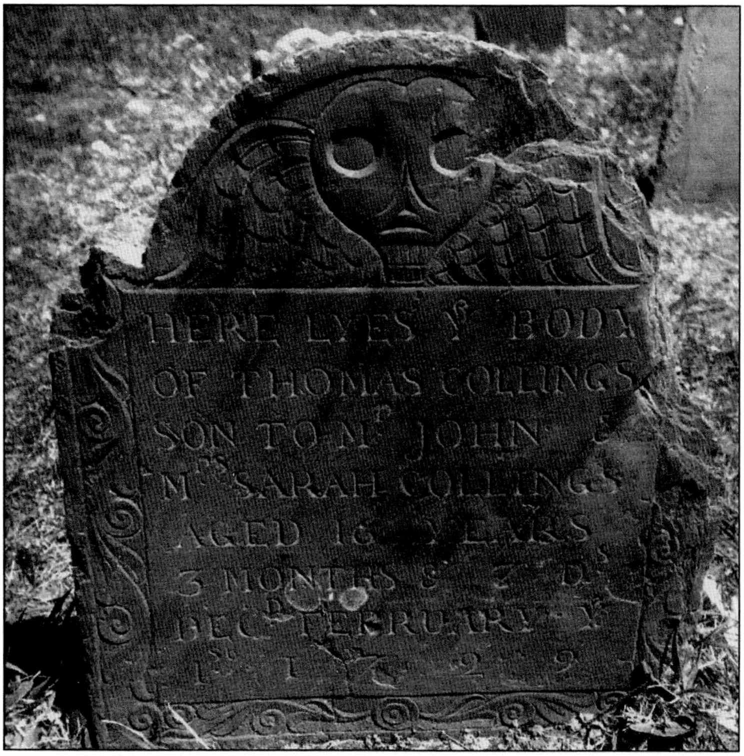

Thomas Collings, 1729, Point of Graves. Little is known about the Collings (also spelled Collins) family. Living at Strawberry Banke, John served on a jury in 1694 and was dead by 1714, when his widow, Sarah, received a tax abatement. In addition to Thomas, the couple had two other sons: John and William. The gravestone shown here was likely carved by James Foster II.

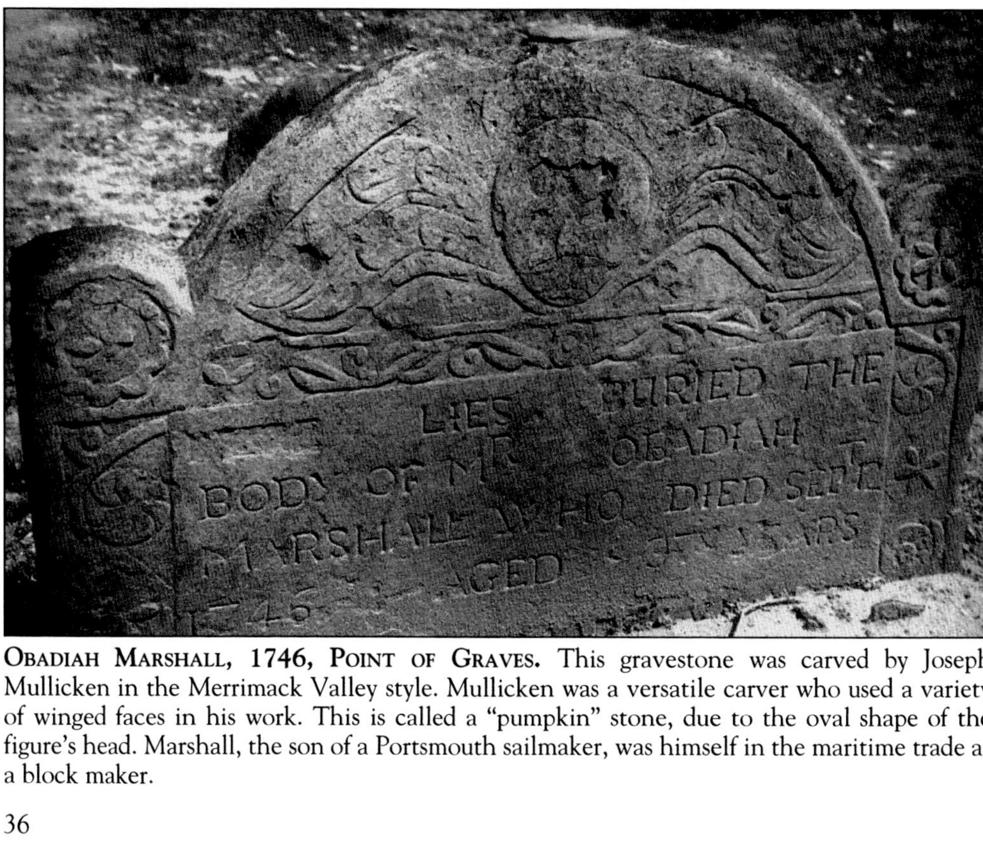

Obadiah Marshall, 1746, Point of Graves. This gravestone was carved by Joseph Mullicken in the Merrimack Valley style. Mullicken was a versatile carver who used a variety of winged faces in his work. This is called a "pumpkin" stone, due to the oval shape of the figure's head. Marshall, the son of a Portsmouth sailmaker, was himself in the maritime trade as a block maker.

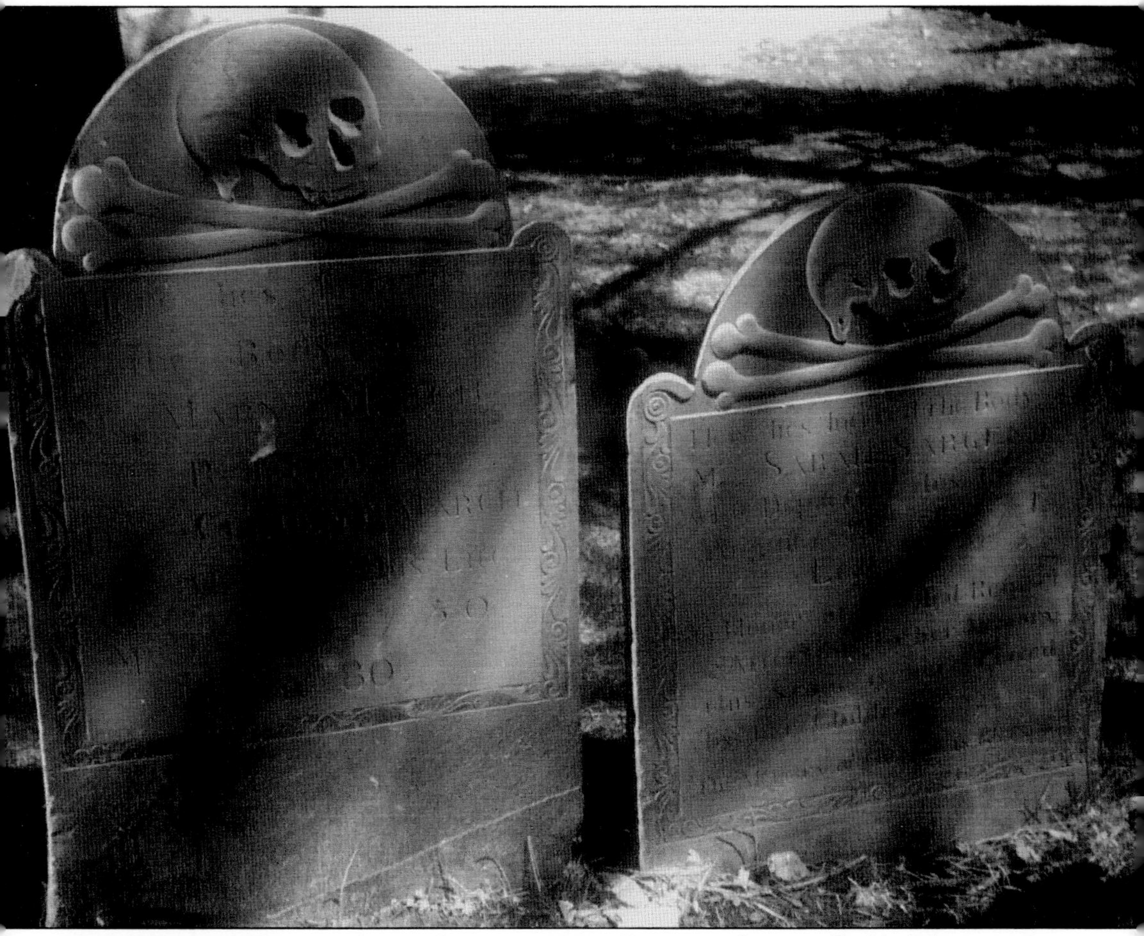

MARY MARCH, 1759, AND SARAH SARGENT, 1771, POINT OF GRAVES. Both of these stones were carved by Capt. John Homer of Boston in a realistically gruesome style all his own. The one to the right memorializes Sarah (Pierce) Sargent, the daughter of Capt. Joshua Pierce and first the wife of John Winslow. Before his death at sea in 1731, they had three children. Her second husband was Dr. Nathaniel Sargent. Sarah's gravestone, likely ordered soon after her death, was "in Honor of the Filial Respect & Affection to her Memory . . . here Placed by her Children." The gravestone to the left is for Mary (Hall) March. Though she died in 1759, her gravestone was not carved until the 1770s. Standing side by side and identical in size, both stones were likely ordered by the same person and carved and erected at the same time. This is not surprising. Sarah's mother was Elizabeth Hall Pierce, a sister of Mary Hall March; Sarah and her aunt Mary may have had a close relationship.

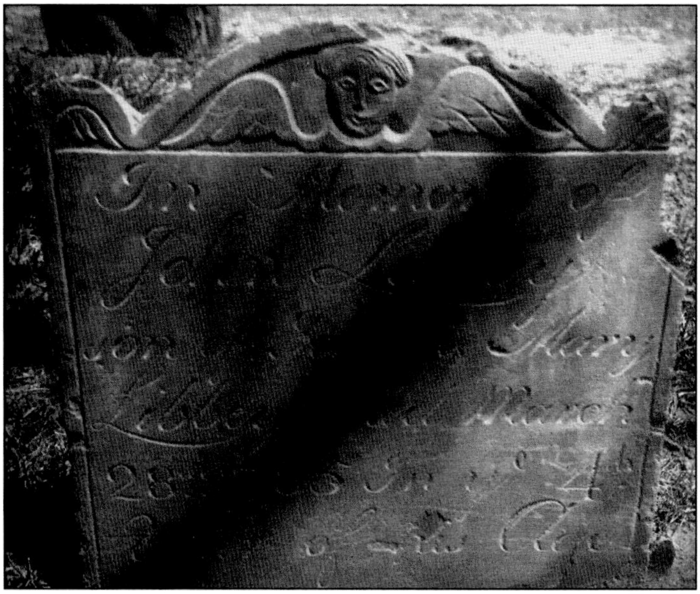

JOHN LIBBEY, 1785, POINT OF GRAVES. The wide-eyed angel depicted here for four-year-old John Libbey is a marked change from the morbid death's-head motif used earlier for children's gravestones within this cemetery. Combined with the elegant cursive script, this comforting stone, carved by a later generation of the Lamson family, surely offered the hope of a heavenly afterlife to John's grieving parents.

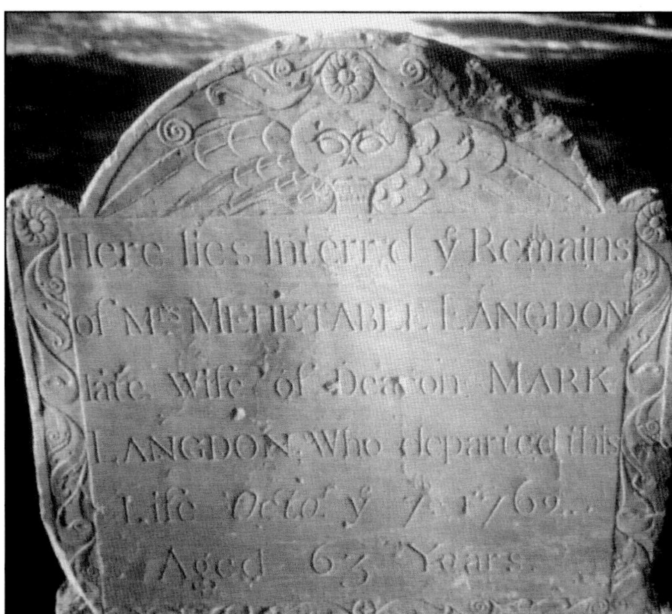

MEHETABLE LANGDON, 1762, POINT OF GRAVES. Mehetable Jackson, from an unidentified branch of this seafaring family in Portsmouth, married Mark Langdon on June 7, 1722. Her husband was both a deacon and town selectman (1736–1738 and 1743–1753). Mehetable's gravestone was carved by the Lamson family of Charlestown, Massachusetts (either Caleb or Nathaniel), and displays their typical death's-head motif.

MARY MANNING, 1773, PLEASANT STREET. This rare gravestone for the wife of a famous Portsmouth mariner is unusual for its depiction of a full skeleton. The grim reaper, armed with a scythe, was carved by Bostonian Capt. John Homer. Mary Purcell Manning's husband, Capt. Thomas Manning, was a famous privateersman during the Revolution, commanding the 18-gun *General Sullivan* and the 10-gun *Diana*. It is highly probable that Manning knew Homer, if not in person, at least by name. Both were sea captains and both were active Sons of Liberty; it is even possible that this gravestone made its way back to Portsmouth on Manning's own ship. Mary Manning's unusual stone was at one time broken into a number of sections and the pieces scattered about. Through the work of local civic groups, it was recently repaired and reset.

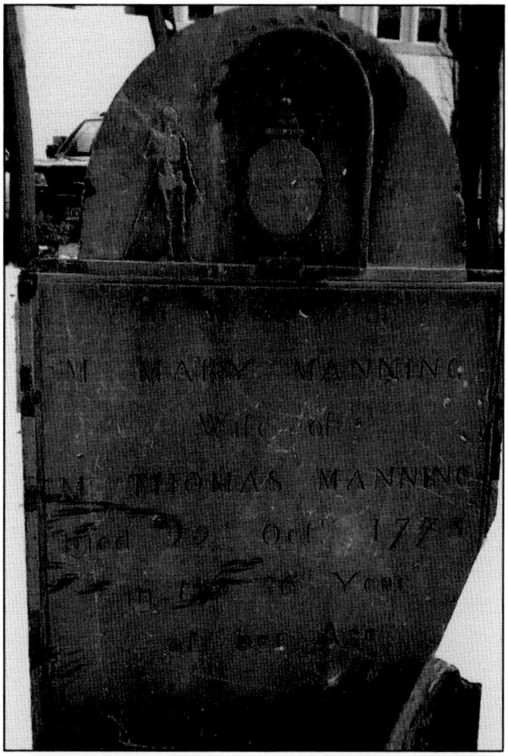

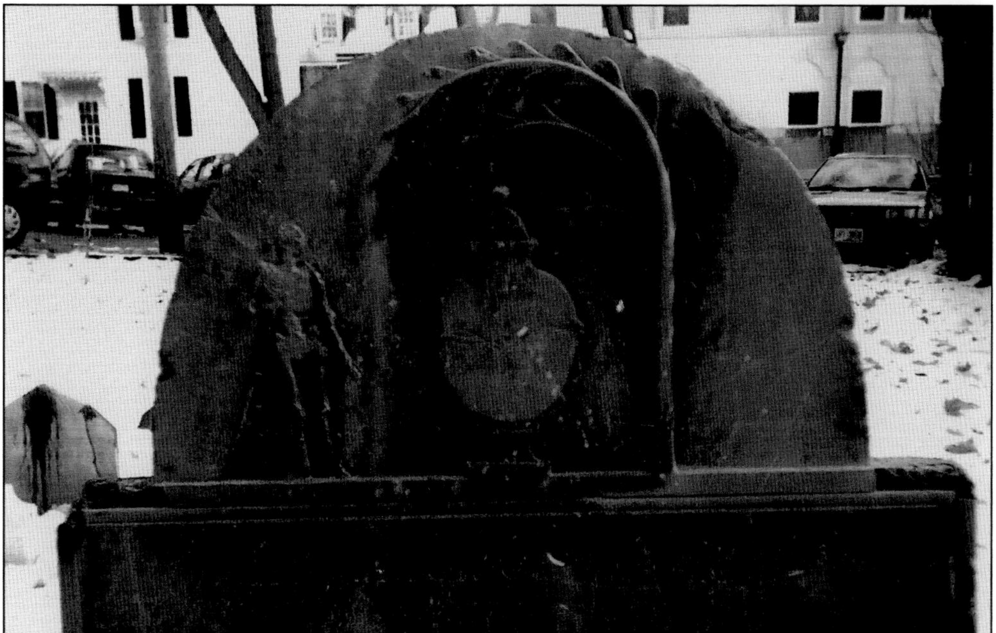

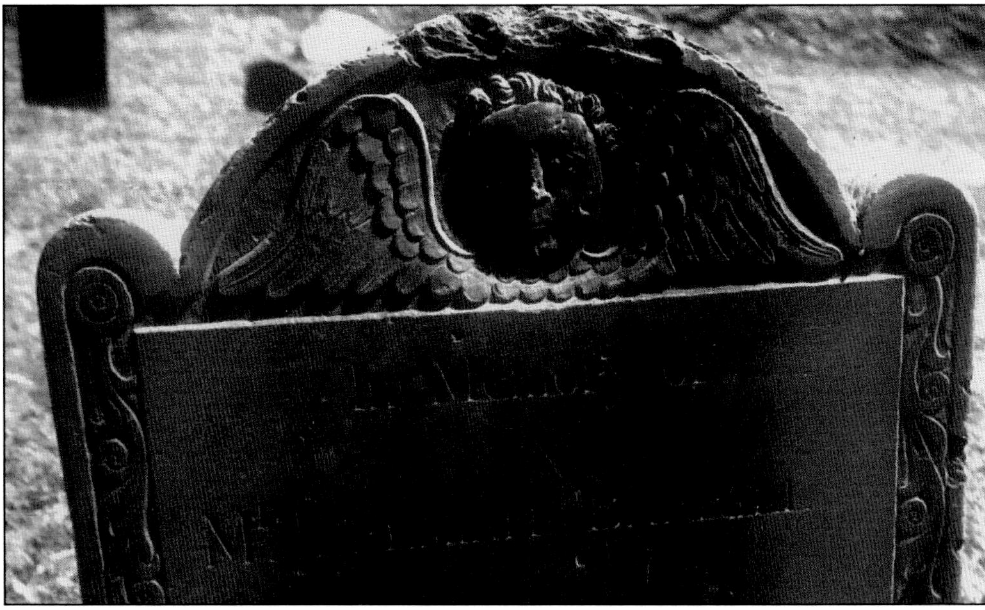

Jeremiah Barrell, 1763, Pleasant Street. This, the oldest extant gravestone here, bears a distinctly male angelic face, the work of a Boston-area carver. Little is known about this young man, who died at the age of 19. One relative by marriage was Elizabeth Langdon Barrell, the sister of future New Hampshire governor John Langdon. The Barrells were a Royalist family during the Revolutionary War.

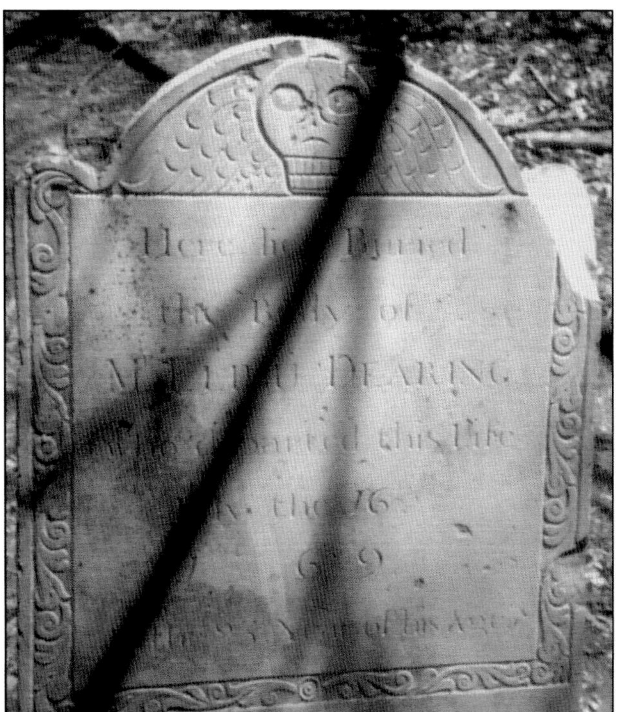

Elihu Dearing, 1769, Pleasant Street. While little is known about Elihu Dearing (also spelled Deering), he was possibly the son of carver William Deering of Portsmouth. William, who likely carved ship's figureheads and other decorative work, had a shop on nearby Water Street. Elihu's gravestone, a conventional death's head, was carved in Boston, possibly by a member of the Geyer family. Note the numeral "1" that looks like the letter "J."

MARY PURVISS, 1799, PLEASANT STREET. This attractive gravestone, utilizing an urn and wreath motif, was carved by Bartlett Adams during his brief stopover in Portsmouth. He was a prolific stonecutter who had originally received his training in Kingston, Massachusetts. The poetic epitaph reads, "Fond, friendly, humane, kind, sincere, A wife, a sister, friend most dear. Ah what avails the heartfelt sigh, These *Charities* were born to die."

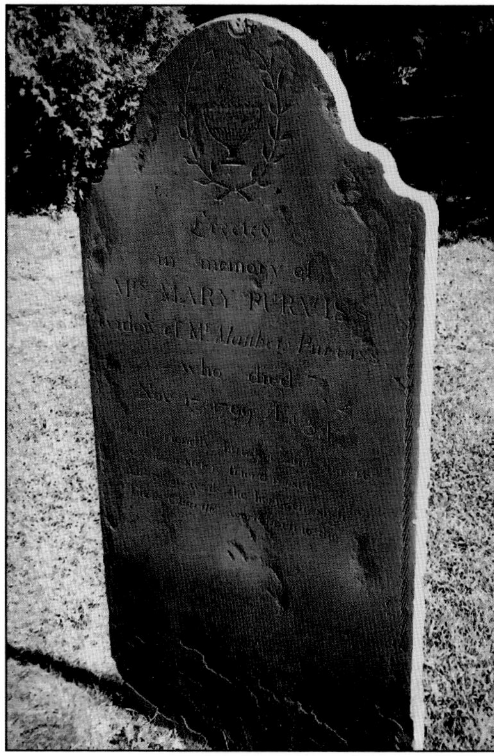

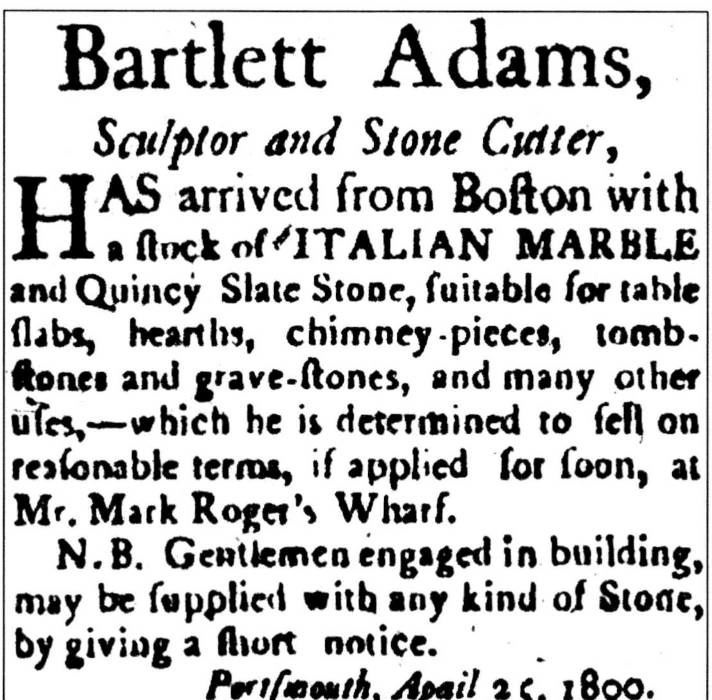

Bartlett Adams,

Sculptor and Stone Cutter,

HAS arrived from Boſton with a ſtock of ITALIAN MARBLE and Quincy Slate Stone, ſuitable for table ſlabs, hearths, chimney-pieces, tomb-ſtones and grave-ſtones, and many other uſes,—which he is determined to ſell on reaſonable terms, if applied for ſoon, at Mr. Mark Roger's Wharf.

N.B. Gentlemen engaged in building, may be ſupplied with any kind of Stone, by giving a ſhort notice.

Portſmouth, April 25, 1800.

A BARTLETT ADAMS ADVERTISEMENT, 1800. Adams learned the carving trade from his brother-in-law Bildad Washburn and later worked with Jonathan Rawson and others in Quincy. As this advertisement from the *Oracle of the Day* implies, he practiced in Portsmouth briefly, perhaps several weeks or a month, before establishing his own permanent shop in Portland, Maine. Note that he operated at wharf-side and that stones could be had "if applied for soon."

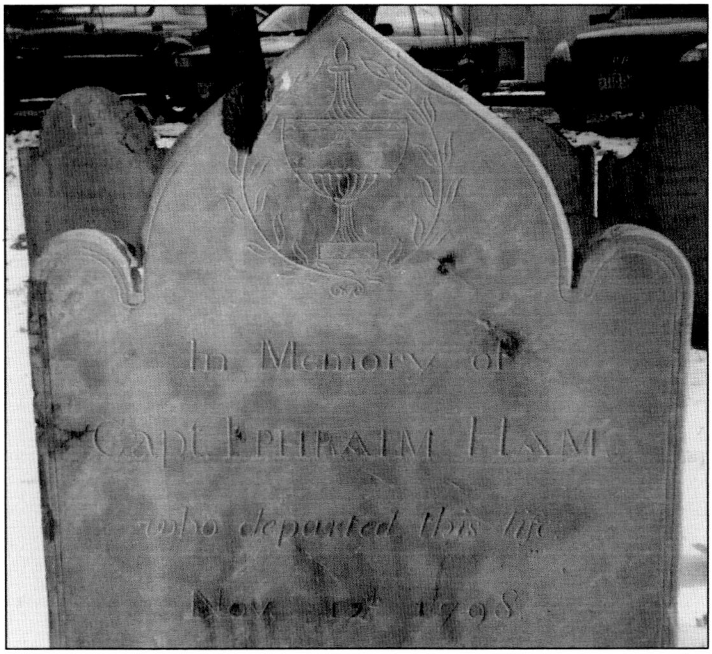

EPHRAIM HAM, 1798, PLEASANT STREET. Capt. Ephraim Ham, one of seven sons of Samuel Ham, was raised on the large family farm at Christian Shore. His back-dated gravestone was carved by Portsmouth's first resident stonecutter, John Marble, who came to town in 1801. It was not uncommon for there to be a delay, often several years, in having a gravestone carved and placed.

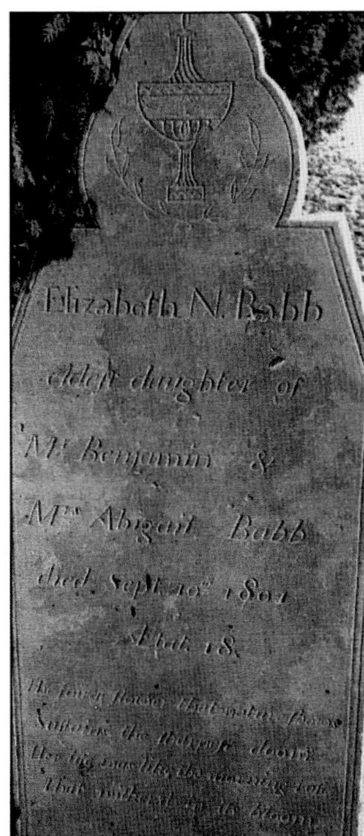

ELIZABETH BABB, 1801, PLEASANT STREET. This unique, coffin-shaped gravestone was crafted by John Marble. The epitaph reads, "The fairest flower that nature shows, Sustains the sharpest doom. Her life was like the morning rose, That witherd in its bloom." Perhaps Elizabeth was named in memory of her ancestor Betsey Babb, who at age 14 was among those killed by Native Americans during the Breakfast Hill Massacre of 1696.

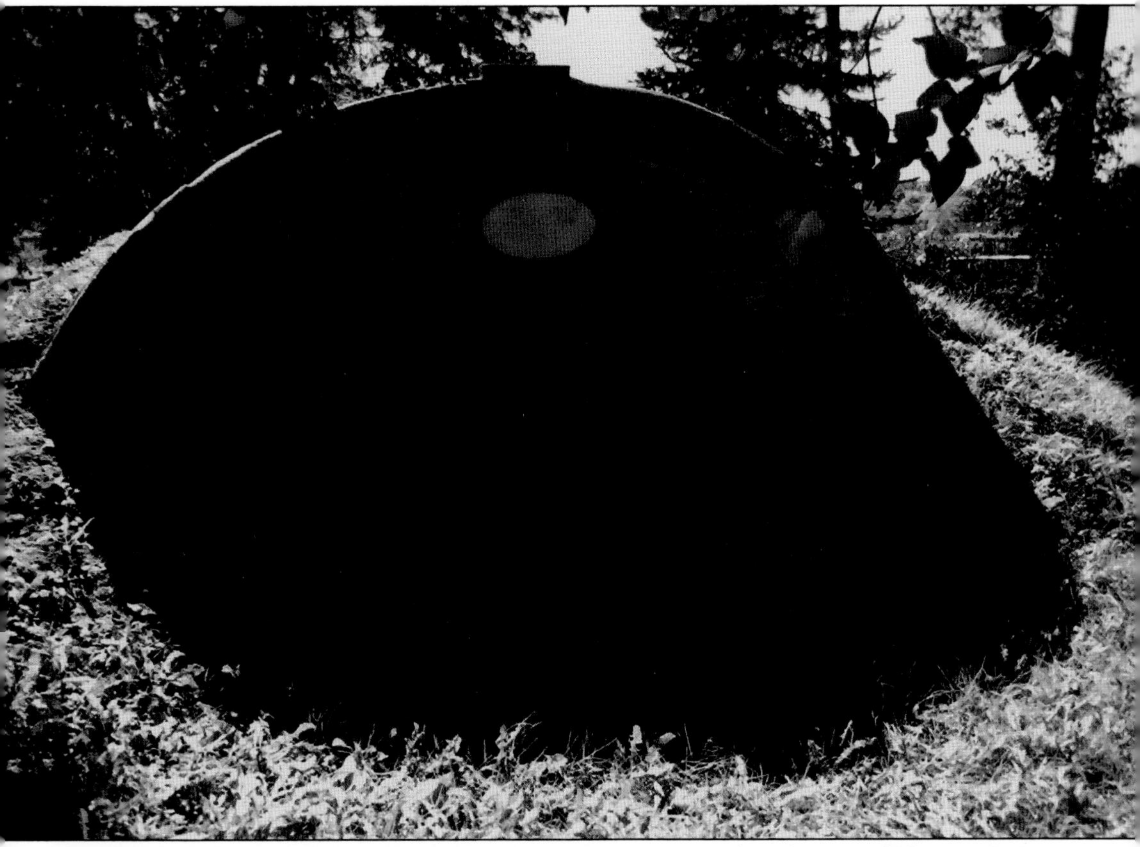

The Wendell Family Tomb, 1818, Pleasant Street. Situated at the rear of Pleasant Street Cemetery, near the waterfront, this tomb was used by members of one of Portsmouth's most successful merchant families. The Wendells originally came to America in 1640, settling in New Amsterdam under the Dutch West India Company. Later generations moved to the Boston area and others subsequently to Portsmouth. The family's most famous member is the poet Oliver Wendell Holmes. This brick-and-earthen structure, with an iron entrance door, was constructed in 1818 as the final resting place for seven family members. Inside, wooden coffins containing the bodies of the deceased were placed on shelves, each with a brass nameplate. Curious historians examined the interior of the tomb in recent years and found that everything within had turned to dust, except the coffin nameplates. The only occupants of the tomb now are the many bats that like its cool darkness. Both the nameplates and the key for the padlocked door are housed at the Portsmouth Athenaeum.

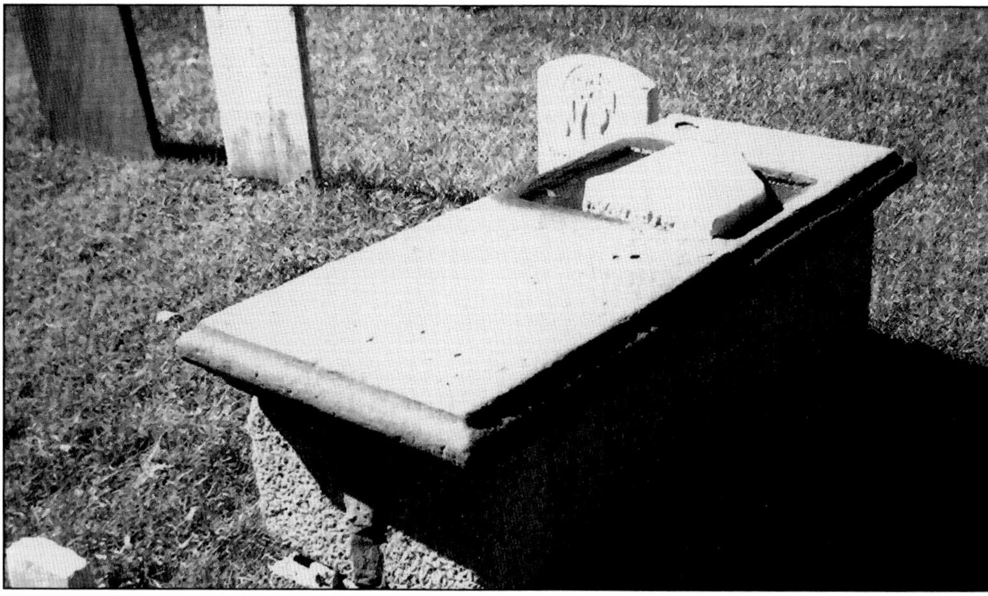

Barrell Tomb, 1802, Pleasant Street. This table stone memorializes members of the Barrell family, including Colburn Barrell, who died in London in 1802, and his wife, Hannah. Its marble inset is now nearly illegible; tombs like this seldom survive intact. Nature's elements take their toll on the top, while vandals eager to look inside cause even more damage to the base.

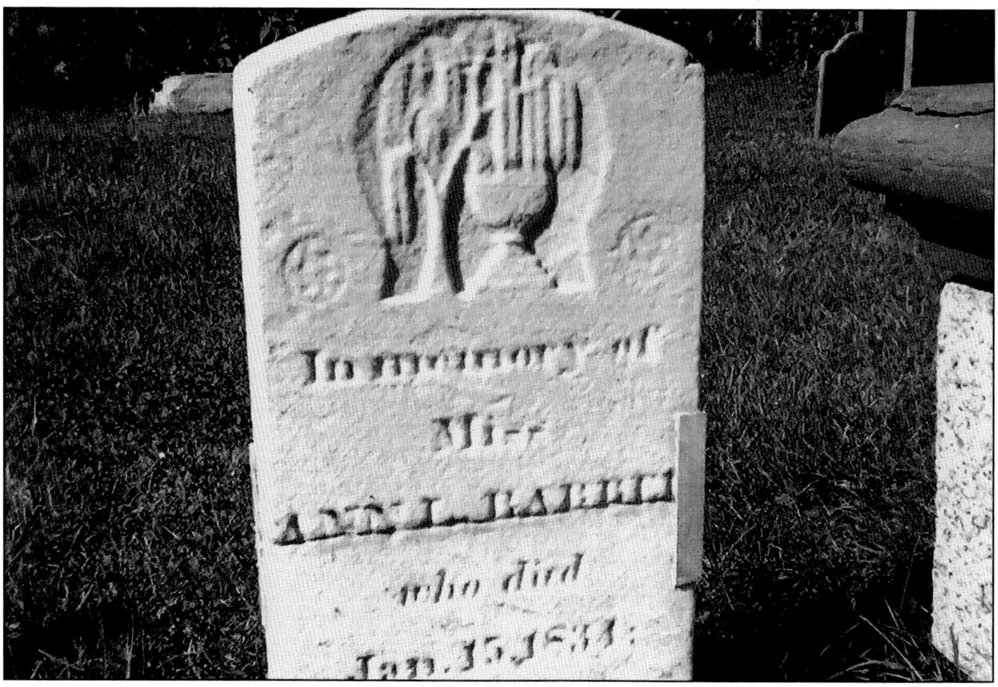

Ann Barrell, 1834, Pleasant Street. Ann, by reason of her title "Miss," never married. She was probably the same Miss Barrell who was a private teacher for young ladies in Portsmouth from about 1804 to 1816, tutoring her pupils in reading, grammar, spelling, and the arts of plain and ornamental sewing and needlework, embroidery, and Dresden. Her marble gravestone, with its urn-and-willow motif, was carved by the Treat family.

Maria Coues, 1797, Pleasant Street. Maria's parents, Capt. Peter Coues and his third wife, Rebecca Elliot Coues, had 13 children, most of whom died young. Like many young girls, Maria learned the art of needlework early. Still extant is a sampler she stitched at age seven in 1795, decorated with her name, a pair of flowering trees, and some verse. Her stone was carved by Daniel Hastings of Newton, Massachusetts.

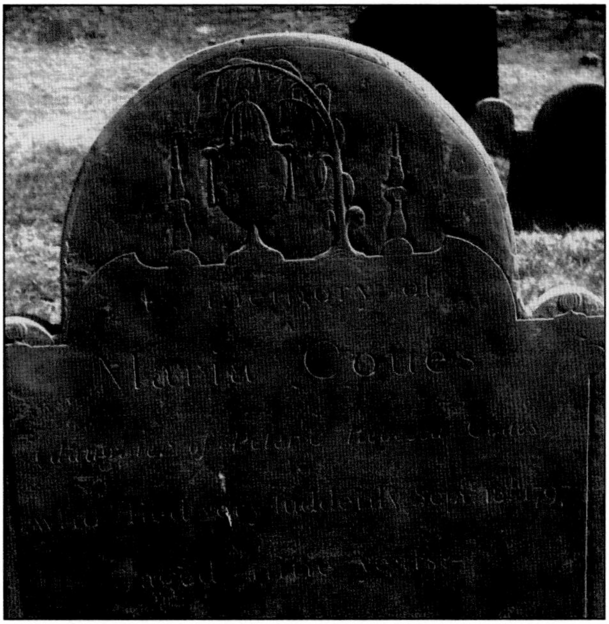

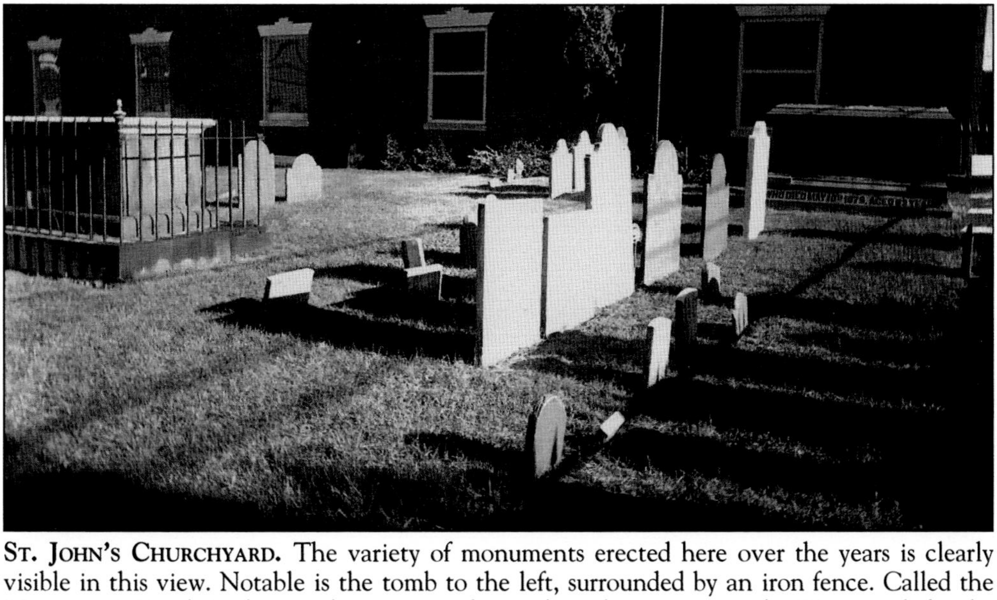

St. John's Churchyard. The variety of monuments erected here over the years is clearly visible in this view. Notable is the tomb to the left, surrounded by an iron fence. Called the "Governor's Tomb," it houses the remains of several royal governors in the Wentworth family. When this tomb was opened around 1809, the coffins were found intact, decorated with coats of arms, lions, and unicorns, and inside one was a sword.

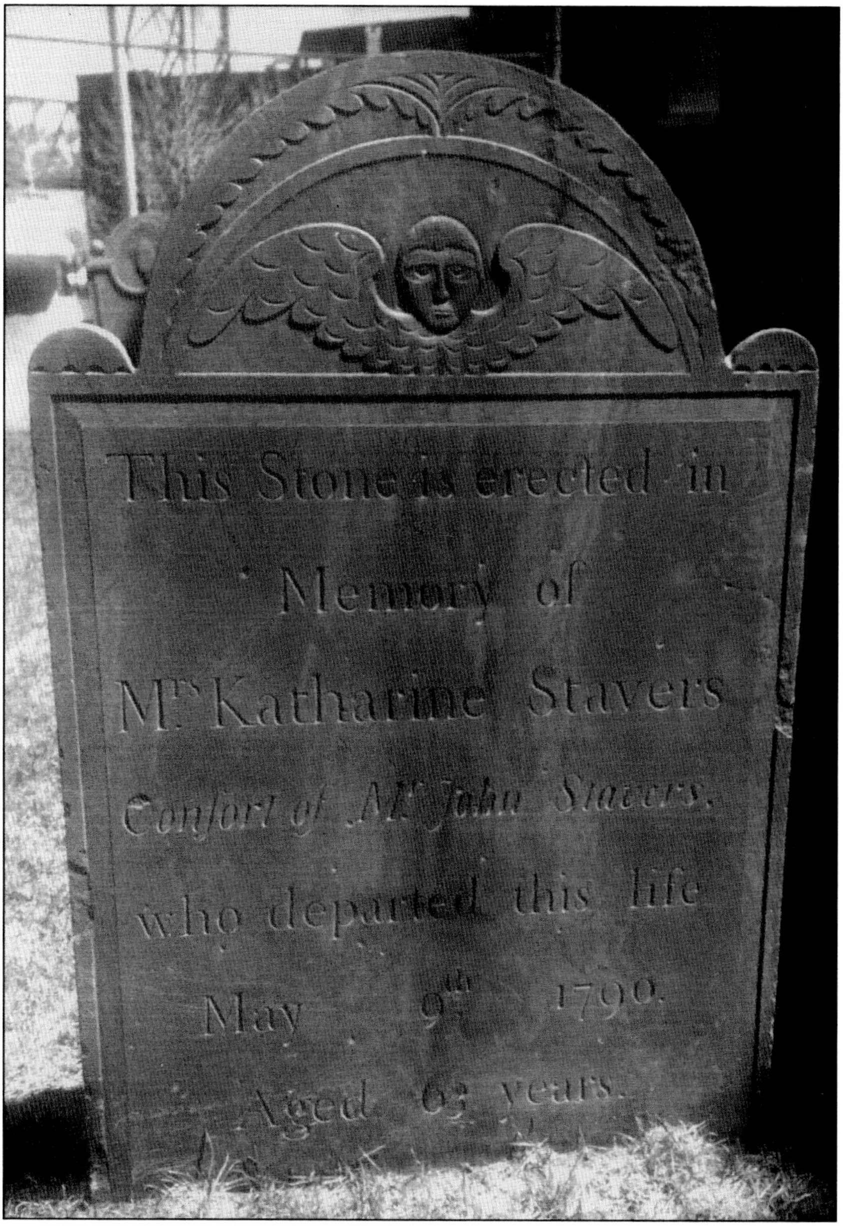

KATHARINE STAVERS, 1790, ST. JOHN'S. Katharine, whose gravestone was carved by Daniel Hastings, was the wife of famous Portsmouth innkeeper John Stavers. An Englishman by birth, he came to America around 1750 and served as a mariner on local vessels. He later went ashore and established the Earl of Halifax Inn on Queen Street. As business grew and the Portsmouth Flying Stage Coach was established with service to Boston, the inn was moved to a larger building on Pitt Street. Katharine was Staver's second wife and was born locally. She and her husband, along with their children and a number of slaves, ran the inn and experienced tumultuous times during the Revolutionary War. In 1775, Stavers's English heritage made him a suspected Tory, and mob violence erupted at his hotel, forcing him to flee Portsmouth. Upon his return, he was jailed, but no doubt helped by his American wife, he willingly took an oath of allegiance to the American cause and changed the name of his inn to the William Pitt Tavern.

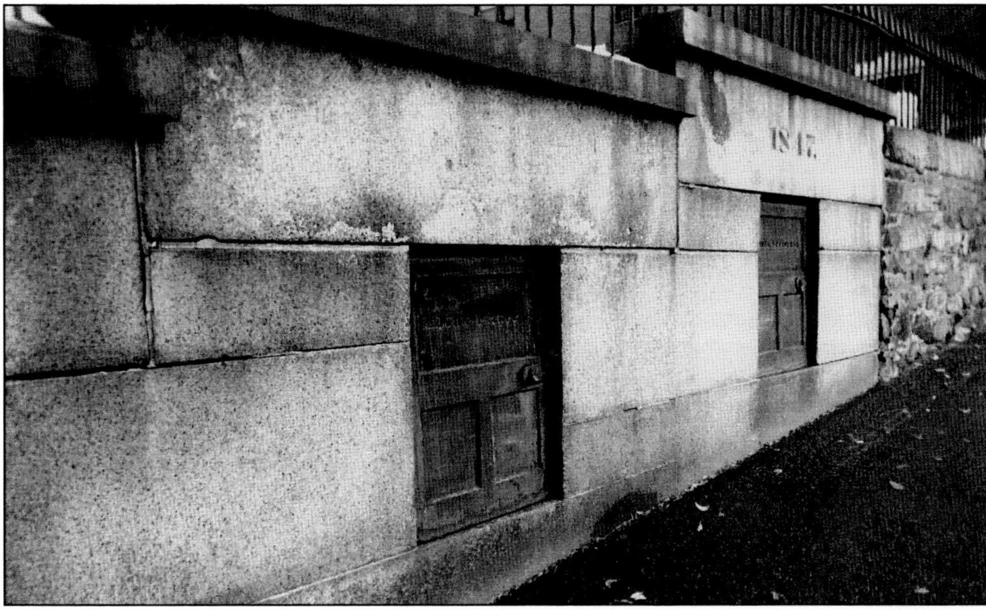

The Peirce and Wentworth Vaults, St. John's. Driving on Chapel Street today, one cannot help but notice these large iron doors. Placed here when the new wall around St. John's was built in 1847, they mark the site of the underground burial vaults. When the wall was built, these tombs were briefly exposed, and some were found to be large, containing the remains of nearly 100 people.

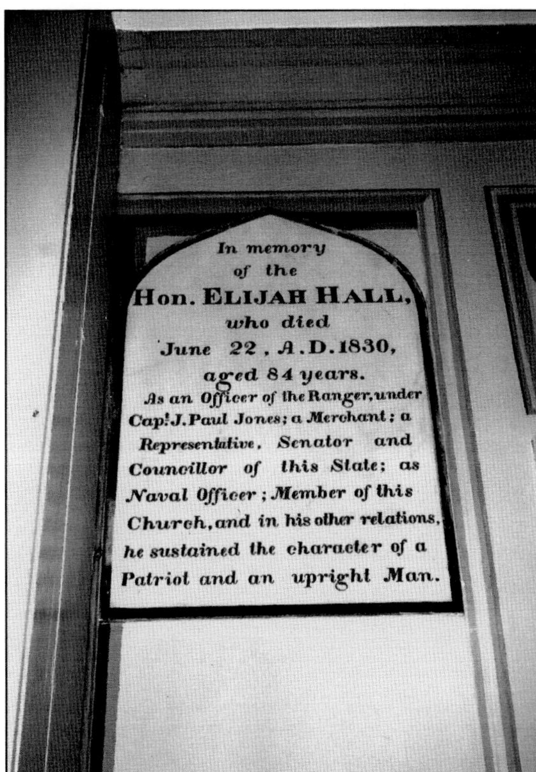

The Elijah Hall Memorial, 1830, St. John's. Some of those who are interred in the underground vaults are memorialized on the walls inside the church itself. When Capt. John Paul Jones and his crew of the *Ranger* captured the HMS *Drake* in the Irish Sea during the Revolutionary War, Hall became her prize commander. (Photograph by Margaret Morrissey; courtesy of Louise Tallman.)

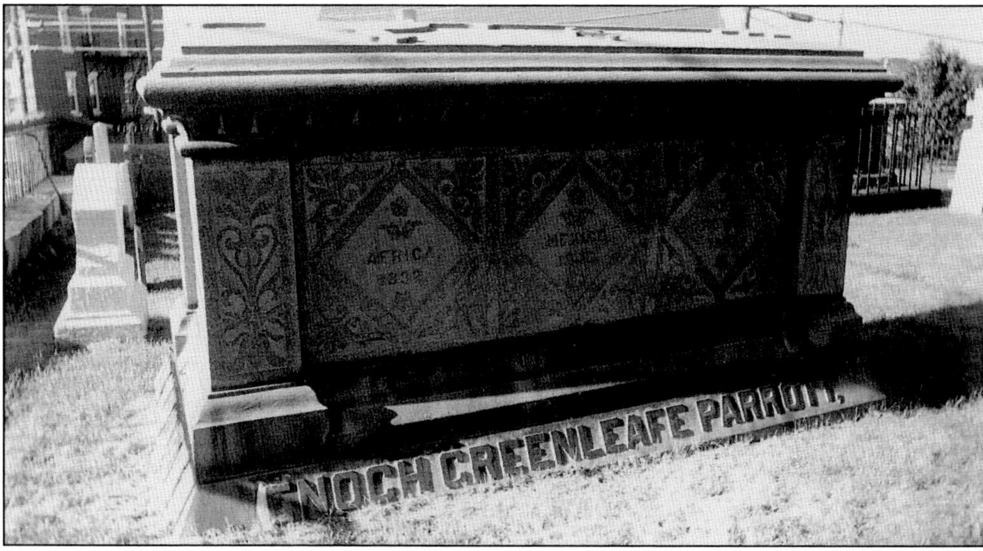

Enoch Greenleafe Parrott, 1879, St. John's. This impressive granite tomb befits the service of this Portsmouth naval officer. A graduate of the Naval Academy, Parrott became a midshipman in December 1831 and soon saw service in Africa. The diamond-shaped designs on his tomb detail his service in various places such as Africa, Mexico, and Port Royal. As the Civil War began, Parrott commanded the new ironclad *Canonicus* in 1863. He served in the Atlantic during the war, a large part of his operations being with the blockade squadrons. In January 1865, Parrot's ship took part in the renewed attack on Fort Fisher in North Carolina, being hit 36 times by enemy fire. In February, Parrot captured the steamer *Deer* trying to run the blockade. After the war, Parrott rose to the rank of commodore and rear admiral and retired from the navy in 1874. By all accounts, he was "a Brave and Loyal Officer," as is carved on his tomb (below).

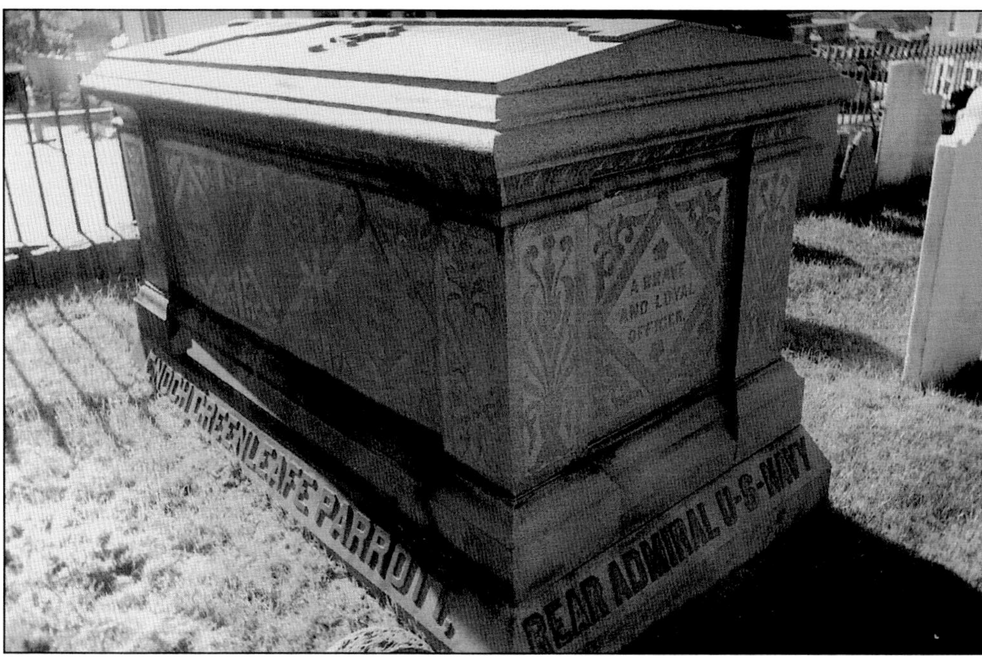

Three

North and Union Cemeteries

North Cemetery is the second oldest of Portsmouth's public burying grounds. It was established in 1753, when the town purchased the land from Col. John Hart, later a commander of a New Hampshire regiment during the French and Indian War, for £150. Placed on the National Register of Historic Places in 1978, North Cemetery is one of the most historic sites in the area for several reasons. The first is the number of prominent men buried here who played an important part in New Hampshire history. These include Gen. William Whipple, an officer during the Revolution and a signer of the Declaration of Independence, and Gov. John Langdon, a signer of the Constitution. Other notables include Dr. Hall Jackson and Capt. Thomas Thompson, commander of the Continental navy frigate *Raleigh*. However, an equally important reason this site is so special is that it reflects Portsmouth's diversity at an early stage of its growth. Buried here are not just the town's important residents of the day, Caucasian and Protestant, but those who gave to Portsmouth the beginnings of the diversity it enjoys today. Within these walls may be found the final resting place of the town's first Jewish resident, Abraham Isaac, as well as Dominick Peduzzi, a man who belonged to the first Roman Catholic parish in the city. Equally telling, though often overlooked, is the fact that a portion of North Cemetery was segregated for the town's early African American residents. While most of the graves for these individuals, many slaves or former slaves, are unmarked, several still remain for such individuals as Prince Whipple, a soldier in the Revolution, his daughter Esther Whipple Mullineaux, and Pomp and Candace Spring.

Less well known is North Cemetery's neighbor, Union Cemetery. Established in 1847, it is often confused as being part of North Cemetery. Though diminutive in size, Union Cemetery is also important. Its monumental sculpture, elegant fencing separating individual family plots, and parklike setting were all features of the rural cemetery movement that started in Boston. In addition, the gravestones and monuments within Union Cemetery are in stark contrast to those found in North Cemetery. Most are made of white marble or limestone and many have a floral motif characteristic of Victorian influences. Important individuals buried here include the family of noted author Thomas Bailey Aldrich, and two of the town's most renowned clipper ship builders. Situated in a waterfront location and once across the way from the elegant Boyd-Raynes Mansion and shipyard, Union was once one of the most beautiful cemeteries in town. Now in poor condition, the Mayor's Blue Ribbon Cemetery Committee has laid the foundation for the restoration of the cemetery by 2007.

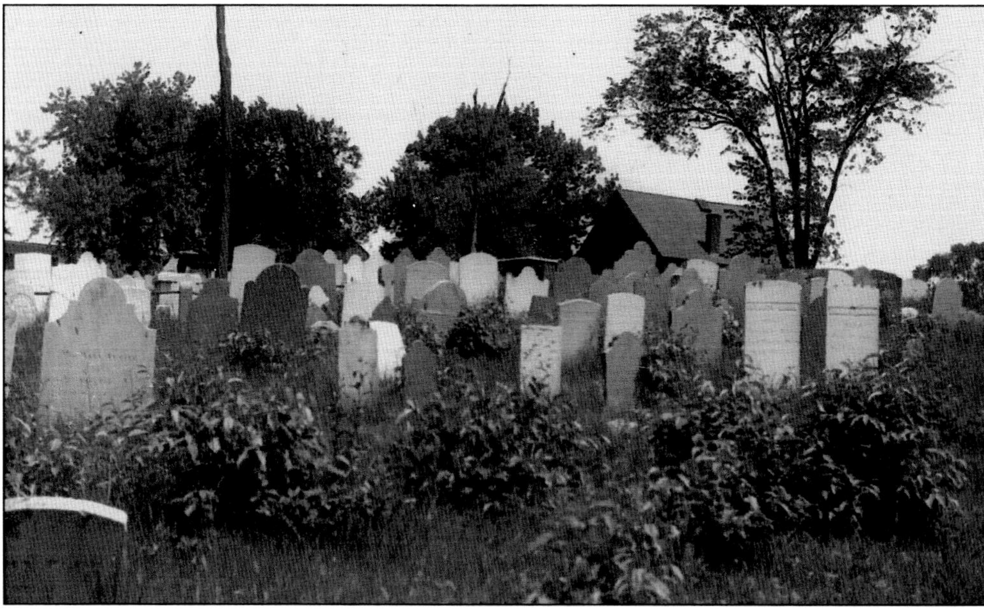

NORTH CEMETERY, 1942. For many years, most of Portsmouth's old burial grounds no longer in active use were sadly neglected, North Cemetery included. This photograph was taken on June 6, 1942, after it had recently been vandalized. Compare this view with the North Cemetery of today, shown on the cover of this book. (Photograph by A. I. Harriman; courtesy of Louise Tallman.)

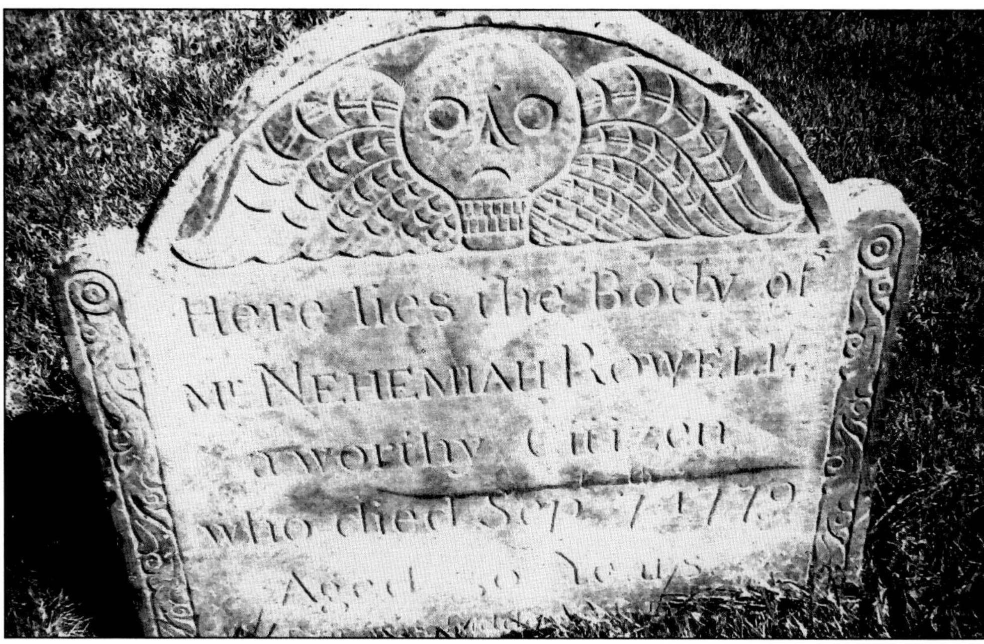

NEHEMIAH ROWELL, 1779, NORTH CEMETERY. Gravestones with the winged-skull motif, usually with a forlorn look, experienced a brief revival during the years of the American Revolution. During this time of economic and political upheaval, "amidst the rage of noise and war," as stated on some gravestones themselves, the public mood was often one of doubt and fear. Note that Rowell's stone calls attention to his standing as a "worthy citizen."

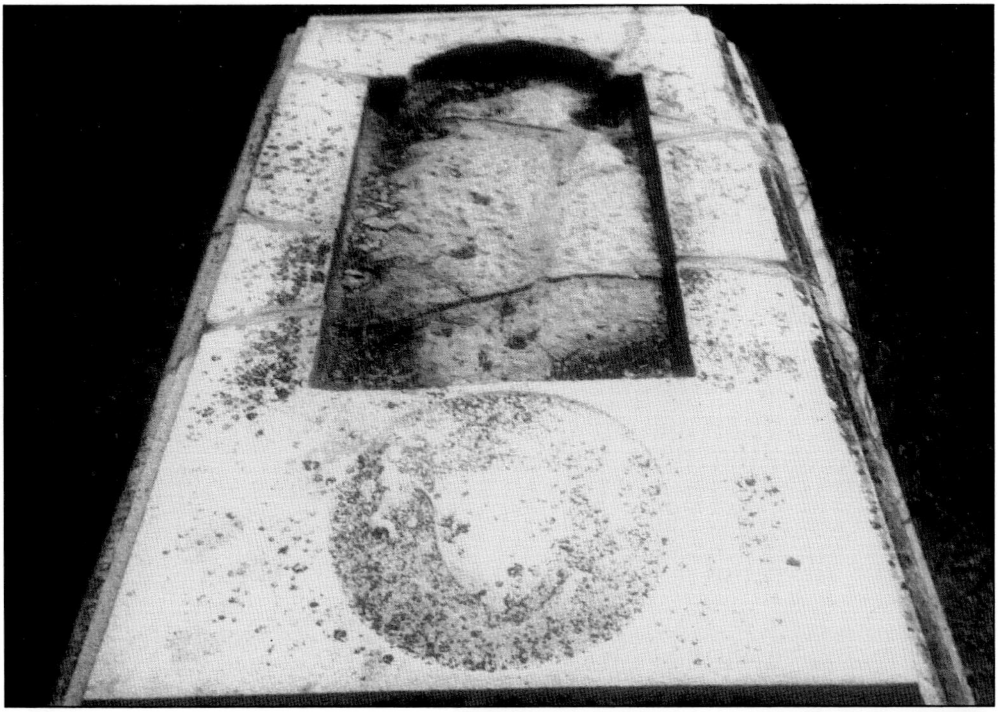

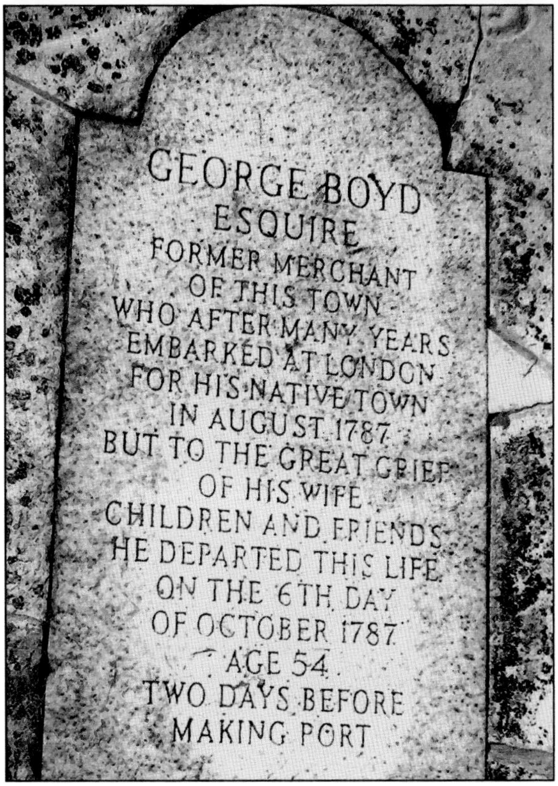

George Boyd, 1787, North Cemetery. George Boyd rose from humble beginnings, first serving as houseboy to merchant Henry Sherburne and working at a ropewalk. Within a few years, he had risen to merchant and shipbuilder, becoming one of the most prolific builders on the Piscataqua River. However, this activity took its toll, and he wrote that building so many new ships was "enough to break the heart of a stone, so much fatigue." With the Revolutionary War approaching, Boyd wanted to preserve his business by remaining neutral; he departed for London in 1774, leaving behind his wife, Jane, and children. At the war's end, Boyd sailed home in August 1787, carrying his table stone, made in England with a blank inset. As his monument states (at right, a replacement for the lost original), he died on the boat within two days' reach of Portsmouth.

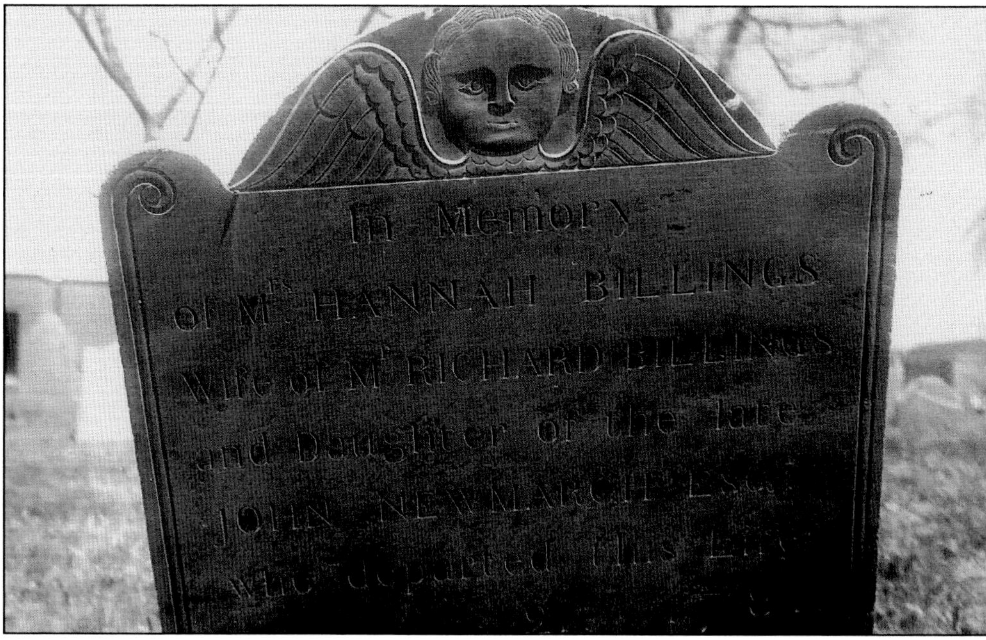

HANNAH BILLINGS, 1781, NORTH CEMETERY. This angel, with its stern visage, was carved for the daughter of prominent merchant John Newmarch. He purchased part of the first South Church meetinghouse and moved it to what is now Congress Street. Hannah and her merchant husband, Richard, once a clerk for John Hancock in Boston, later lived there.

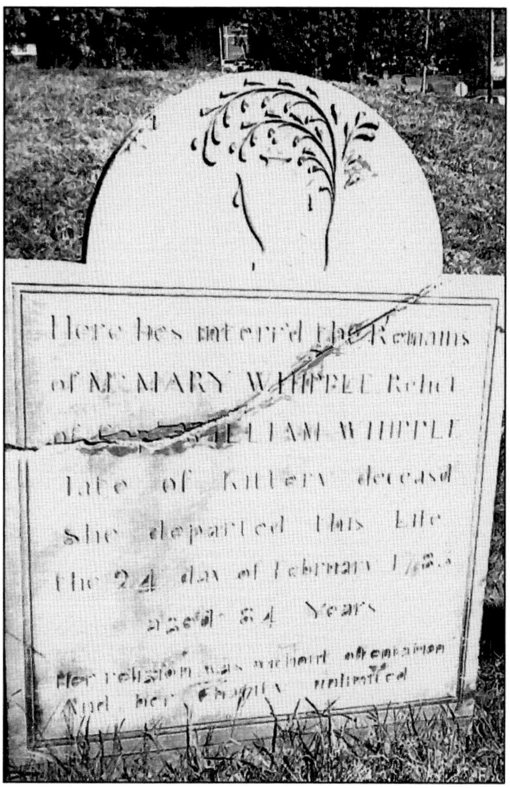

MARY WHIPPLE, 1785, NORTH CEMETERY. Mary was the daughter of Portsmouth merchant John Moffat. Her husband, William Whipple, was a merchant, slave trader, and sea captain who played a prominent part in the American Revolution in New Hampshire. Interestingly, Mary's gravestone, carved by John Homer, uses the title of captain for her husband, rather than his rank of general. Her epitaph reads, "Her religion was without ostentation And her Charity unlimited."

CLARISSA AND ANDREW MCINTIRE, 1791, NORTH CEMETERY. The fragility of childhood life in the 18th century is demonstrated by this gravestone for the McIntire children. Neil McIntire was a tobacconist in Portsmouth for many years. The use of a winged skull, especially for children, at this late date may be indicative of the shock and grief experienced by Neil and Mary at the loss of their infants.

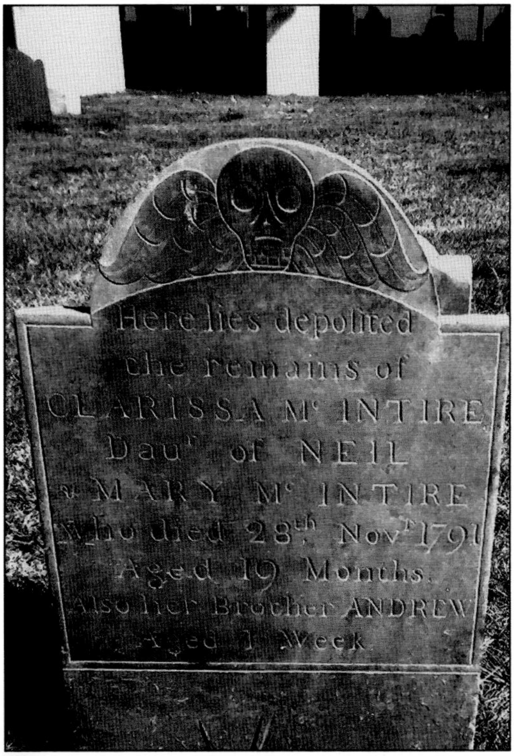

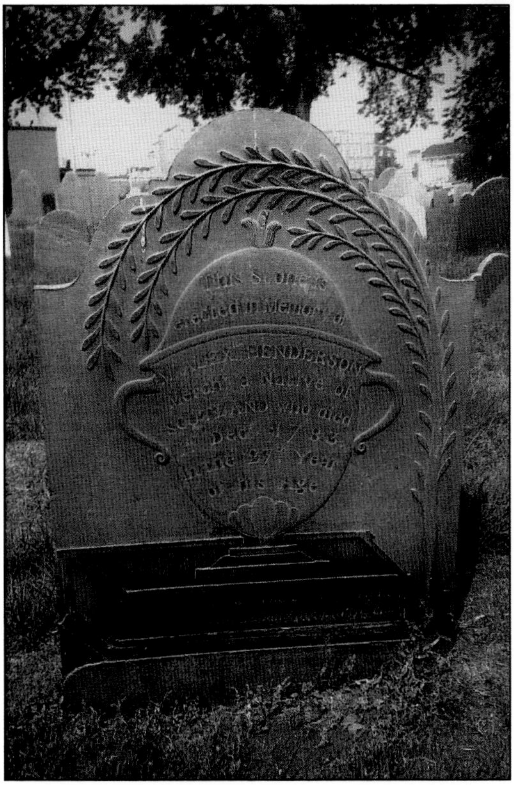

ALEXANDER HENDERSON, 1783, NORTH CEMETERY. This "Native of Scotland" was related to Portsmouth merchant Hugh Henderson, a dealer in English and West Indian goods around the time of the Revolution. The Hendersons were tied to the well-known Sheafe family by marriage. Because of their foreign birth, they were suspected of being Royalists during the war, a charge that proved unfounded. This striking stone was carved by John Homer of Boston.

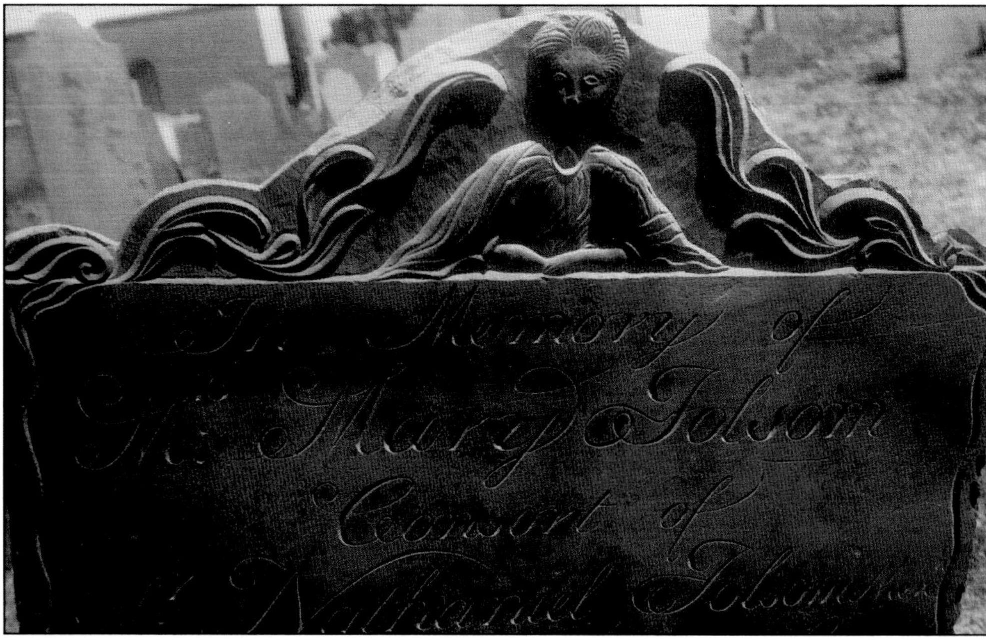

MARY FOLSOM, 1782, NORTH CEMETERY. This gravestone is a beautiful example of the portrait style, intended as an idealized likeness of the deceased. Note the finely coiffed hair and tiny hand. Gravestones like this could only be afforded by the wealthy. Mary was the daughter of Portsmouth innkeeper James Stoodley. She married merchant and ship owner Nathaniel Folsom in 1771, and the wealth he accumulated from his privateering enterprises during the American Revolution no doubt helped to pay for his wife's marker.

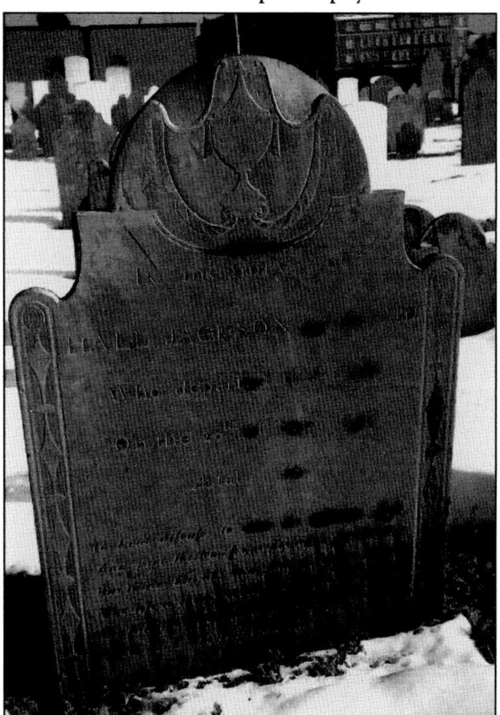

HALL JACKSON, 1797, NORTH CEMETERY. Dr. Hall Jackson, whose gravestone carver was Daniel Hastings, made important contributions to both the political and medical arenas in Portsmouth. He was a staunch supporter of the American cause during the Revolution and commanded an artillery regiment. However, Jackson's greatest contribution was his work in introducing the drug digitalis to American medicine, a drug still used today to treat those with heart ailments.

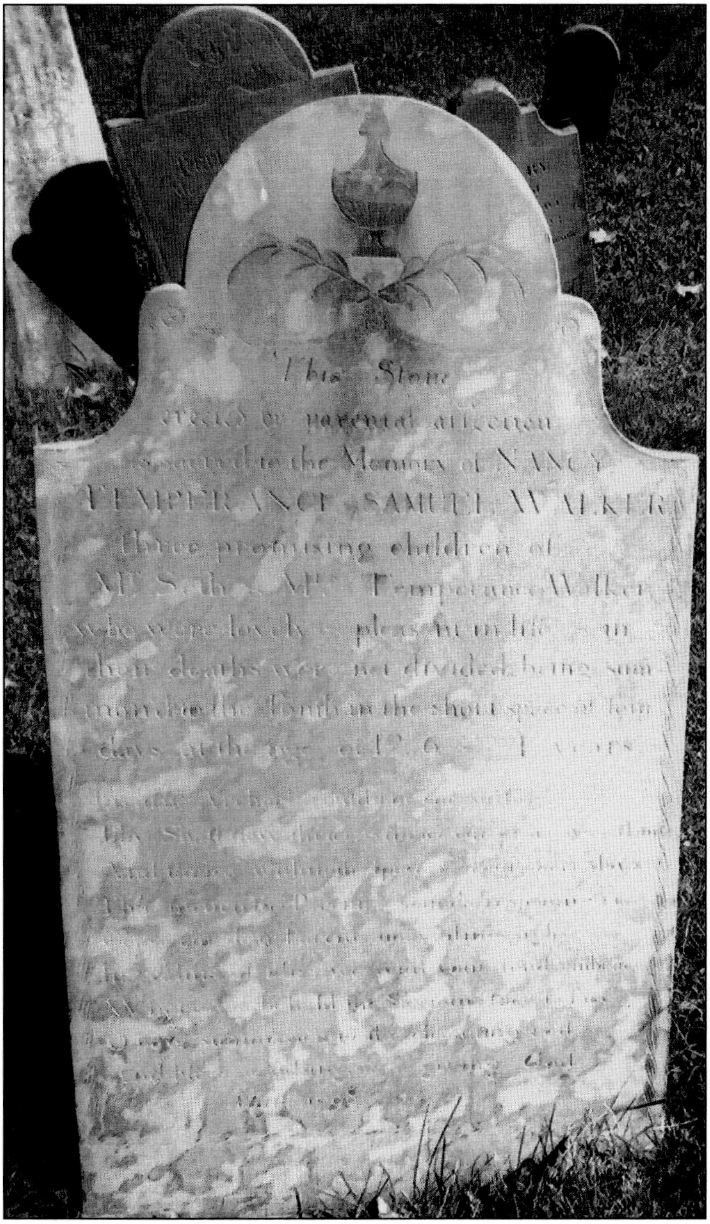

THE WALKER CHILDREN, 1798, NORTH CEMETERY. This gravestone is surely one of the most heart-wrenching in all of Portsmouth, detailing the deaths of Nancy, Temperance, and Samuel, the children of Seth and Temperance Walker, in March 1798. These "three promising children . . . who were lovely & pleasant in life & in their deaths were not divided: being summoned to the Tomb in the short space of four days: at the age of 12, 6 & 4 years." The parents' grief comes through clearly in the extensive epitaph, which was carved by Bartlett Adams while in Portsmouth and reads as follows: "Insatiate Archer could not one suffice? Thy Shaft flew thrice & thrice our peace was slain. And thrice within the space of four short days Thus mourn the Parents; sounds responsive rise. Cease our dear Parents sighs. In realms of bliss we wait your fond embrace; Where we behold the Saviour face to face. O bow submission to the chastising rod, And bless a taking as a giving God." The cause of the sudden deaths is unknown.

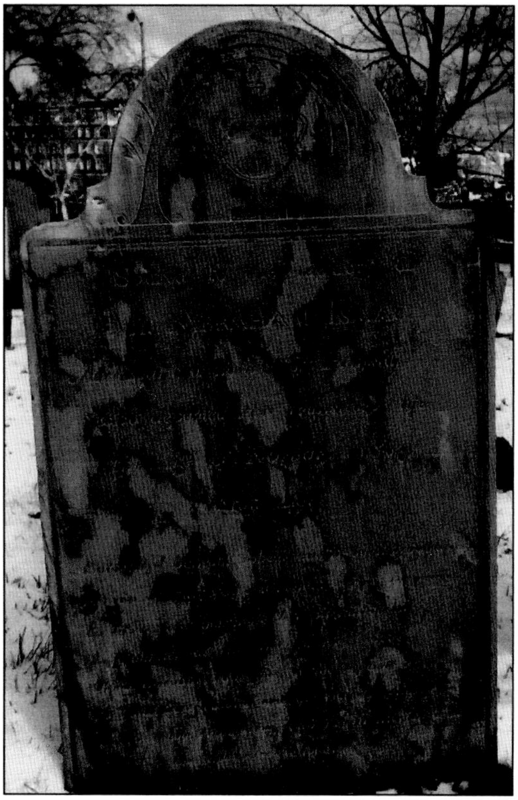

ABRAHAM ISAAC, 1803, NORTH CEMETERY. Isaac is important in Portsmouth history as the first Jewish settler in town. Tradition describes him as orthodox, always closing his shop on Saturdays, the Jewish day of worship. Because there was no established temple in town, he worshiped at home. Isaac's store, "at the sign of the Golden Tea-Pot," according to an October 31, 1795, *Oracle of the Day* advertisement (below), sold a wide variety of items from feathers to crockery. He was highly regarded by his fellow townsmen, and his gravestone (left) was carved locally by John Marble. The fact that Isaac's epitaph was written by local poet Jonathan Mitchell Sewall speaks volumes about his character. It reads, "A son of faithful Abra'm sleeps in peace. . . . Through various toils his active spirit ran, A faithful steward and an honest man."

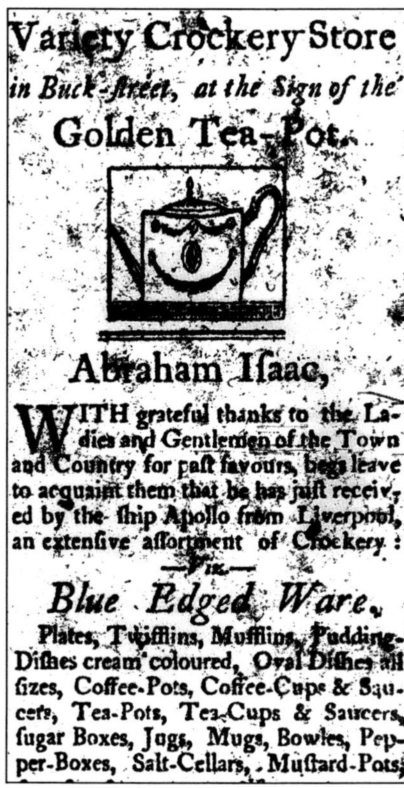

Variety Crockery Store
in Buck-ſtreet, at the Sign of the
Golden Tea-Pot.

Abraham Iſaac,

WITH grateful thanks to the Ladies and Gentlemen of the Town and Country for paſt favours, begs leave to acquaint them that he has juſt received by the ſhip Apollo from Liverpool, an extenſive aſſortment of Crockery:

—Viz.—

Blue Edged Ware.

Plates, Twifflins, Mufflins, Pudding-Diſhes cream coloured, Oval Diſhes all ſizes, Coffee-Pots, Coffee-Cups & Saucers, Tea-Pots, Tea-Cups & Saucers, ſugar Boxes, Jugs, Mugs, Bowles, Pepper-Boxes, Salt-Cellars, Muſtard-Pots,

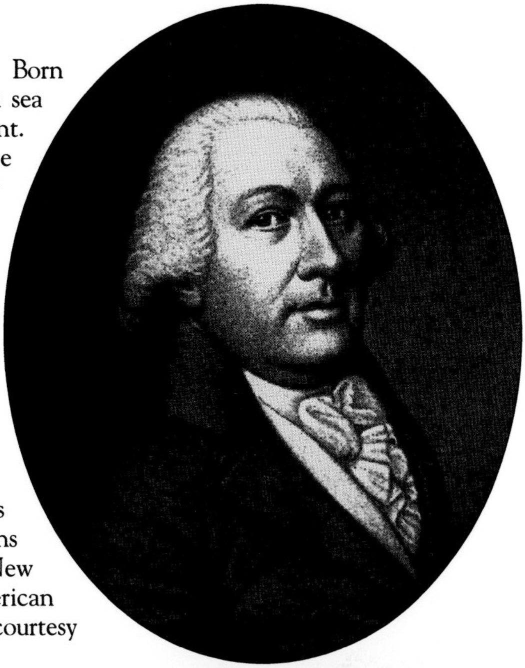

John Langdon, 1819, North Cemetery. Born in Portsmouth in 1741, Langdon was first a sea captain and then a ship owner and merchant. During the Revolution, he served as marine agent for the state and was responsible for building the frigate *Raleigh*. He also served in the military, heading his own militia units at Saratoga and Rhode Island. Langdon later became president of New Hampshire, signer of the Constitution, U.S. senator (1789–1801), and governor of New Hampshire (1810–1812). One of the most respected men of his day, he counted among his friends and admirers Thomas Jefferson and George Washington. His modest tomb (below) looks neglected in this 1942 view and is much the same today. Plans for its restoration are now under way by the New Hampshire Society of the Sons of the American Revolution. (Photograph by A. I. Harriman; courtesy of Louise Tallman.)

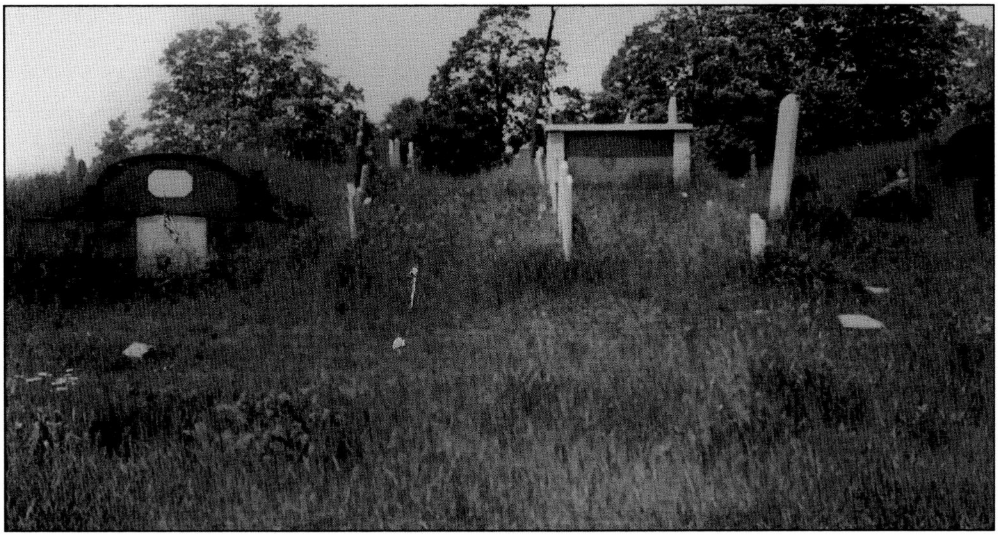

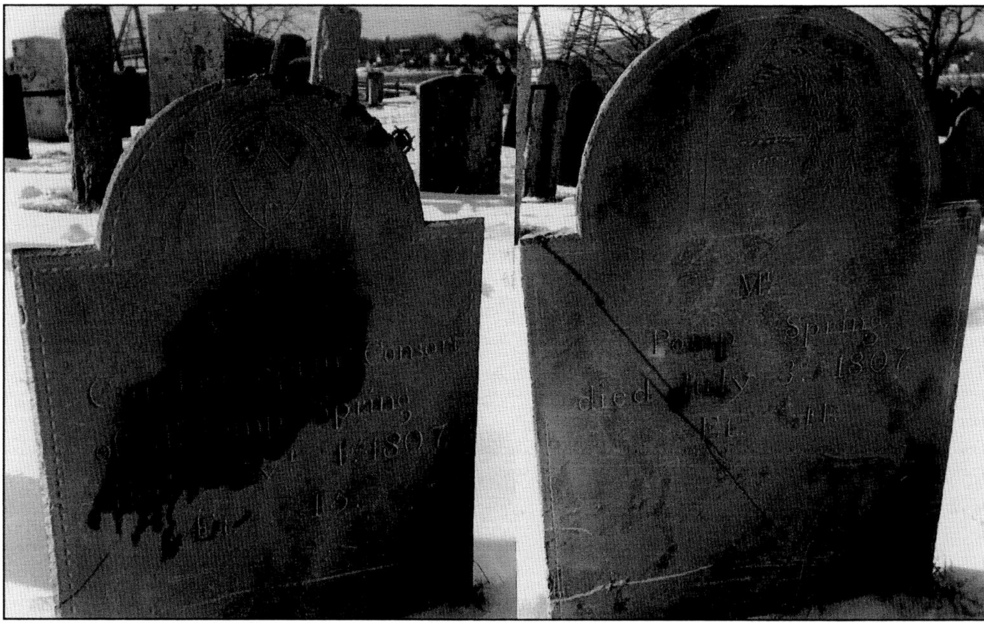

POMP AND CANDACE SPRING, 1807, NORTH CEMETERY. Pomp Spring married Candace Wentworth in November 1793. This free black couple, both former slaves, owned a house on Church Lane in Portsmouth, where Pomp established his own business as a baker. Together, they were part of the town's thriving African American community. Pomp's high regard is demonstrated by his position as president of the African Society.

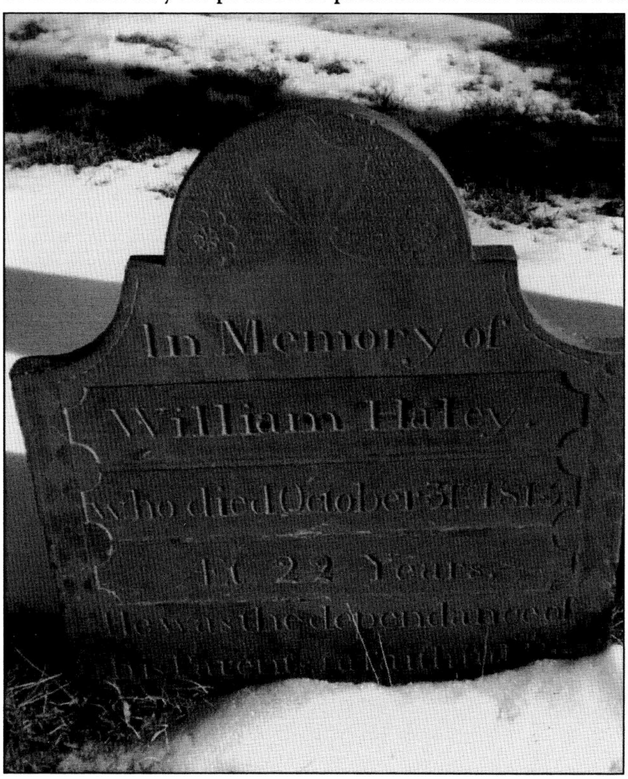

WILLIAM HALEY, 1815, NORTH CEMETERY. This attractive stone, with its urn-and-flower motif, bears interesting diamond-patterned borders. Likely carved by Samuel Treat, the epitaph reads, "He was the dependence of his Parents & a faithful Brother." Note that Treat misjudged the space he had to work with, and that the "other" part of the word "Brother" was carved in smaller letters between the two lines.

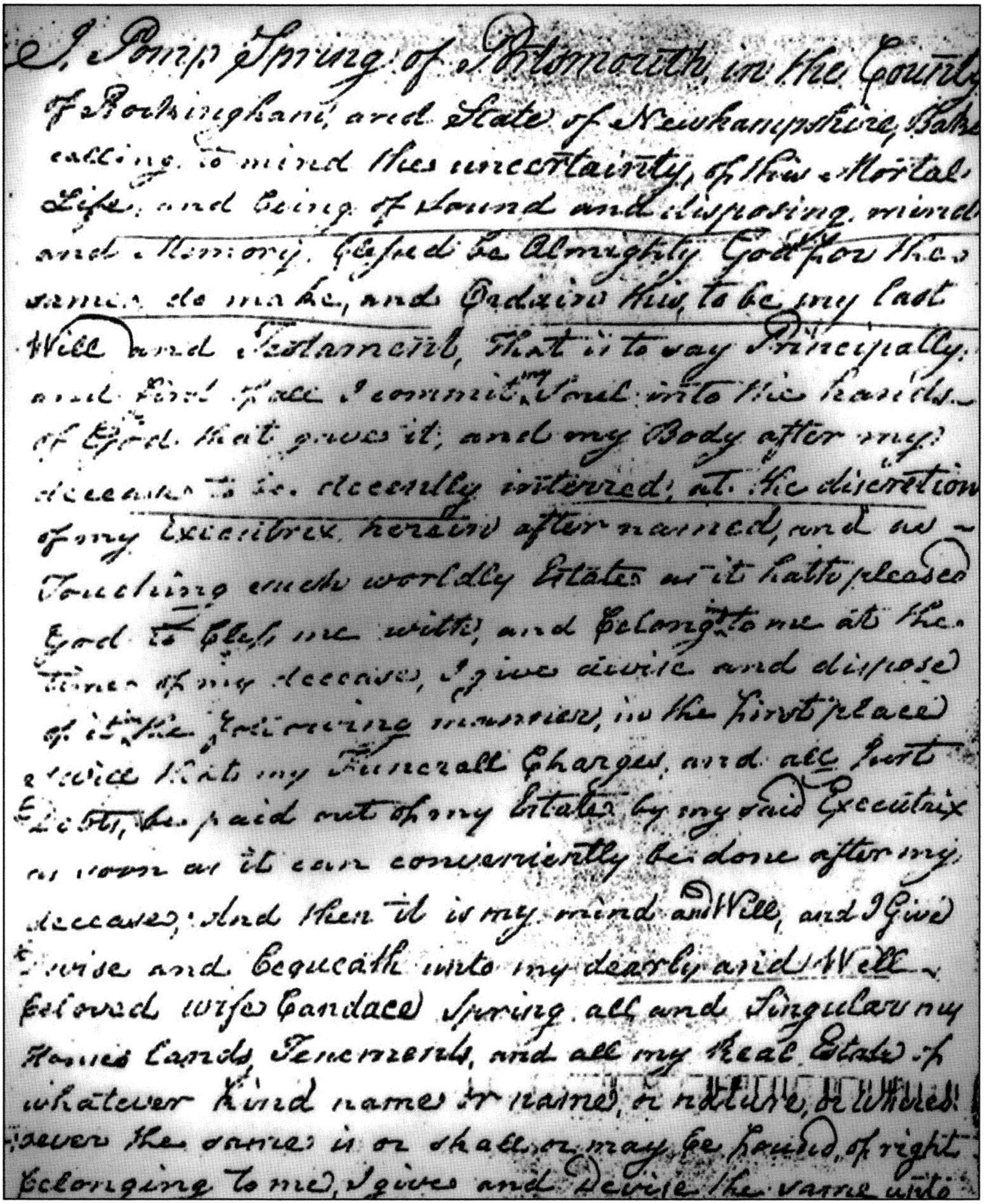

I, Pomp Spring of Portsmouth in the County
of Rockingham, and State of Newhampshire, Baker
calling to mind the uncertainty of this Mortal
Life, and being of sound and disposing mind
and Memory, Blessed be Almighty God for the
same, do make and ordain this to be my last
Will and Testament, That is to say Principally
and first of all I commit my Soul into the hands
of God that gives it; and my Body after my
decease to be decently interred; at the discretion
of my Executrix hereinafter named, and as
Touching such worldly Estates as it hath pleased
God to bless me with; and belong to me at the
time of my decease, I give devise and dispose
of it in the following manner, in the first place
I device that my Funerall Charges and all Just
Debts, be paid out of my Estate by my said Executrix
as soon as it can conveniently be done after my
decease; And then it is my mind and Will, and I Give
devise and bequeath unto my dearly and Well
beloved wife Candace Spring all and Singular my
Houses Lands Tenements, and all my Real Estate of
whatever kind name or nature, or wheresoever
the same is or shall or may be found, of right
belonging to me, I give and devise the same unto

Pomp Spring's Will, 1807. This will is rare for the time. Life was difficult for free African Americans, and few who had gained their freedom had enough holdings to record a will. Pomp Spring, however, aided by his wife, Candace, was a successful baker and homeowner. This document is telling; the first practical matters Pomp addressed were that his body was "to be decently interred" and that "my Funerall Charges and all Just Debts" be paid "as soon as it can conveniently be done after my decease." Spring was undoubtedly aware that many in Portsmouth's African American community were not "decently interred," lacking gravestones to mark their final resting place. His wishes for both himself and his wife, who died four months later, were followed by the administrator of their estate, Caesar Whidden. Their stones (see previous page) were likely carved by Samuel Treat. (From Rockingham County Probate Records, Reel 18, No. 7780.)

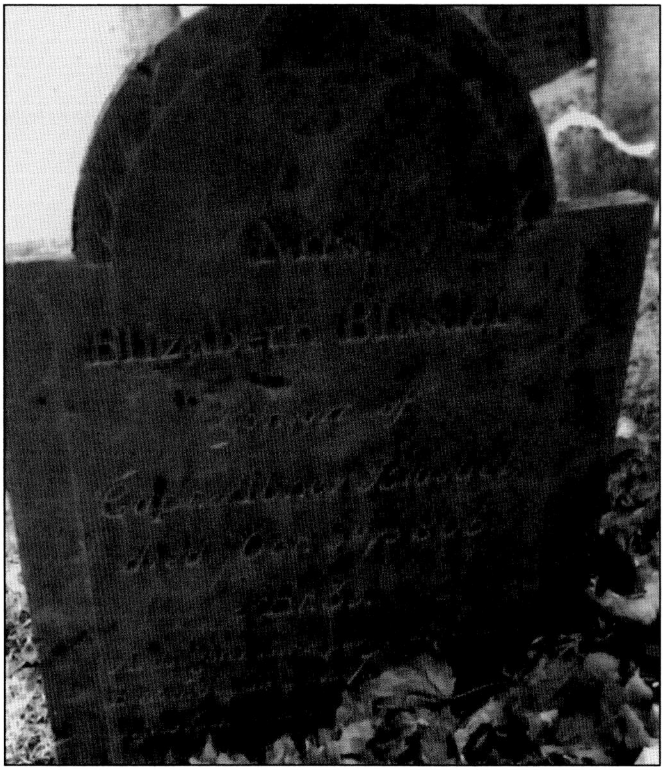

ELIZABETH BLASDELL, 1805, NORTH CEMETERY. This stone for the wife of Captain Blasdell (often spelled Blaisdell) was carved by John Marble. It displays his oft used half-circle side borders and ropelike edging at the top. More unusual is the sunburst disk at the top. Blasdell, probably a former ship captain, operated a grocery on Spring Hill, very close to where Marble's shop was located, and was possibly well acquainted with the carver.

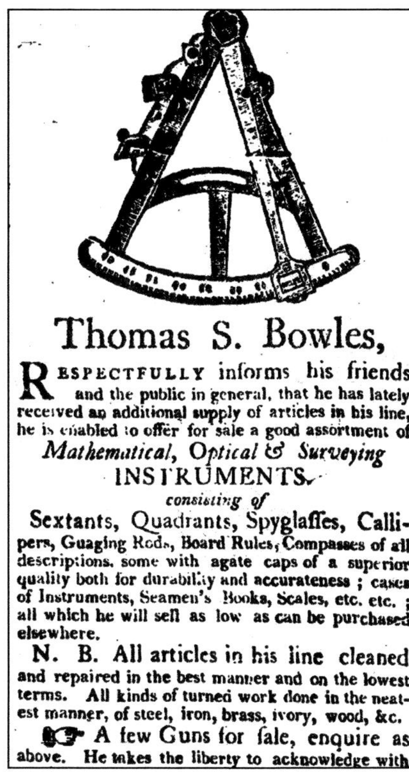

Thomas S. Bowles,

RESPECTFULLY informs his friends and the public in general, that he has lately received an additional supply of articles in his line, he is enabled to offer for sale a good assortment of

Mathematical, Optical & Surveying
INSTRUMENTS,
consisting of

Sextants, Quadrants, Spyglaſſes, Callipers, Guaging Rods, Board Rules, Compasses of all descriptions, some with agate caps of a superior quality both for durability and accurateness; cases of Instruments, Seamen's Books, Scales, etc. etc.; all which he will sell as low as can be purchased elsewhere.

N. B. All articles in his line cleaned and repaired in the best manner and on the lowest terms. All kinds of turned work done in the neatest manner, of steel, iron, brass, ivory, wood, &c.

☞ A few Guns for ſale, enquire as above. He takes the liberty to acknowledge with

A THOMAS BOWLES ADVERTISEMENT, 1807. Thomas Bowles was a dealer in a variety of specialized instruments, as indicated by this advertisement that appeared in the June 21, 1807, edition of the *Oracle of the Day*. He was no doubt kept busy both selling and repairing sextants, quadrants, and other nautical instruments in this seafaring town. His wife and child (see next page) are buried in North Cemetery. (Courtesy of the Portsmouth Public Library.)

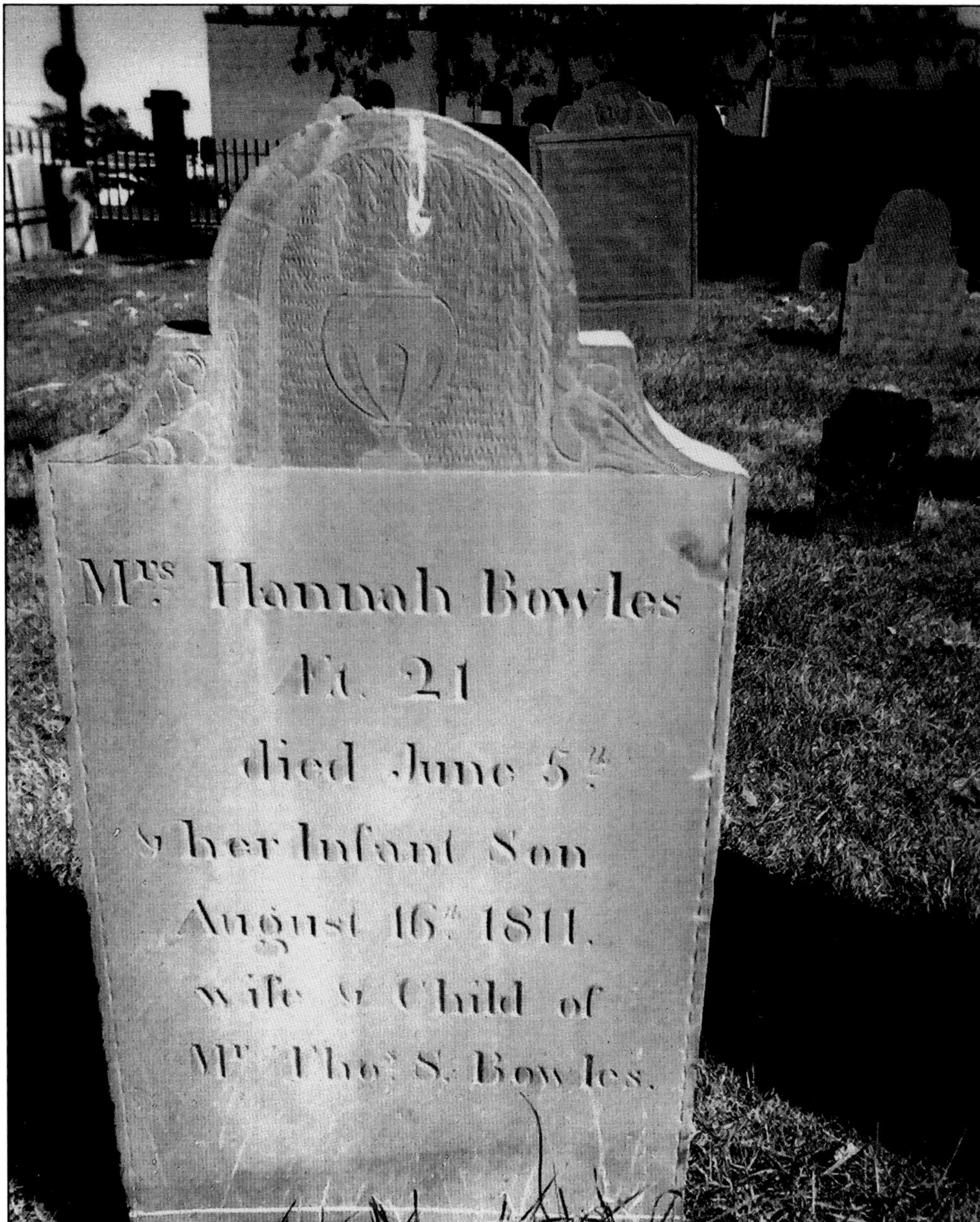

HANNAH BOWLES AND CHILD, 1811, NORTH CEMETERY. This gravestone, likely carved by Samuel Treat, tells the story of an all too common family tragedy. Hannah Bowles likely died from the rigors of childbirth, and her son survived for less than three months. Whether he died from birth complications or another malady is unknown. The deaths of Hannah and her son are symbolized by the floral motifs in the upper corners of the stone. The broken flower bud on the left indicates the two lives cut tragically short, while the flower at right may be interpreted as a symbol of both life's frailty and immortality in the afterlife. The fact that a name for the Bowles infant is absent on this stone is interesting. Because of Thomas Bowles's grief and the business affairs he had to manage, his sickly infant was likely cared for by others, perhaps female relatives. Due to these factors, the infant may never have been named.

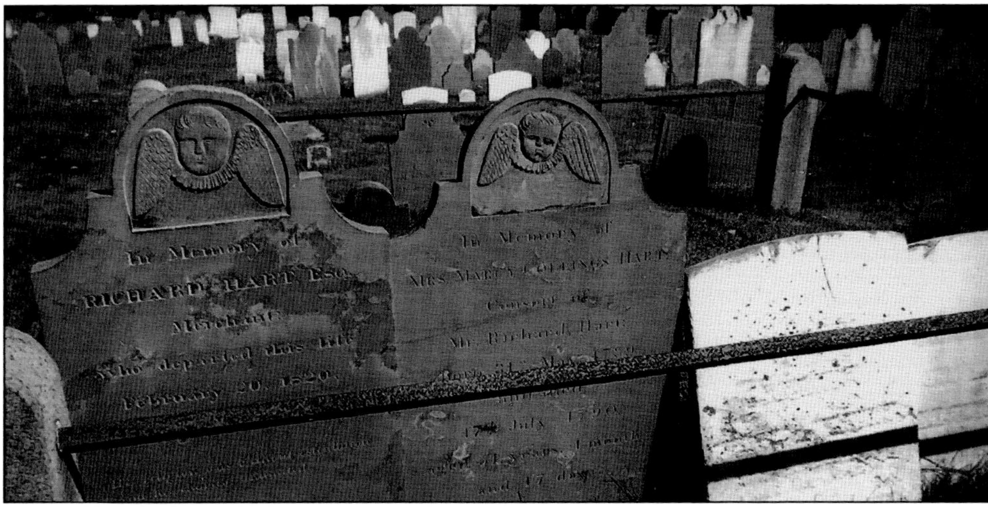

RICHARD, 1820, AND MARY HART, 1790, NORTH CEMETERY. Though widely separated in date, these unusual stones were both carved around 1820, likely by local stonecutter Samuel Treat. Richard Hart was the son of Col. John Hart. The background of Mary Collings Hart is uncertain, but she may have been the daughter of Portsmouth mariner Capt. John Collings.

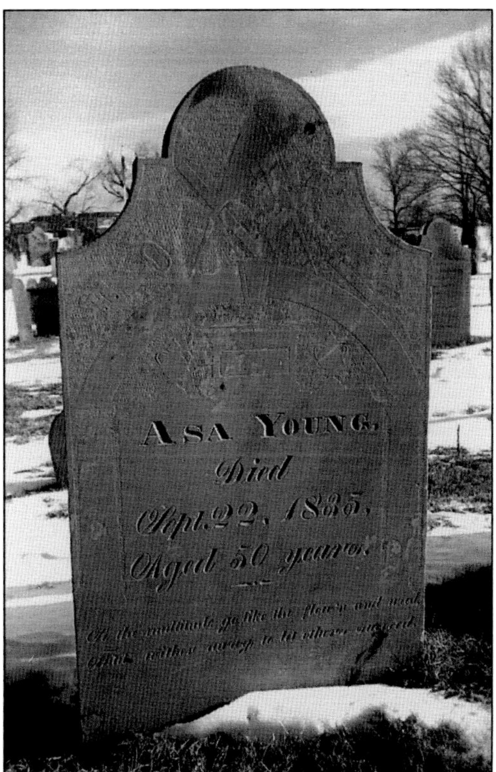

ASA YOUNG, 1835, NORTH CEMETERY. The themes on this gravestone are quite varied. The Masonic emblems, with a large compass and square flanked by a key and square, are unmistakable. Below the keystone and under the compass sits a sarcophagus with a stalk of wheat lying on top. This device is flanked on both sides by urns. The carver of this stone, possibly local, is not positively known.

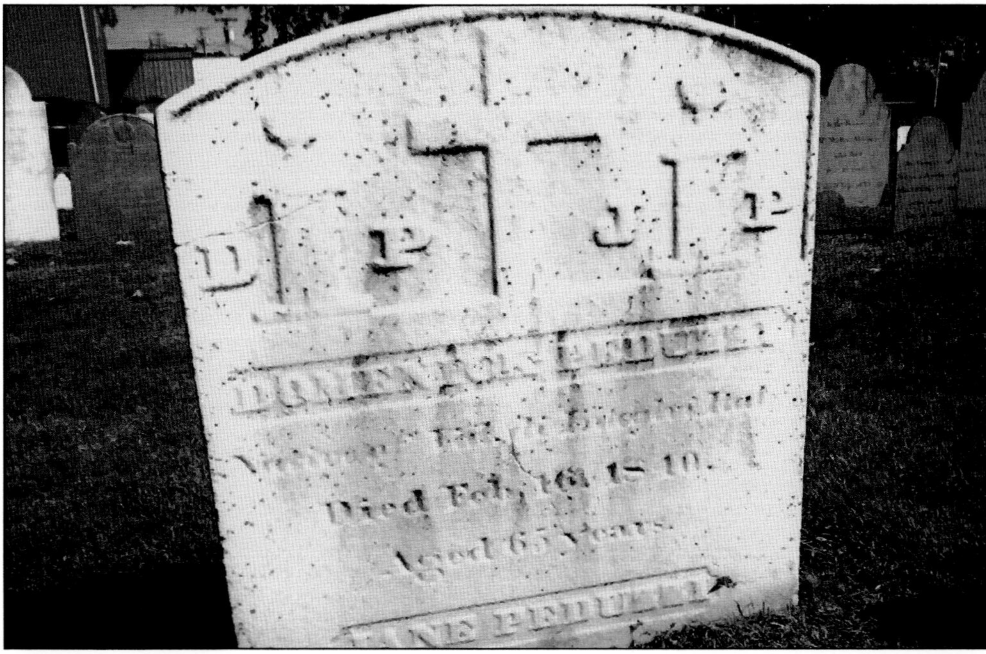

DOMENICK, 1840, AND JANE PEDUZZI, 1811, NORTH CEMETERY. This stone was carved by the Treat family in Portsmouth around 1840. Jane was Domenick's first wife, and his second wife, Margaret, is buried nearby. Peduzzi emigrated from Italy and operated a confectioners shop. At his building on Congress and High Streets, the first services were held for the future St. Mary's Roman Catholic Church.

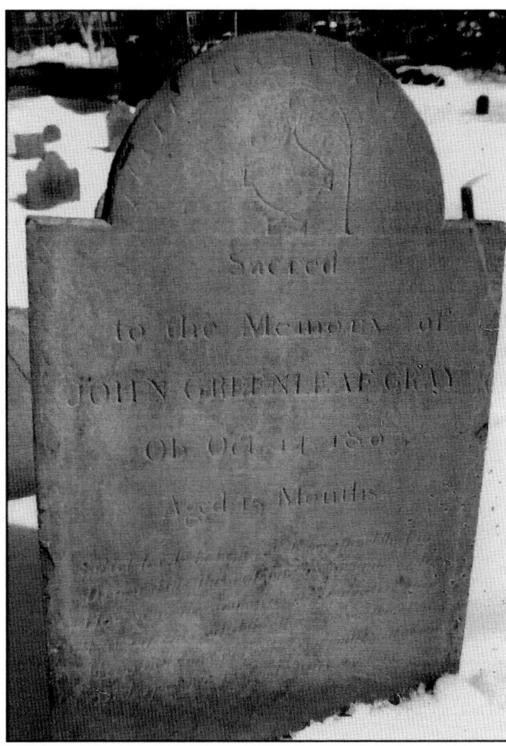

JOHN GRAY, 1803, NORTH CEMETERY. While little is known about the infant for whom this gravestone was made, its creator is interesting. Gray's stone is attributed to carver Levi Maxcy, a native of Attleboro, Massachusetts. Born in 1770, he worked in eastern Massachusetts, later moved to South Carolina, and died at Edisto Island in 1822. His brother Jonathan Maxcy was the first president of the University of South Carolina.

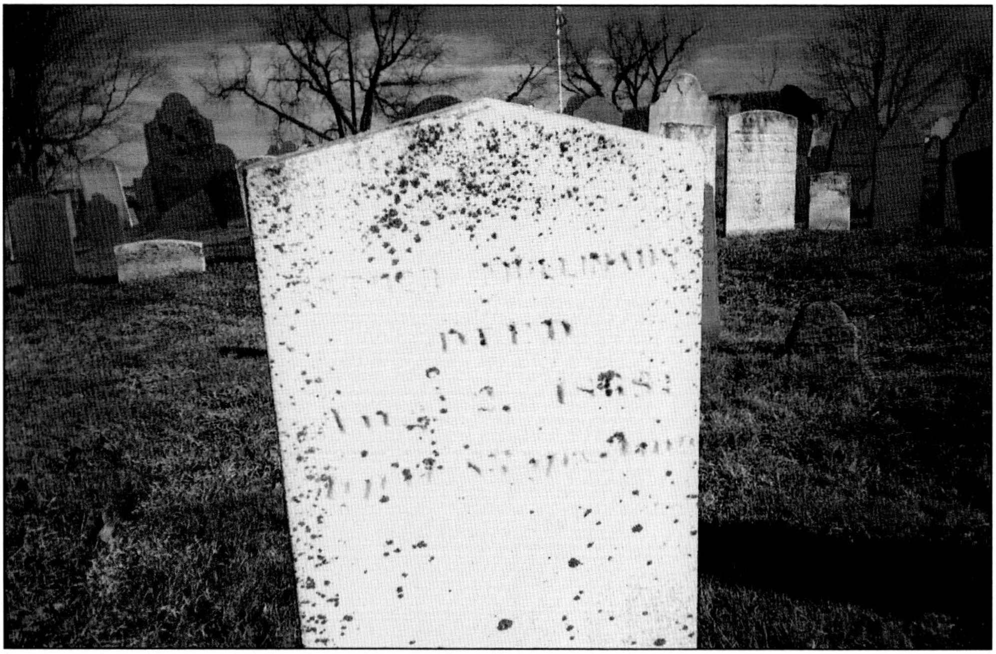

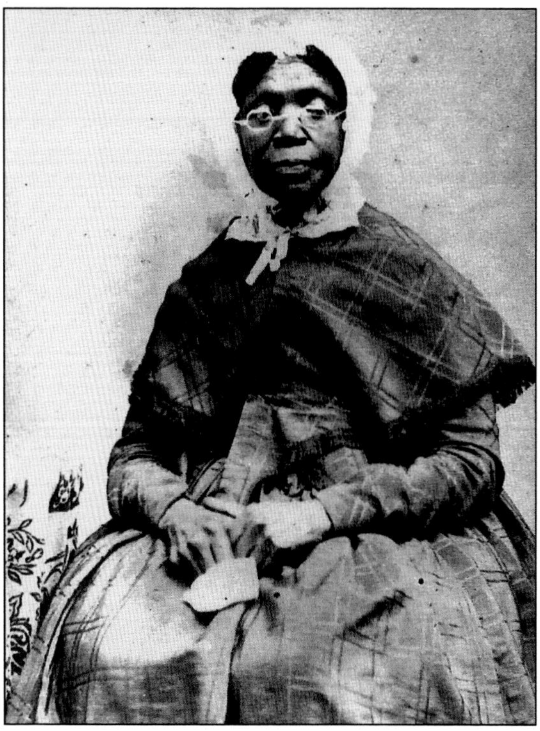

ESTHER MULLINAUX, 1868, NORTH CEMETERY. Esther Whipple Mullinaux (left) was the daughter of former Revolutionary War soldier Prince Whipple and his wife, Dinah. Both were slaves who later gained their freedom. Esther married William Mullinaux, a free black who was likely a mariner, in 1801. Whether he left her or was lost at sea is unknown, but Esther remarried and was again a widow by 1827. Life was difficult for Esther, but she worked hard as a laundress and saved enough money to buy her own house on Walden Lane in 1851. For all her life, she was a devout member of North Church. Her death severed one of Portsmouth's last links to its Revolutionary past, and her gravestone was purchased by North Church.
(Left, courtesy of North Church and the African American Resource Center, via Valerie Cunningham.)

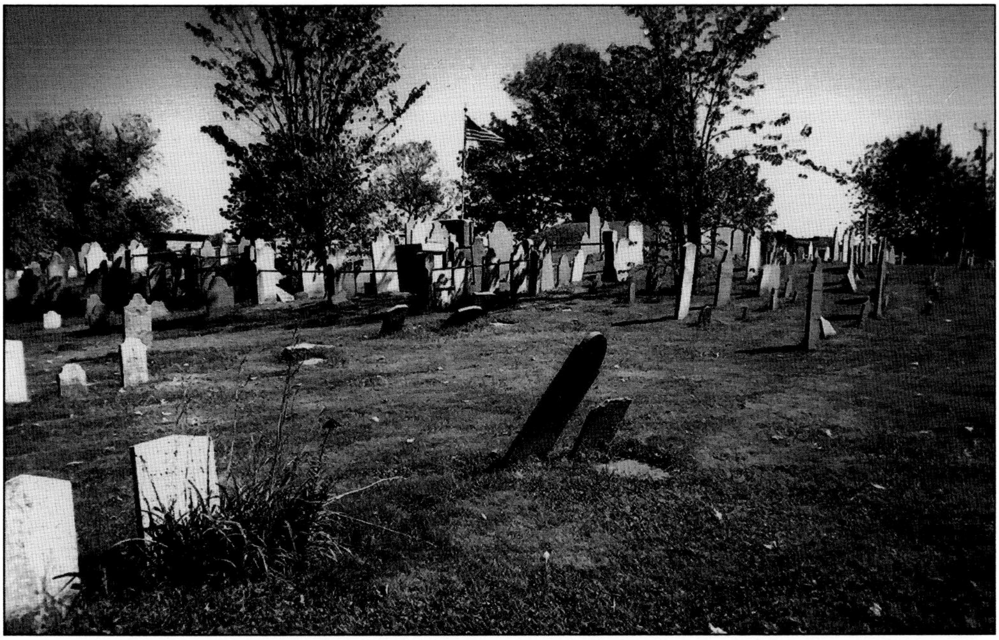

North Cemetery. The back half of North Cemetery, close to the waterfront, is shown in this view. A number of gravestones in this area have either been lost or heavily damaged, and work on this section is in progress. Plans have been made to restore or reset most of the stones that have been damaged or upset.

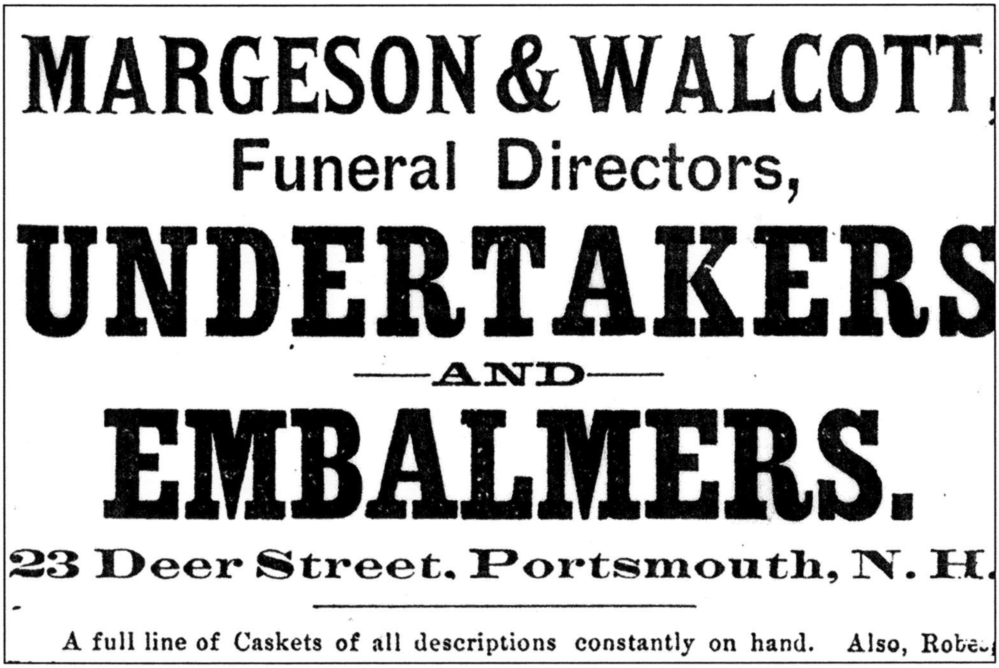

A Margeson and Walcott Advertisement, 1892, Portsmouth. The area around North and Union Cemeteries was a logical place for those associated with the funeral business. Pictured here is a city directory advertisement for an undertaker and casket supplier on nearby Deer Street. (Courtesy of the Portsmouth Public Library.)

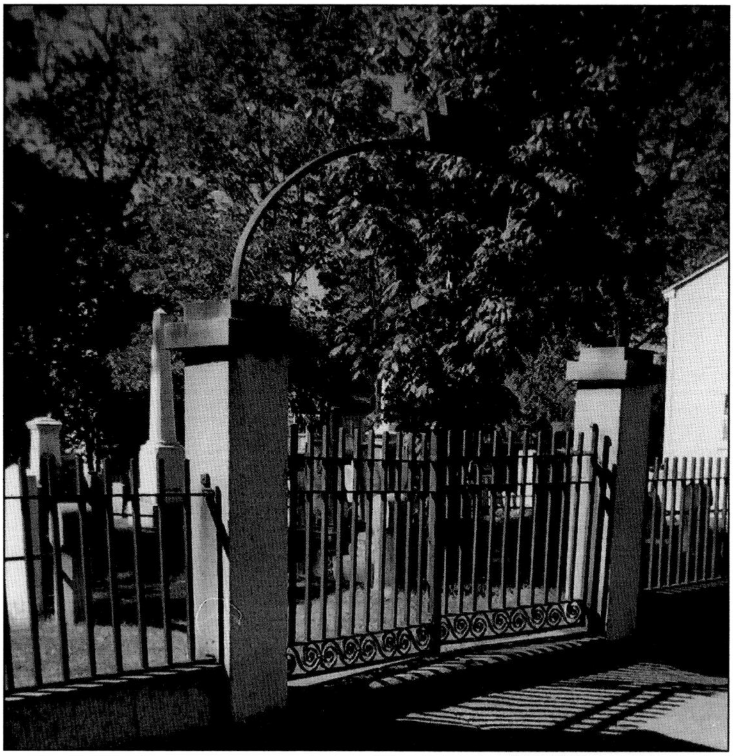

The Union Cemetery Gate. Like many other cemeteries established in the mid-1800s, Union Cemetery is fronted by an elaborate wrought-iron fence and gate. The keystone at the top of the arch over the gate bears the date 1847 and is made of stone.

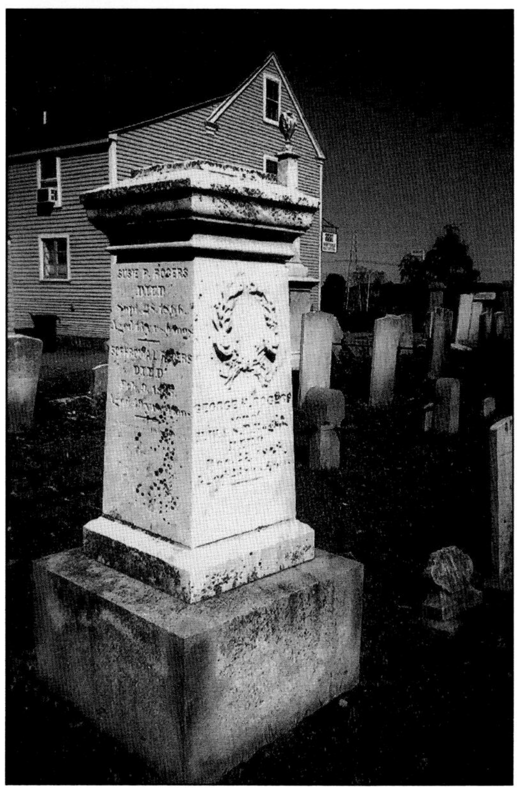

The Rogers Monument, c. 1865, Union Cemetery. Marble monuments such as this were common at the time for many family plots. This version, which stands about five feet tall, sits on a granite base and sports a floral-wreath motif that was quite popular. More elegantly styled monuments, like the one in the background, were often taller and topped off with an urn or other decorative device.

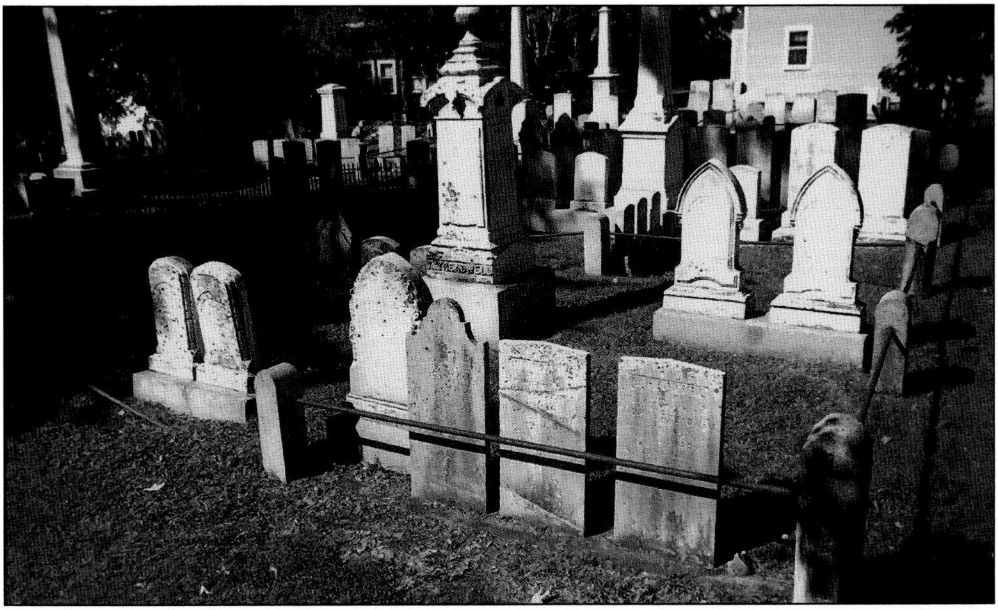

The Treadwell Family Plot, Union Cemetery. This view shows a main feature of the rural cemetery movement: fenced-in family plots. Prior to the 1830s, family members in public cemeteries were often buried near each other, but rarely in such specifically designated enclosures. Within these plots, several generations are usually found buried together, often with a central monument that is larger in size than those that came after.

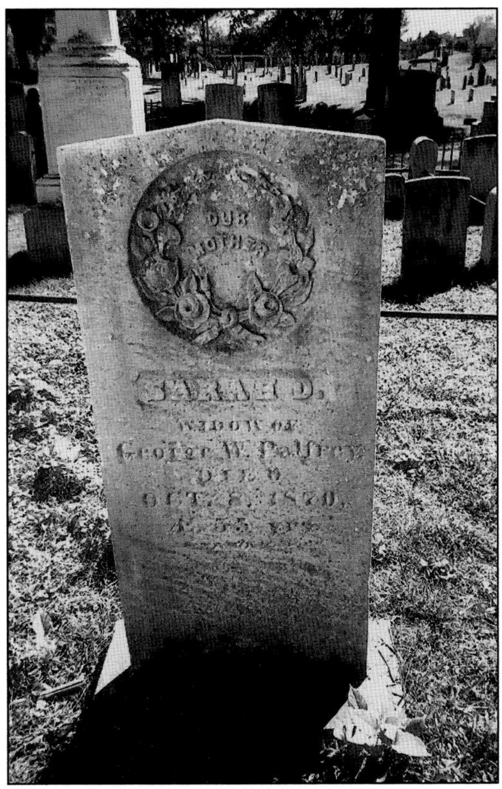

Sarah Palfrey, 1870, Union Cemetery. The influence of Victorian era ideals is immediately discernible in this attractive yet simple gravestone. Note the floral-wreath motif consisting of roses, morning glories, and pansies. All are symbolic of such ideas as love, remembrance, and heavenly joy. The fact that this stone was chosen by Sarah's adoring children is denoted by the wording of "Our Mother" within the wreath.

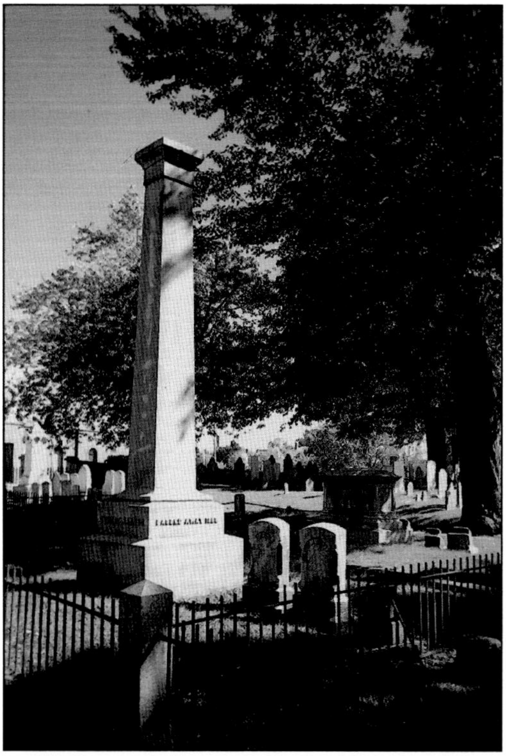

GEORGE RAYNES, 1855, UNION CEMETERY. The fact that George Raynes and his family are buried here (left) is not all that surprising. His famous shipyard and mansion were just across the way, where the Portsmouth Herald building now stands. Born in York, Maine, in 1799, Raynes launched his shipbuilding career in the 1820s at the yard of Jacob Remick in Portsmouth's north end. The first ship he built was the *Planet* in 1828. In 1832, he bought the old Boyd Mansion and shipyard and soon established himself as the premier shipbuilder in Portsmouth. Raynes would build more than 50 ships there before his death, including some of the finest clipper ships on the Piscataqua River. These include the long-lived *Coeur De Lion*, *Sea Serpent*, *Tinqua*, *Wild Pidgeon*, *Witch of the Wave* (below), and several others.

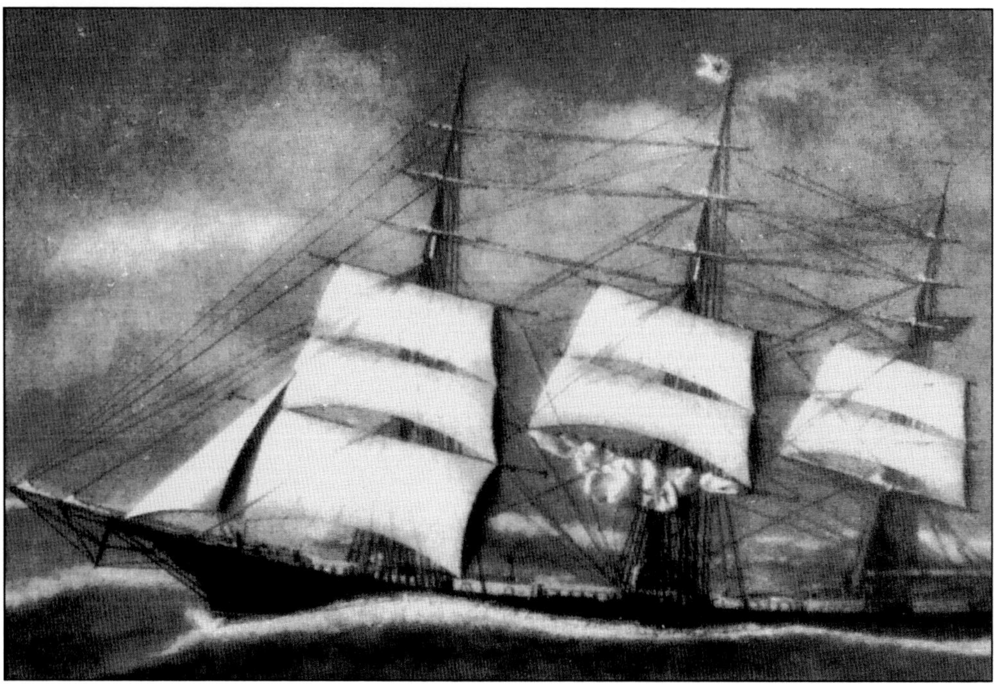

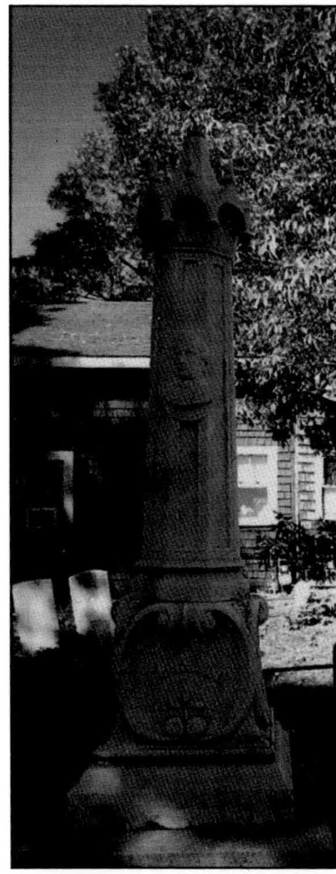

Frederick Fernald, 1855, Union Cemetery. It is appropriate that Fernald, who died 18 days after George Raynes, is buried close to his rival. He built his first ship, the *Harriet Rockwell,* in 1835 at age 24. Fernald took over the Badger shipyard in 1837 and, in 1844, partnered with William Pettigrew, building some 30 vessels. The clipper ships built by Fernald were much the equal of those built by Raynes and include such notables as *Midnight* (below), *Typhoon*, *Noonday*, *Dashing Wave*, and *Red Rover*. Interestingly enough, while the monument for George Raynes is the larger of the two, Fernald had the upper hand in terms of ship size. His largest clipper was the *Typhoon* (1,612 tons), slightly besting that of Raynes's *Sea Serpent* (1,402 tons).

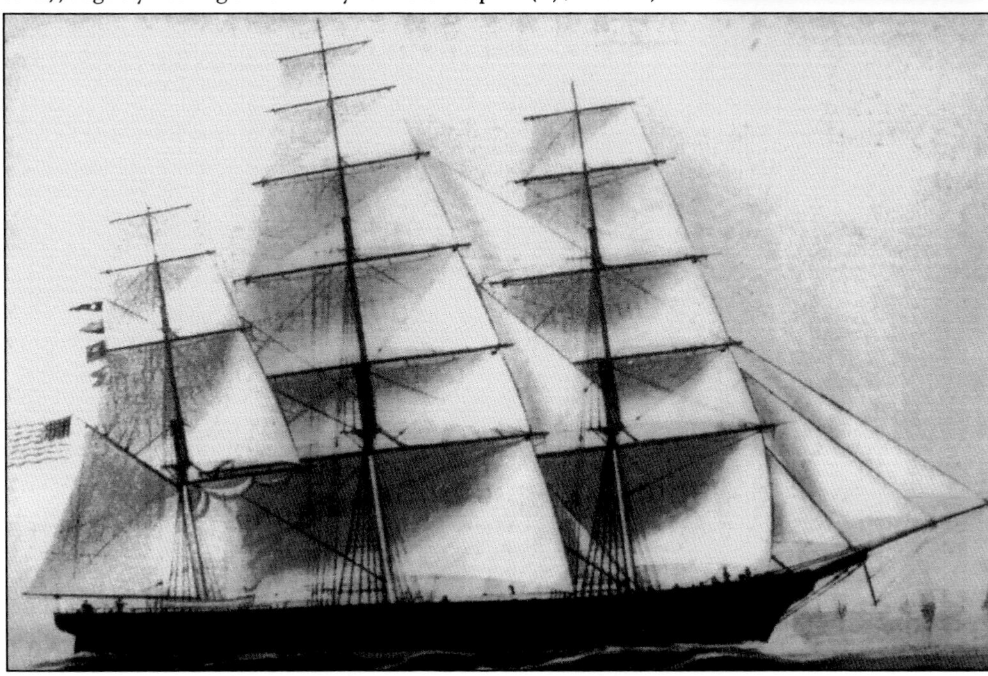

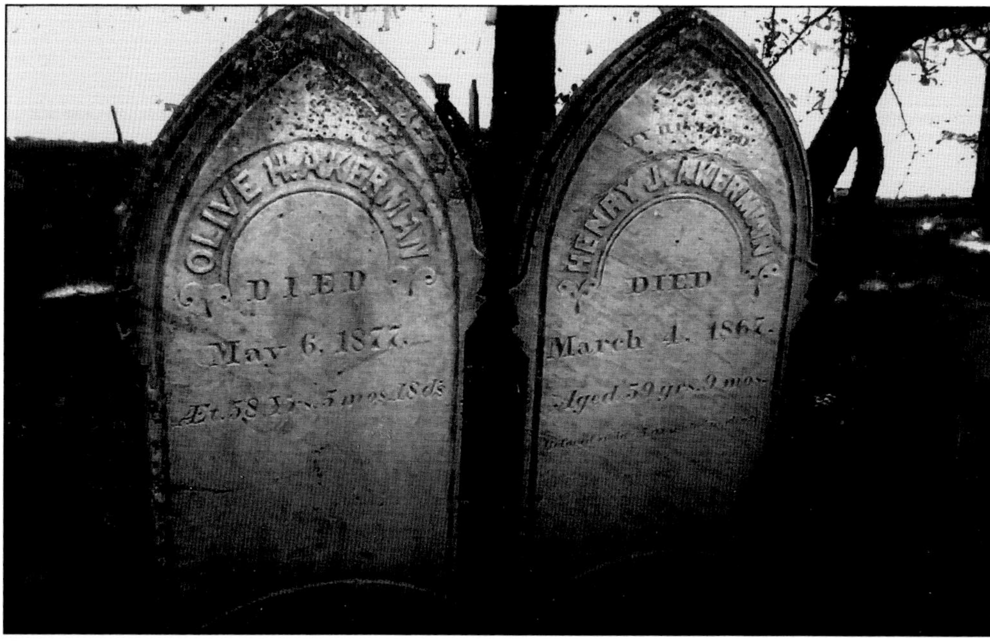

OLIVE, 1877, AND HENRY AKERMAN, 1867, UNION CEMETERY. These Gothic-arch gravestones are adorned with just a few decorative scrolls. Though attractive, they reflect the time's growing trend toward a minimalist approach in both wording and decoration. Such a trend would not reach its zenith until the early decades of the 20th century.

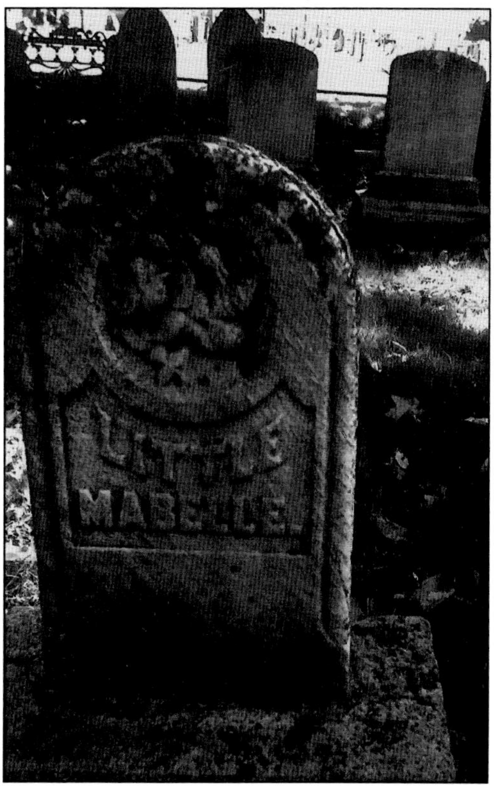

LITTLE MABELLE, UNION CEMETERY. One of the joys in exploring cemeteries is coming upon a mystery stone. The wording and broken floral motif tell of a well-loved girl, a life tragically cut short. Who was Mabelle, and why did she die so young? Research might answer some of these questions, but sometimes just contemplating the fragile nature of life may provide all the information one really needs.

Four

South Street Cemeteries

The cemetery complex that is located at the junction of South Street and Sagamore Avenue is one of the largest of its kind in the seacoast. While many people visit on a daily basis to go for a peaceful walk, fly a kite, or ice-skate, few realize how much history is encompassed within its grounds. One of the most infamous events to take place here was the public execution of Ruth Blay of South Hampton. She was sentenced to hang for concealing the death of her illegitimate child on December 30, 1768. In front of a huge crowd, Blay was executed for her crime by High Sheriff Thomas Packer, despite the fact that a last-minute reprieve had been granted by the royal governor.

What may look to most people like one big cemetery is actually a series of five, established between c. 1671 and the present, and the addition of one entire family cemetery relocated from its original site, making six in all.

The oldest part of this area is the Cotton Cemetery, located off South Street in the northern corner. This cemetery lies on land granted to "Goodman" William Cotton in 1671. The area was used for burials prior to 1671, as evidenced by that part of the agreement with Cotton that reads, "The said land shall still remayne for a trayning field and to bury dead in." After the land was abandoned as a training field for local militia, it was designated as the "Minister's Pasture" for the old South meetinghouse.

The next section to be established here was Proprietor's Burying Ground (later called Proprietor's Cemetery). It was laid out in 1831, the same year as Boston's famous Mount Auburn Cemetery. Sitting on the corner of South Street (formerly Auburn Street) and Sagamore Avenue, it is distinguished by its elaborate monuments and fenced-in family plots, all key elements of the burgeoning rural cemetery movement.

The complex at South Street expanded in size in 1847 with the opening of Harmony Grove Cemetery directly adjacent to Proprietor's. It too is noted for its monumental sculpture, heavily influenced by the Victorian era. The cemeteries at South Street grew even larger in size in 1871, when Sagamore Cemetery was established at the southeastern end of the area off Sagamore Avenue. Another interesting addition came to South Street in 1875, when the Cutts-Penhallow family cemetery, formerly on Green Street, was relocated to an area between Proprietor's and Harmony Grove that now stands under a small grove of lofty pine trees.

The final addition to the cemeteries at South Street came after 1900, when the portion named Elmwood Cemetery was opened. Still in use today, it overlooks an inlet of the Piscataqua River.

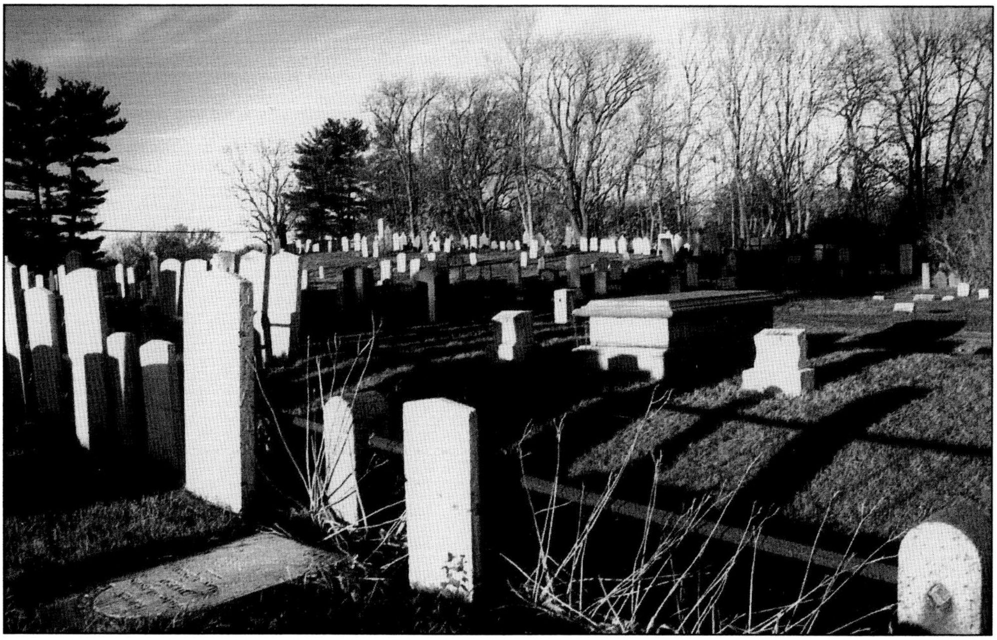

PROPRIETOR'S AND COTTON CEMETERIES. In the foreground in this view are several gravestones located in Proprietor's Cemetery. Note the large table stone at center right. Just beyond and sitting on a hill is Cotton Cemetery. This is the oldest area within South Street used for burials.

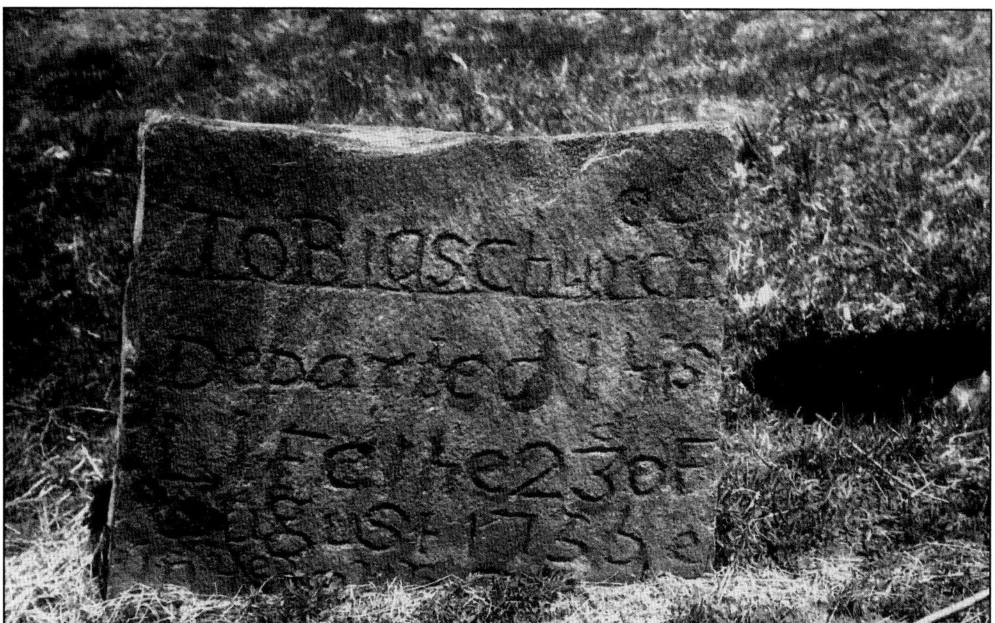

TOBIAS CHURCHEL, 1756, COTTON CEMETERY. This rough-hewn gravestone was not professionally carved but made by a friend or family member. Note the crude lettering, and the last two letters of the deceased's surname at upper right, carved there after the stoneworker had run out of room. Churchel (usually spelled Churchwell or Churchill) was likely the son of John Churchwell.

ELIZABETH JACKSON, 1764, COTTON CEMETERY. This death's-head gravestone was likely carved by a Boston-area professional, perhaps a member of the Lamson family. Carrying a simple, yet rather ominous look, it is the only design of this type found in Portsmouth. With a few exceptions, all of the winged-skull gravestones in South Street are found in the Cotton Cemetery section.

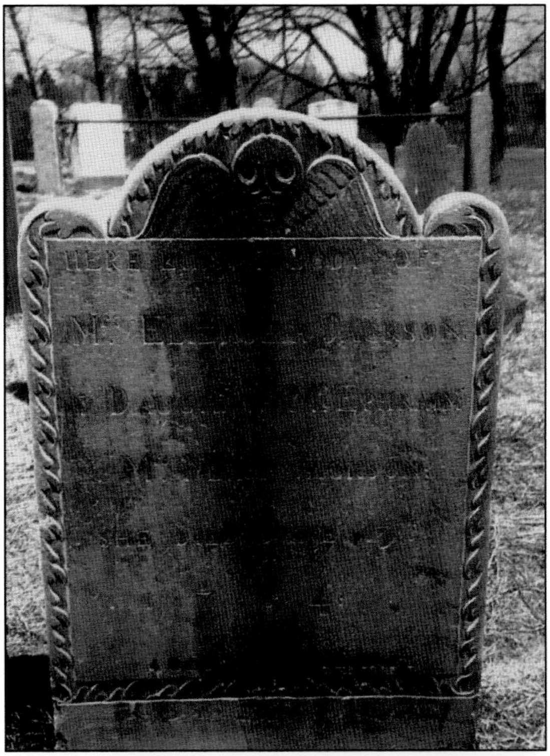

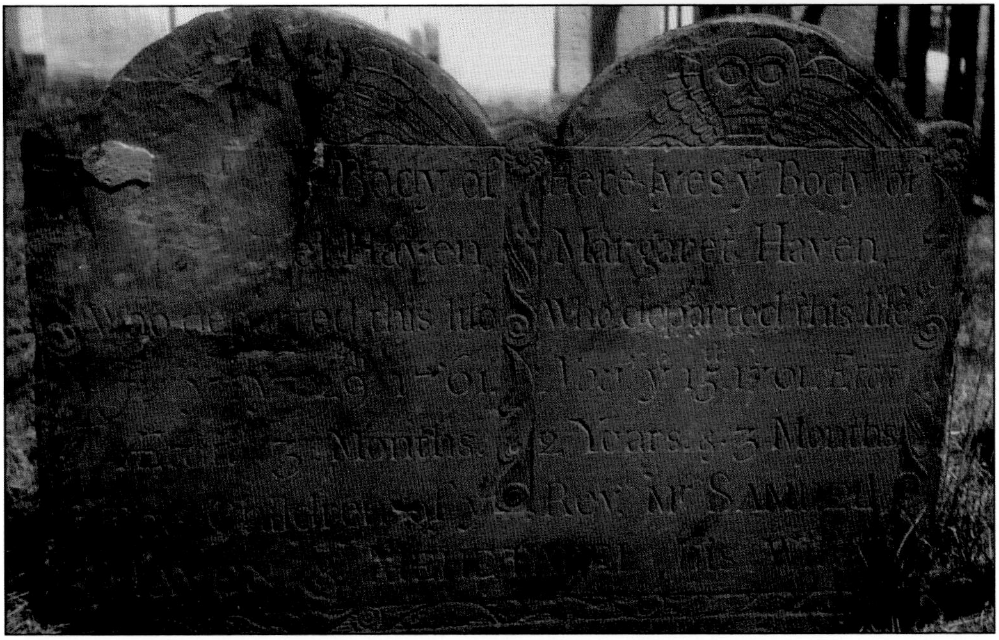

SAMUEL AND MARGARET HAVEN, 1761, PROPRIETOR'S CEMETERY. A work carved by the Lamson family, this double gravestone for the Haven children originally stood at the site of the old South Church. When the church was destroyed in the 1850s, the remains of several ministers and their families were relocated to Proprietor's Cemetery. The beloved Rev. Samuel Haven served as South Church pastor from 1752 until his death in 1806.

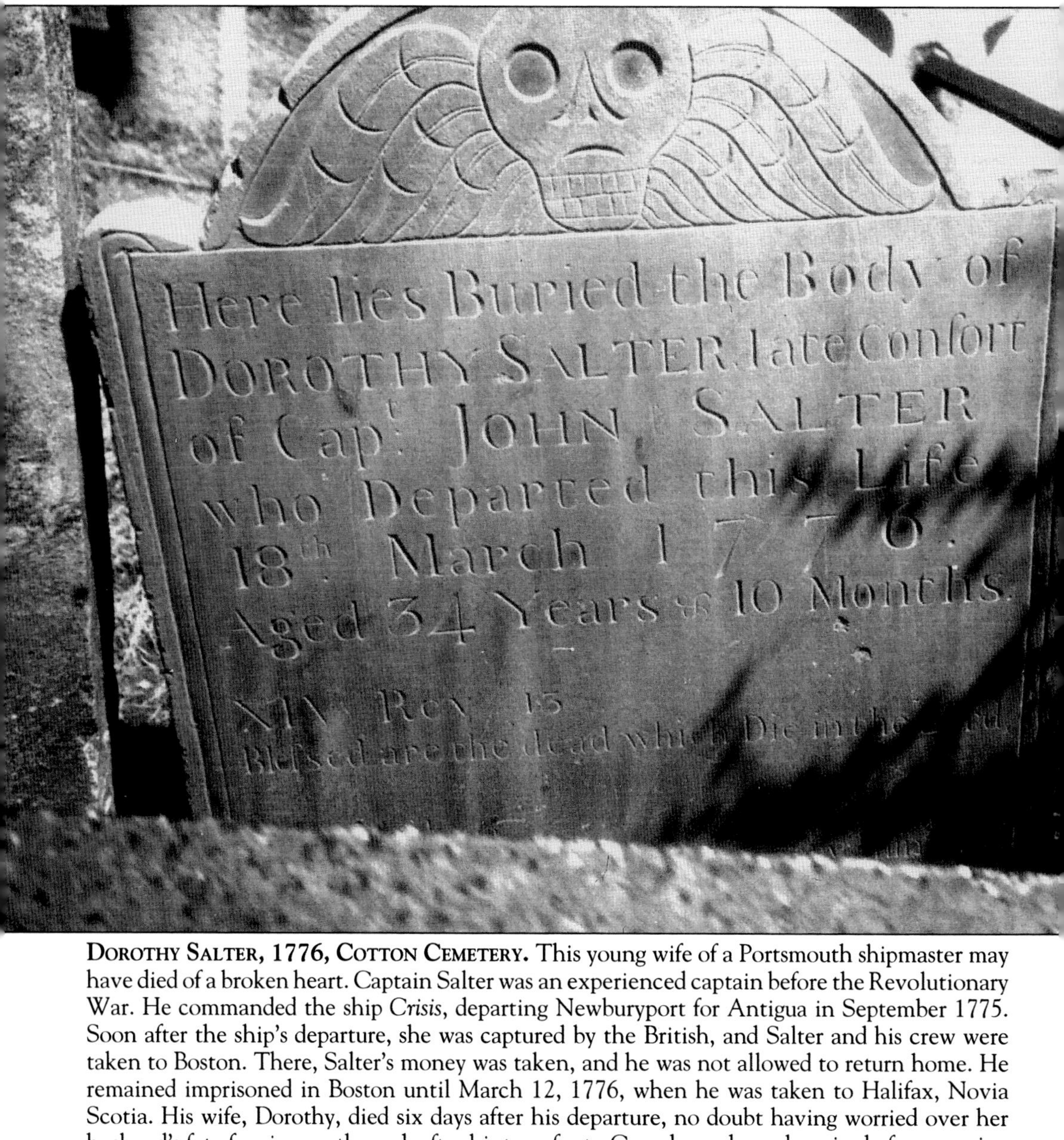

DOROTHY SALTER, 1776, COTTON CEMETERY. This young wife of a Portsmouth shipmaster may have died of a broken heart. Captain Salter was an experienced captain before the Revolutionary War. He commanded the ship *Crisis*, departing Newburyport for Antigua in September 1775. Soon after the ship's departure, she was captured by the British, and Salter and his crew were taken to Boston. There, Salter's money was taken, and he was not allowed to return home. He remained imprisoned in Boston until March 12, 1776, when he was taken to Halifax, Novia Scotia. His wife, Dorothy, died six days after his departure, no doubt having worried over her husband's fate for six months and, after his transfer to Canada, perhaps despaired of ever seeing him again. After being kept in chains and later imprisoned ashore, Captain Salter was suddenly released on April 28, 1776. He finally returned to Portsmouth in late May only to find that his wife was dead. Broken by the terrible news, combined with his lengthy ordeal, he remained ashore for the duration of the war.

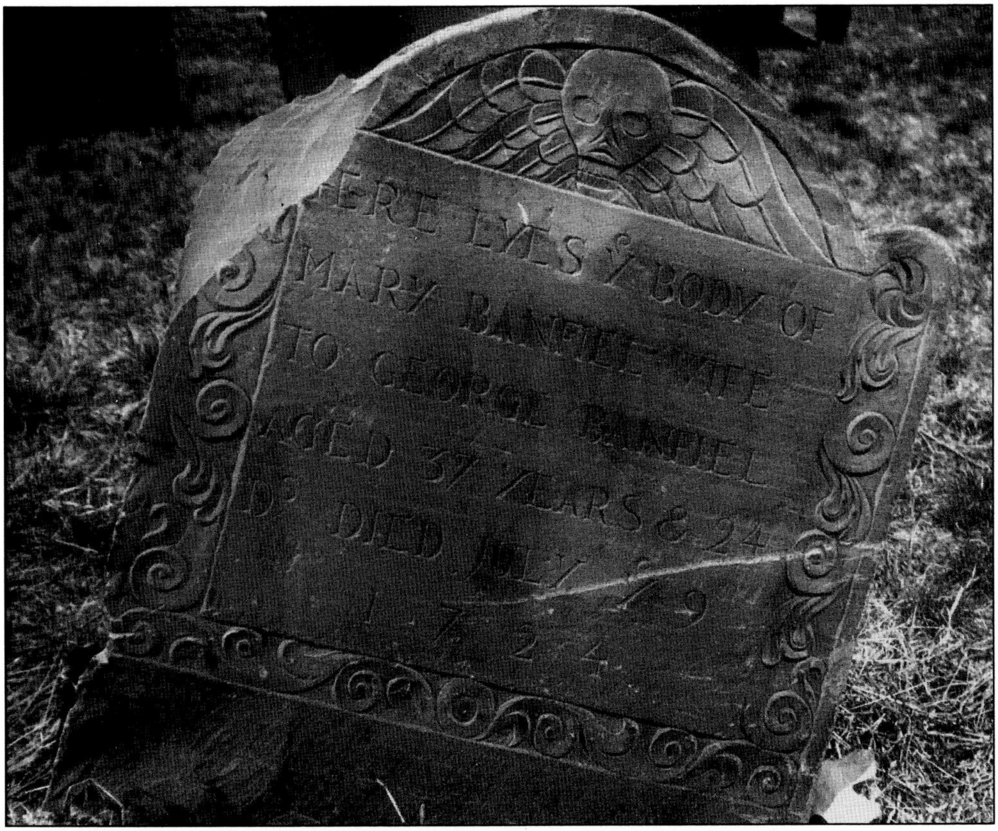

MARY BANFIEL, 1724, CUTTS-PENHALLOW PLOT. This gravestone, carved by a Boston stonecutter, is one of the oldest found in South Street. Mary was the wife of George Banfield, whose family of mariners and fishermen had arrived in Portsmouth by 1667. Though uncertain, Mary may have been the daughter of Jethro Locke of Rye and a member of the church in Greenland prior to 1712.

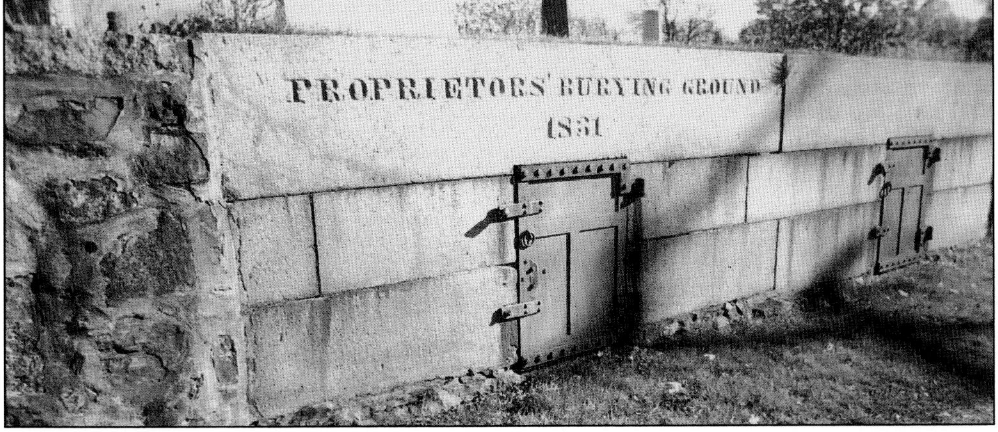

PROPRIETOR'S BURYING GROUND. This wall is located at the corner of South Street and Sagamore Avenue. Note the original designation of "Burying Ground." The iron doors mark the entrance not to individual graves but rather to holding tombs. Such places were used to store coffins of the deceased during the winter months, when the ground was too frozen to dig graves.

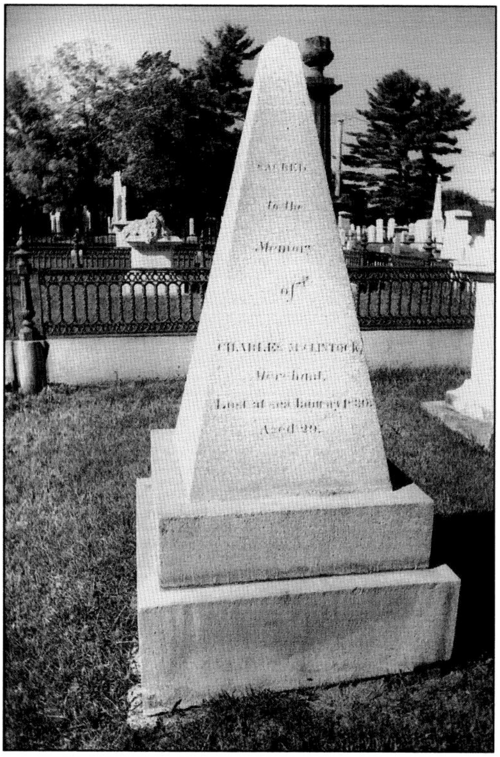

CHARLES McCLINTOCK, 1830, PROPRIETOR'S CEMETERY. The actual date this monument was erected is uncertain but was likely years after McClintock died. Note that Proprietor's Cemetery was not established until 1831. Memorial stones like this are common in seafaring towns such as Portsmouth.

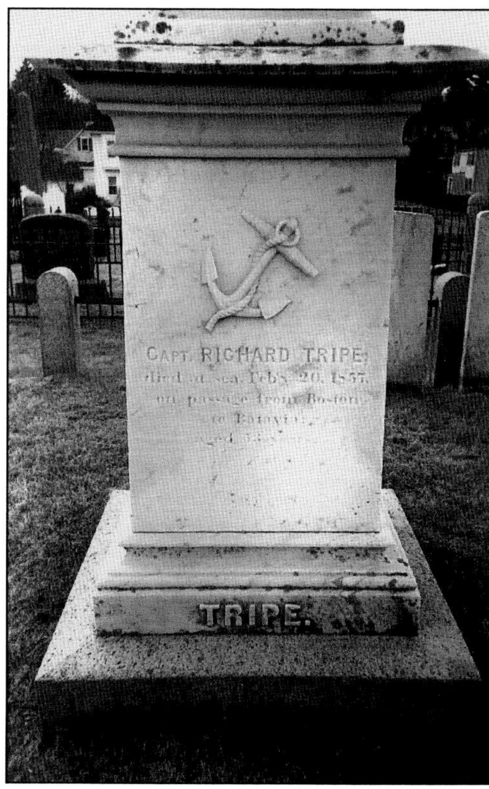

RICHARD TRIPE, 1857, PROPRIETOR'S CEMETERY. The anchor is often used on sailor memorials. Tripe was likely the namesake son of Capt. Richard Tripe, who built a 60-ton schooner in Dover in 1785. The death of this latter-day captain and his subsequent burial at sea on the long voyage to Batavia was likely due to illness, but on what ship is unknown.

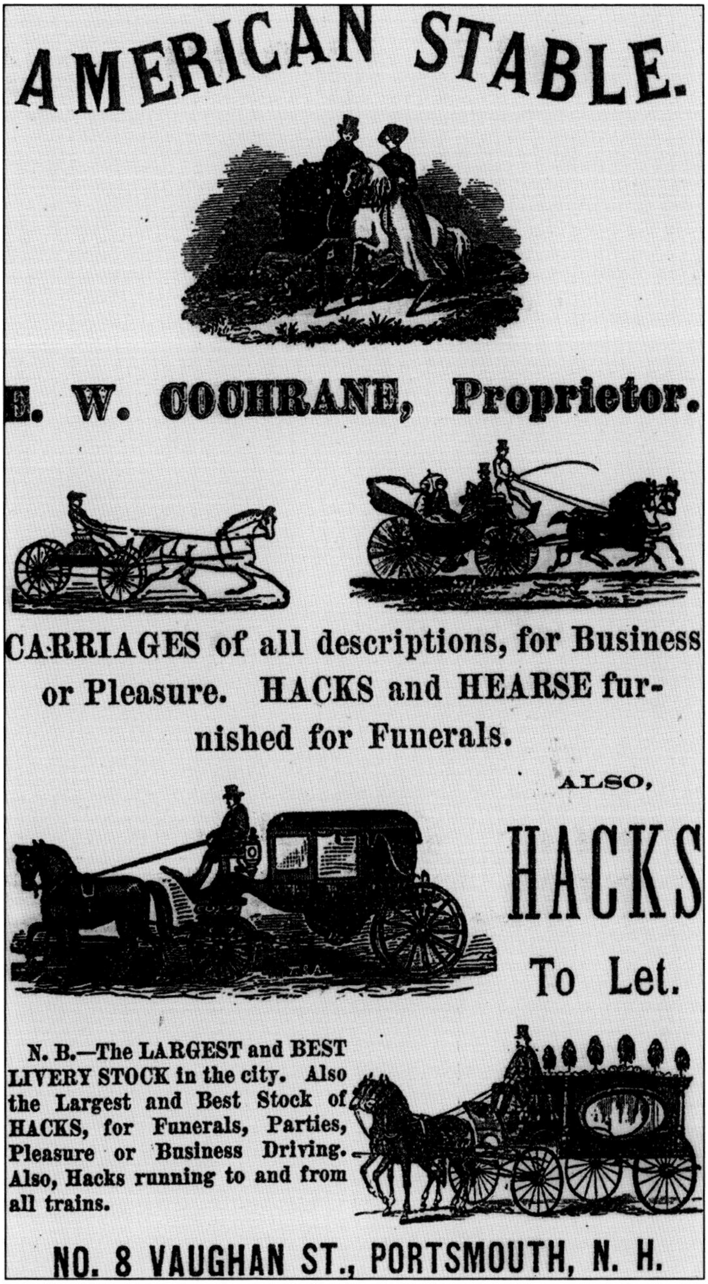

AN AMERICAN STABLE ADVERTISEMENT, 1875. This advertisement appeared in a city directory publication and demonstrates that even in olden days, just like today, the funeral business was a diverse and profitable one. In earlier times, it was stables and liveries such as this one that supplied horse-drawn vehicles "furnished for funerals." The elegant vehicle at the bottom of this ad is a hearse that was used to transport the deceased to the cemetery, while the coach above it was used to transport those who attended the funeral. More so than in today's society, the wealth and standing of the deceased dictated how elaborate his funeral procession would be. Vehicles such as those depicted here would not have been affordable to those of lesser means. (Courtesy of the Portsmouth Public Library.)

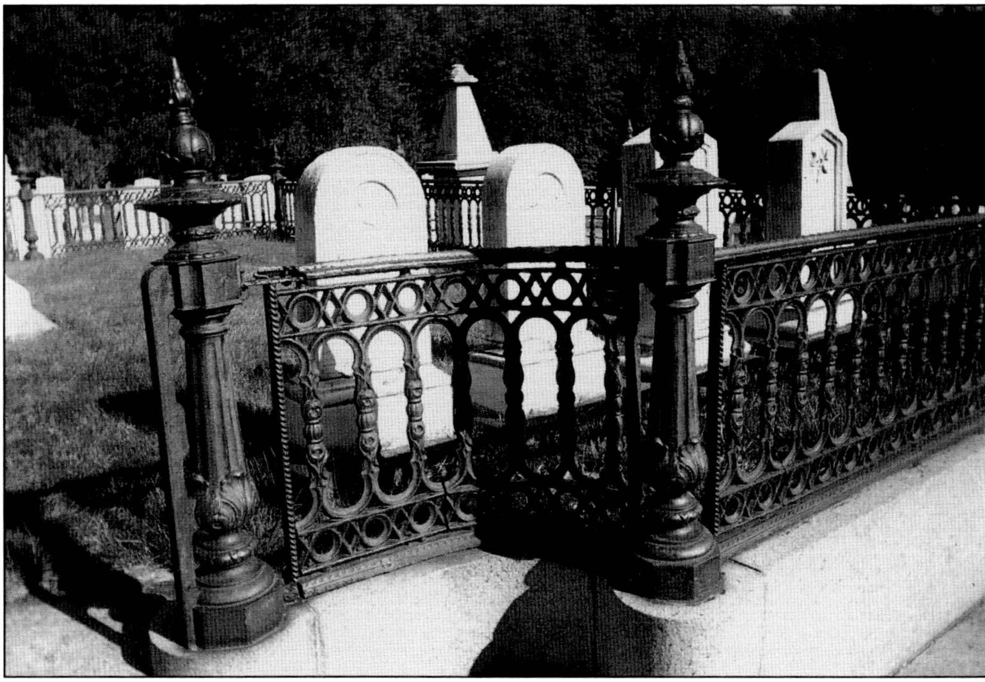

WROUGHT-IRON WORK, PROPRIETOR'S CEMETERY. An attractive aspect of this cemetery is the numerous fenced-in family plots. The ironwork executed on many of these enclosures are works of art in and of themselves, sometimes more interesting than the stones within. The Rice family plot (above) displays a simple yet attractive style distinguished by its circle and diamond border patterns along the top and bottom. The Hill family plot (below) shows ironwork that is more delicate in nature and scrollwork reminiscent of the Victorian era.

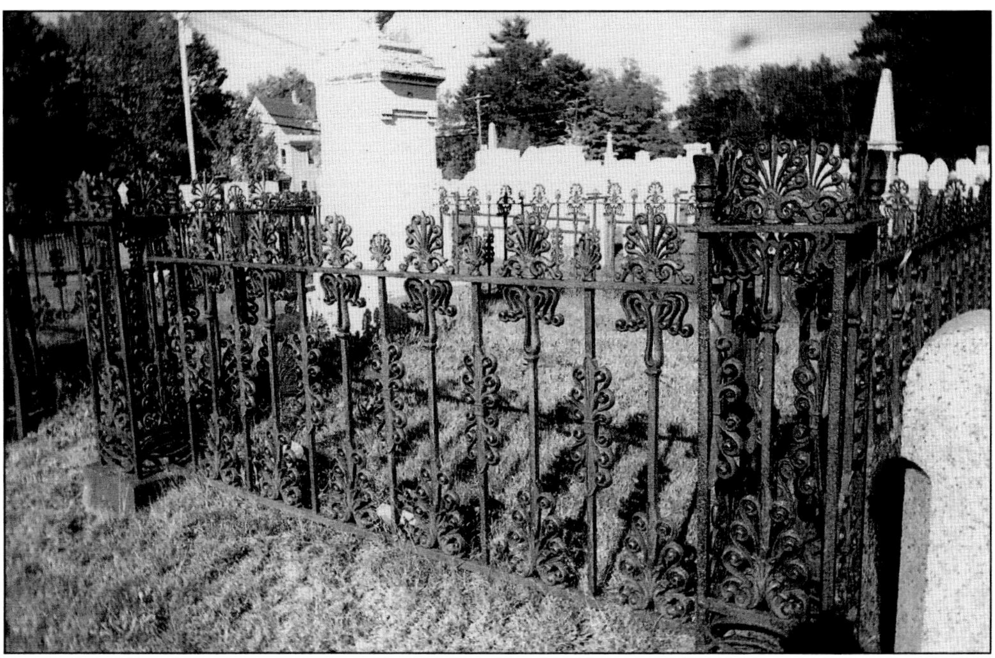

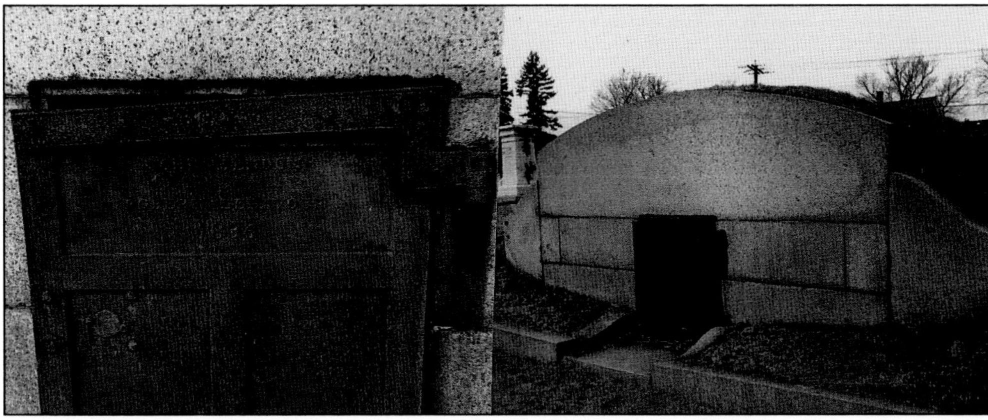

JOHN MENDUM AND ROBERT LEFAVOUR, 1836, PROPRIETOR'S CEMETERY. This masonry-and-earthen tomb is like those at the North and Pleasant Street Cemeteries. However, this modern version uses granite for its façade rather than brick. In the photograph to the left, note the iron hinge on the entrance door, as well as the small keyhole and its sliding cover. It was common for interrelated families and friends to share tombs such as this.

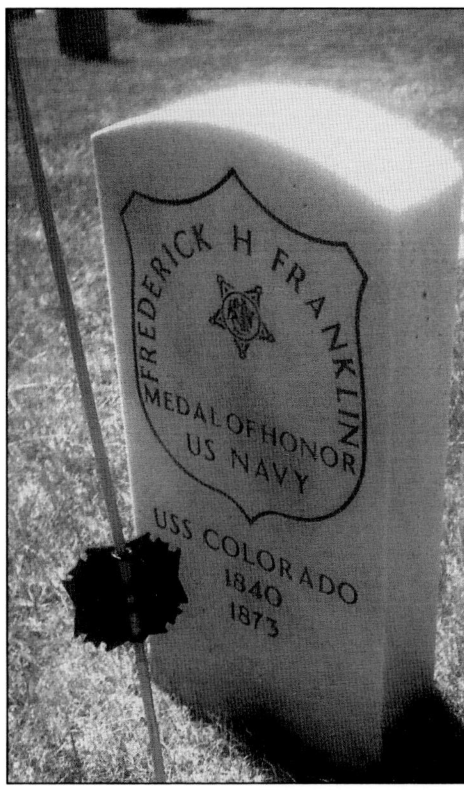

FREDERICK FRANKLIN, 1873, PROPRIETOR'S CEMETERY. Franklin is one of five Medal of Honor winners buried in Portsmouth, three of whom are in South Street. A quartermaster on the battleship *Colorado*, Franklin earned his medal during an attack on Korean forts on June 11, 1871. He was cited for assuming control of Company D after its commander, Lieutenant McKee, was wounded, handling the company with "great credit."

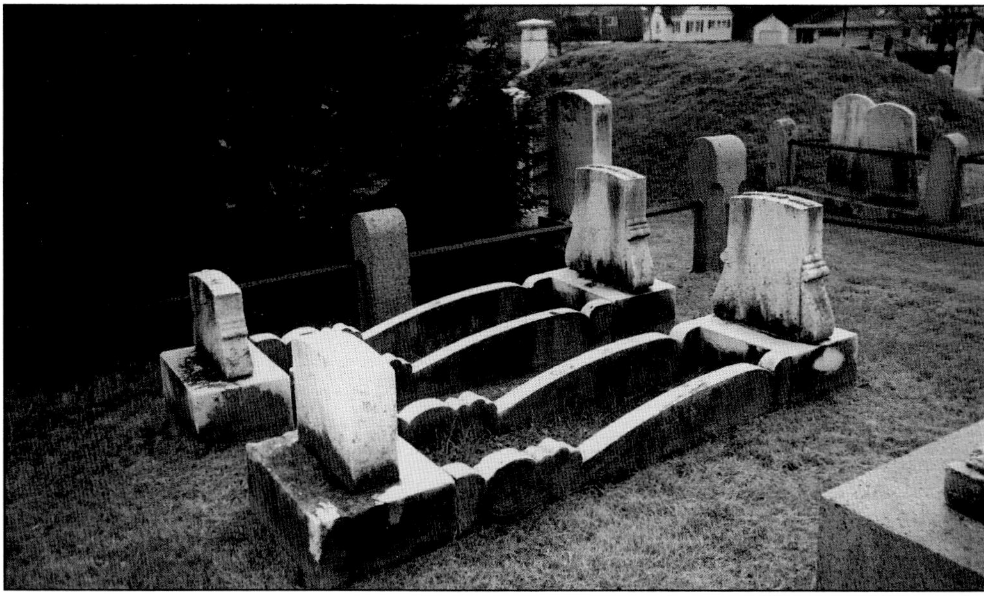

Lucy, 1850, and Elisha Hill, 1852, Proprietor's Cemetery. This view of the Hill family plot is striking, revealing how the headstones and footstones are connected by decorative marble work. By physically connecting the two stones, the ideal of being "laid to rest," as if the deceased were merely asleep in a bed, is fully realized. Lucy Hill was 68 years old at the time of her death. Elisha Hill, born in 1776, was a merchant in town, as is shown by this advertisement appearing in the *Oracle of the Day* in 1807. Vital information about the Hills is carved on a monument at the center of the family plot, while the graves for Elisha and his wife are simply marked "Our Father" and "Our Mother." (Below, courtesy of the Portsmouth Public Library.)

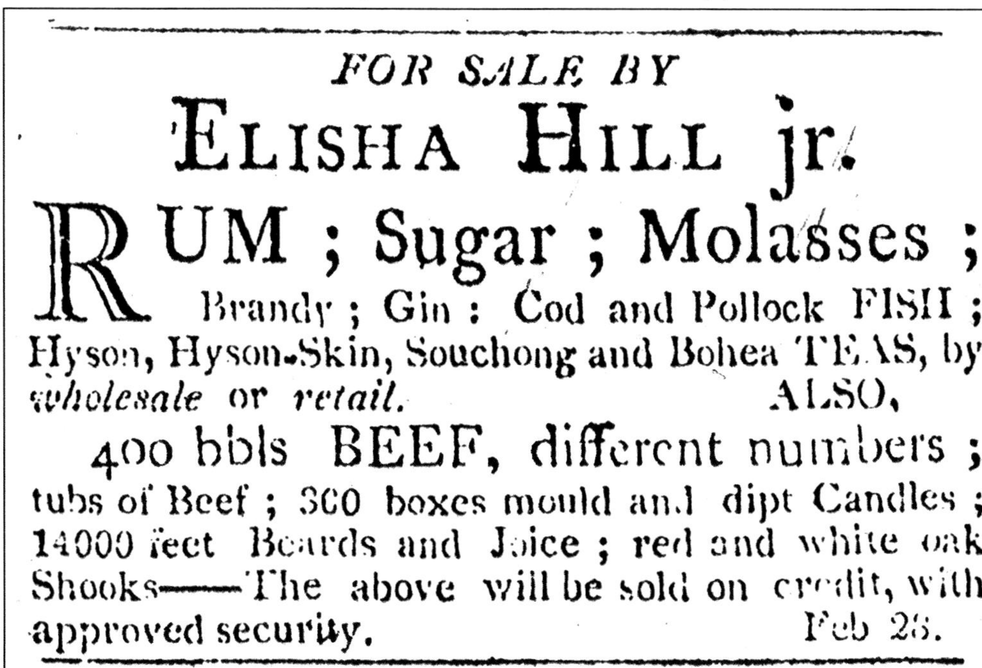

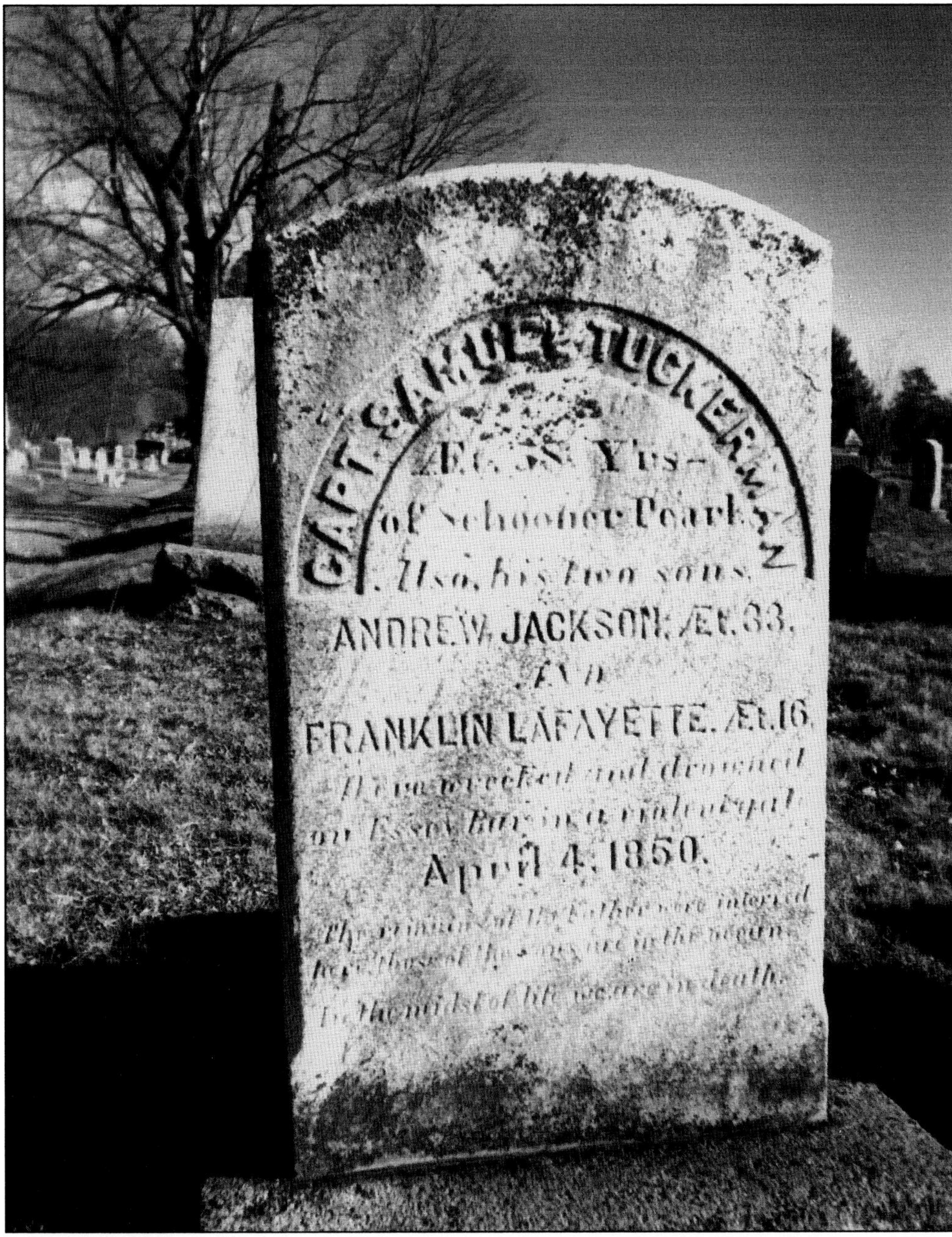

SAMUEL, ANDREW, AND FRANKLIN TUCKERMAN, 1850, HARMONY GROVE CEMETERY. Monuments relating a disaster at sea or a shipwreck are common in coastal towns throughout New England and the eastern seaboard. Each gravestone that records these events is unique and can make for quite compelling reading. This stone marks the death at sea of Captain Tuckerman and his two patriotically named sons. While sailing in the coastal schooner *Pearl* off Massachusetts, all were "wrecked and drowned on Essex Bar in a violent gale." It is unknown whether Captain Tuckerman and his sons were brought home to rest in Portsmouth or buried in Massachusetts. The shock of this tragedy to the Tuckerman family and friends must have been great, reflected in the last line on the gravestone: "In the midst of life we are in death."

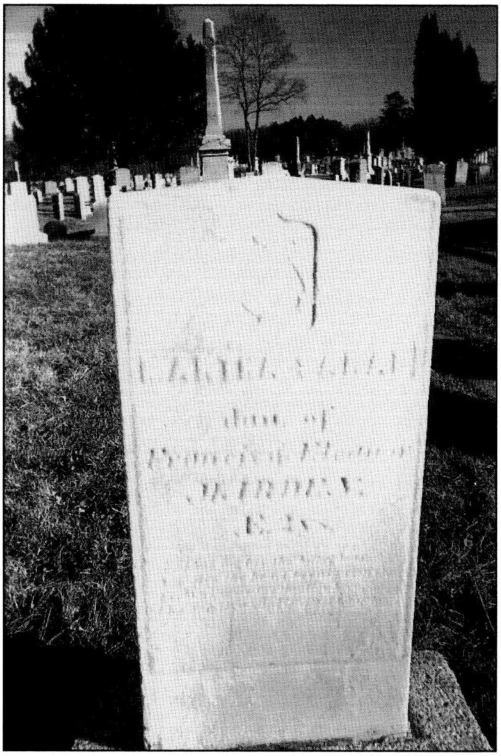

Martha Sarah Marden, Harmony Grove Cemetery. The date of death for this two-year-old child, likely the daughter of Irish immigrants, is uncertain. The harp that adorns her poignant gravestone conveys several different meanings, both of which may be applicable to young Martha. Its use may be indicative of Irish heritage, as this musical instrument is Ireland's national symbol. The harp is also a symbol of hope.

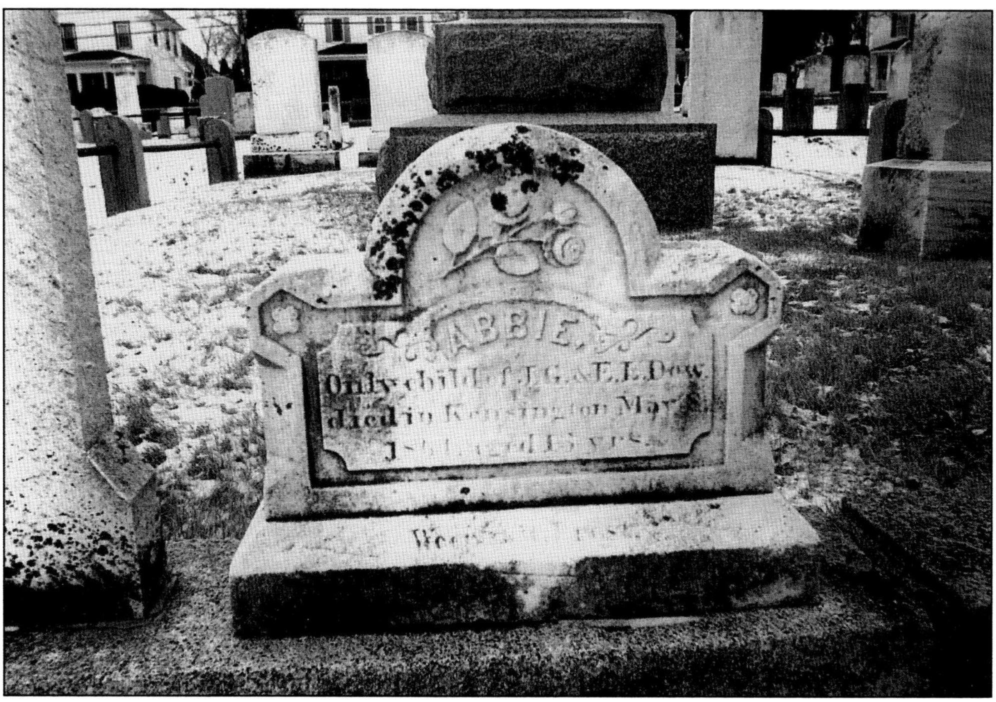

Abbie Dow, 1864, Proprietor's Cemetery. Three roses, symbols of love and purity, adorn this touching gravestone of a 13-year-old girl who died in Kensington on a spring day in May. Her simple epitaph reads, "Weep not. I rest."

JOHN CORNELIUS, 1866, PROPRIETOR'S CEMETERY. A pair of shepherd's crooks adorn this gravestone for a Portuguese native who "died at this city." This motif symbolizes the ideal of charity and is found on few other gravestones in Portsmouth. Nothing is known about Cornelius; however, this stone was erected by his children, as evidenced by the small line of verse at the bottom reading, "Father we miss thee."

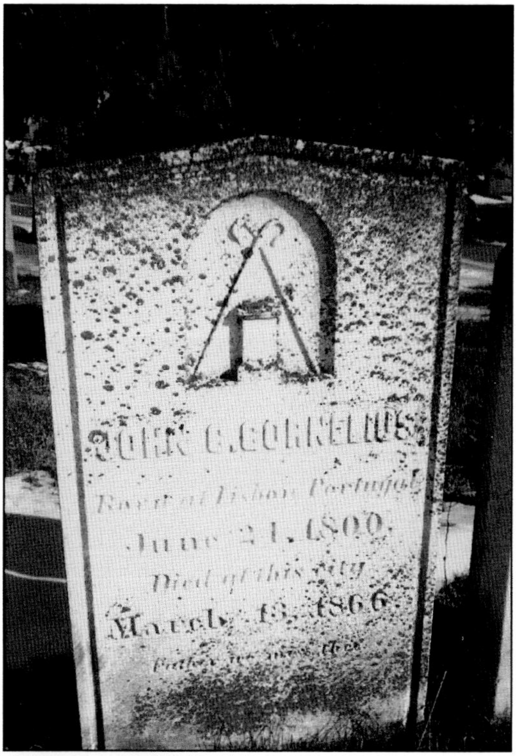

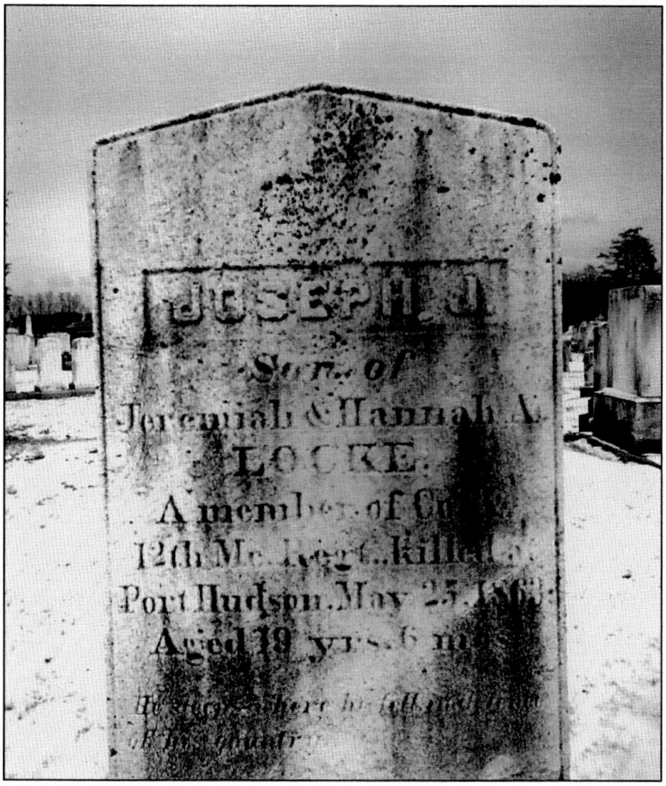

JOSEPH LOCKE, 1863, HARMONY GROVE CEMETERY. Locke joined the 12th Maine Regiment at Portland in 1861. He died early on during the siege on the Confederate fort at Port Hudson, Louisiana. This siege lasted 48 days and was one of the longest in American military history. Joseph Locke, who "sleeps where he fell in defence of his country," was one of 5,000 Union casualties at Port Hudson.

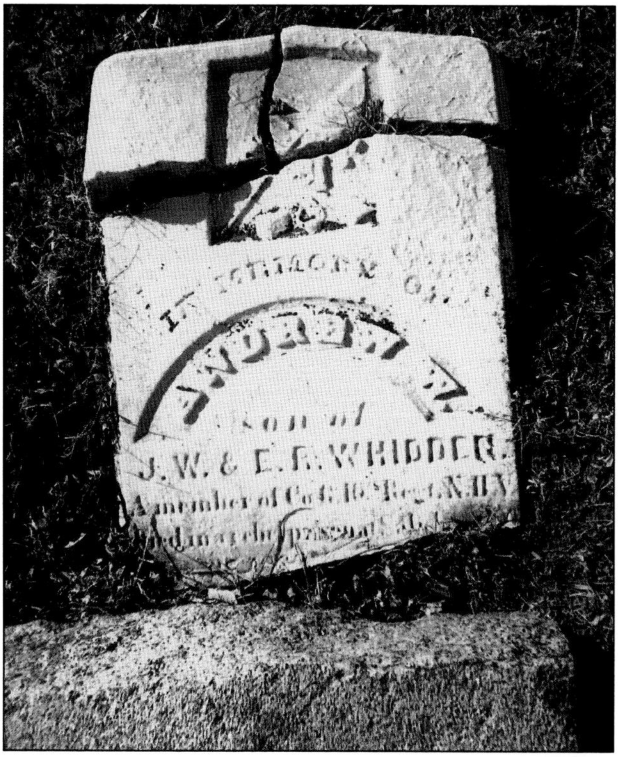

Andrew Whidden, 1865, Harmony Grove Cemetery. This young soldier of the 10th New Hampshire Regiment was captured at the Battle of Fair Oaks, Virginia, in October 1864. He "died in a rebel prison at Salisbury, North Carolina," on January 27, 1865, one of 5,000 Union soldiers to die there. His epitaph, now lost, read, "His body lies not here. There is rest in heaven for the weary and suffering soldiers."

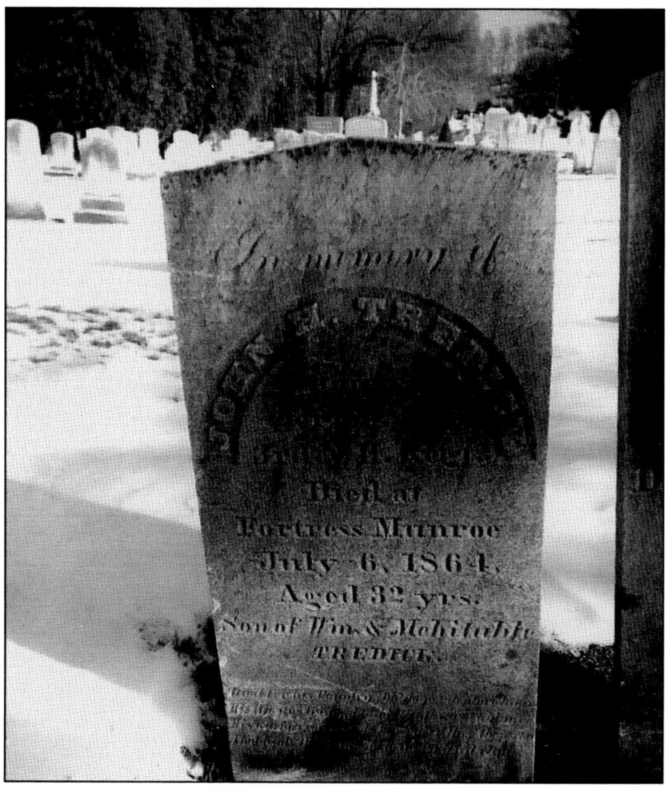

John Tredick, 1864, Harmony Grove Cemetery. A lieutenant in the 3rd New Hampshire Regiment, Tredick was severely wounded at Weir Bottom Church, Virginia, on June 16, dying shortly thereafter at Fortress Monroe. The son of William and Mehitable Tredick, he was one of 352 men of his regiment to die during the war.

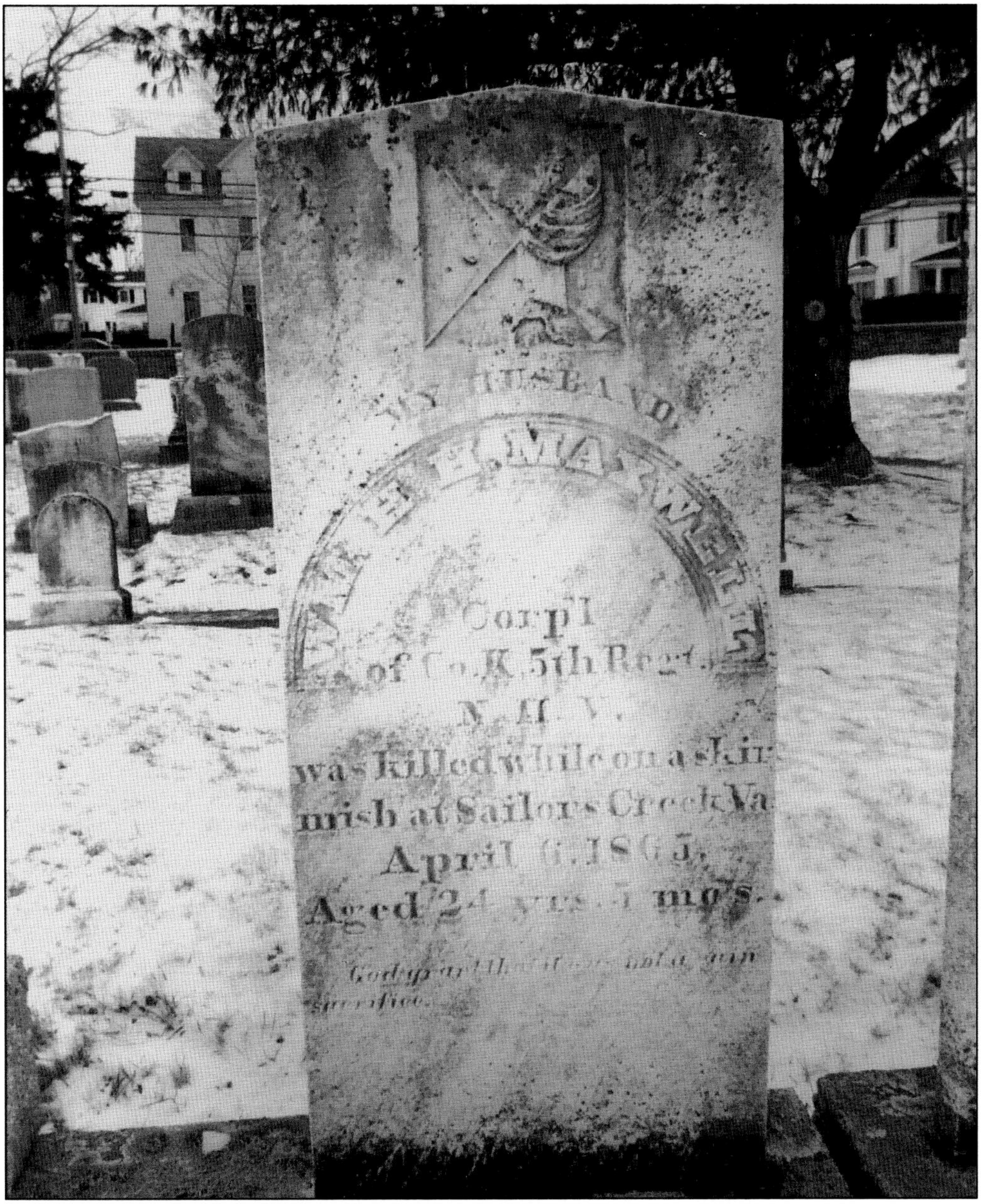

William Maxwell, 1865, Harmony Grove Cemetery. The circumstances in which Maxwell died make this stone historically and personally interesting. His death at "Sailors" Creek on April 6 marked the last-ditch effort of the Confederate army. Robert E. Lee lost 8,000 men at Saylors Creek, while Union losses were relatively light. Unfortunately, one of them was this young New Hampshire corporal. By the time that news of his death reached home, the war was reported as over. Just three days after the battle in which Maxwell was killed, Lee surrendered to Grant at Appomattox Courthouse. The grief of a young widow is reflected in this epitaph, reading, "God grant that it was not a vain sacrifice." Interestingly, Maxwell's 5th New Hampshire Regiment suffered more casualties during the entire war than any other Union regiment, with 1,051 men killed or wounded. A closeup view of the military motif on this stone can be seen on page 26.

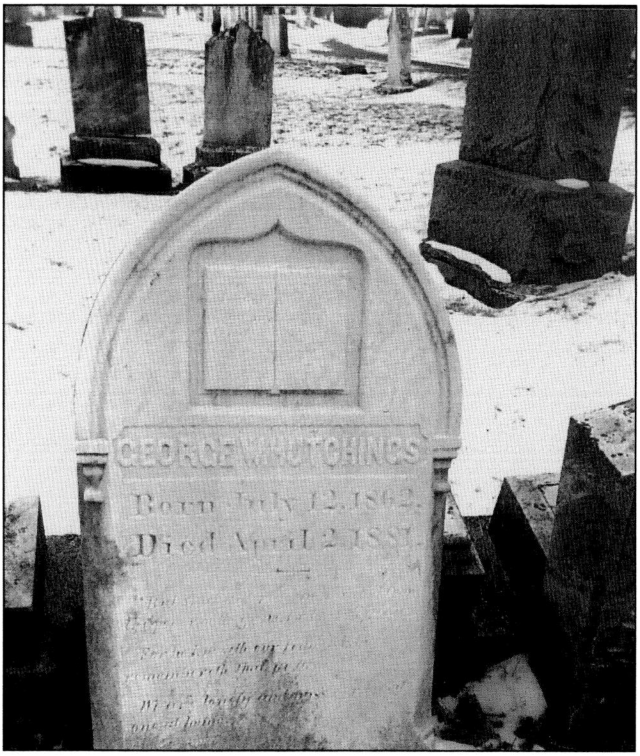

George Hutchings, 1881, Elmwood Cemetery. This marble gravestone, with its Gothic-arch and open-book motif, is one of the oldest to be found in this portion of South Street. The open-book motif can have dual meaning, signifying "the Divine word" from the Bible or the deceased's accomplishments. The former meaning is probably intended here, based on Hutchings's youth and the extent of scriptural verse on his stone.

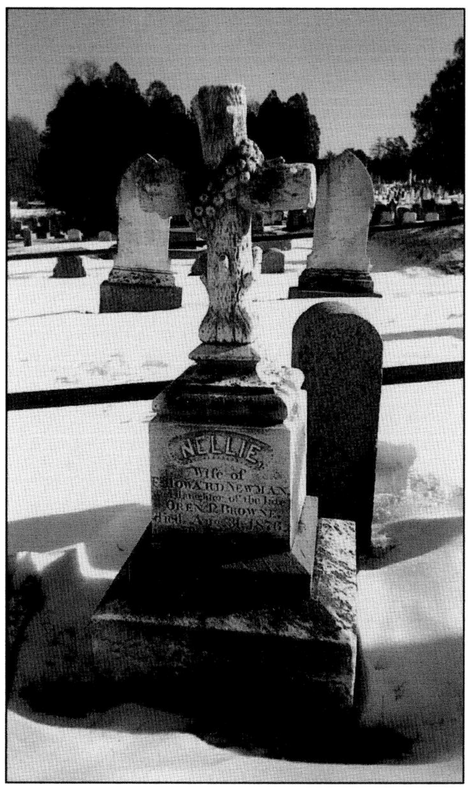

Nellie Newman, 1876, Harmony Grove Cemetery. Called a "tree-stump" marker, this type of monument is not widely found in Portsmouth. The style is representative of the rustic movement that became popular in the country in the mid-19th century. This "back-to-nature" approach was idealized in book and verse by such writers as Henry David Thoreau and was practically applied with the establishment of the rural cemetery movement.

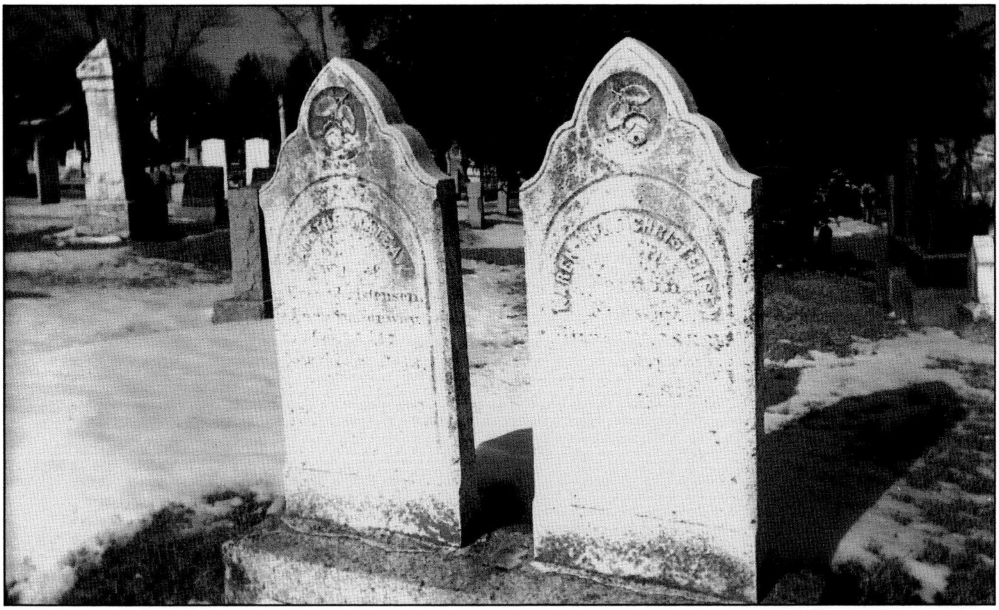

ANETHE MATEA AND KAREN ANNE CHRISTENSEN, 1873, HARMONY GROVE CEMETERY. These Norwegian women, sisters-in-law who arrived at the Isle of Shoals in 1871–1872, were killed by Louis Wagner in what became famous as "the Smuttynose Murders." Their sad story has remained popular to this day. Anethe was described as "fair and merry, with thick, bright sunny hair," while Karen was "melancholy from the loss of a lover and lonesome."

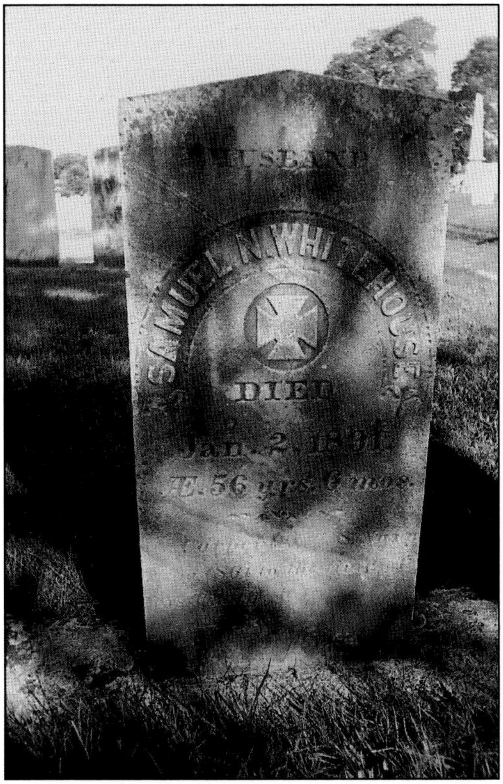

SAMUEL WHITEHOUSE, 1891, HARMONY GROVE CEMETERY. Whitehouse's stone describes him as a carpenter in the U.S. Navy "from 1861 to the time of his death." The Maltese cross adorning his stone is a symbol dating back many centuries in Europe and is commonly found on gravestones from the mid- to late 1800s.

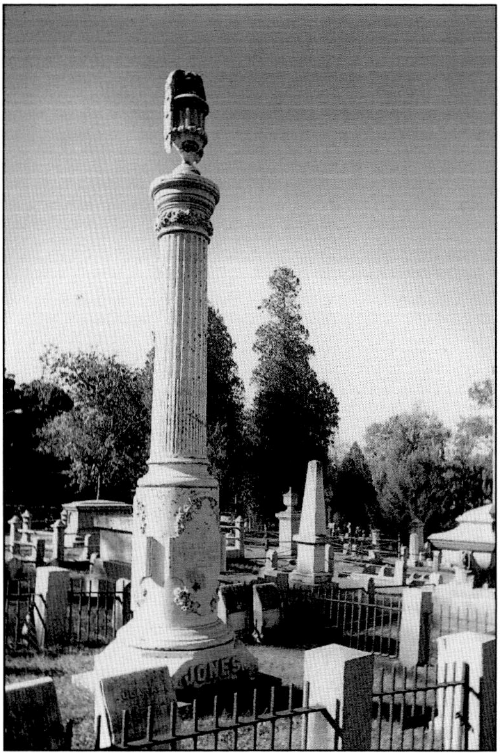

William Jones, 1855, Harmony Grove Cemetery. The importance of the person buried here is indicated by this lofty monument. Jones was a Portsmouth ship owner who had full or part interest in many of the ships constructed here, including the square riggers *Arethusa* and *Franconia* and the Raynes-built clipper ship *Emily Farnum.*

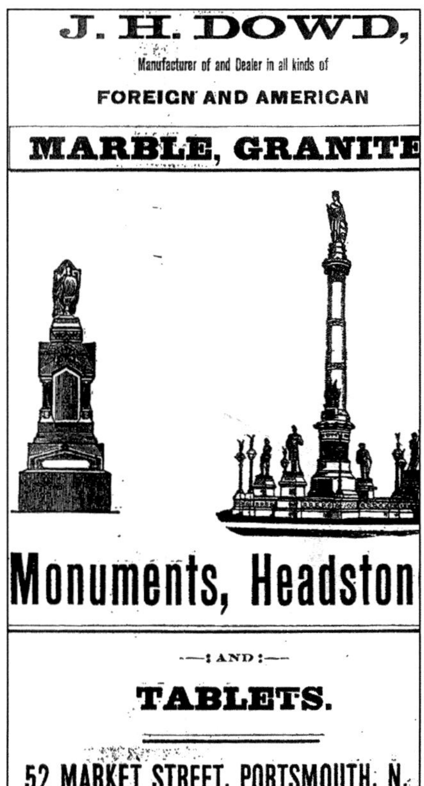

J. H. Dowd Advertisement, 1892. John Dowd established his monument company in Portsmouth the same year this advertisement appeared in a city directory. Though he specialized in elaborate marble and granite works, he supplied simpler gravestones when called upon to do so. His company operated until around 1950 and was surpassed in town only by the Treat family in years of service in the stonecutting profession.

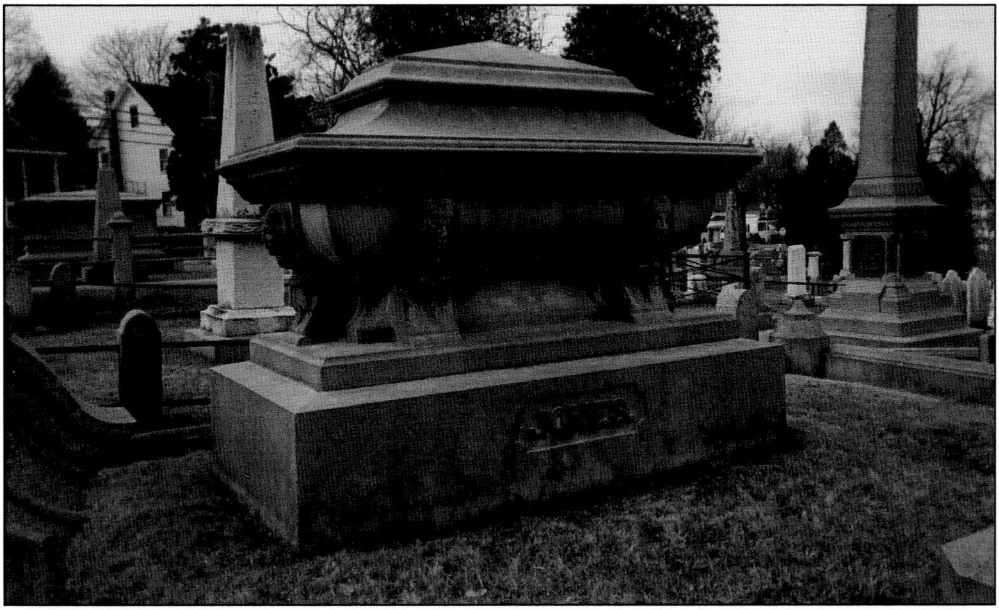

Albert Jones, 1870, Harmony Grove Cemetery. Jones was born in 1830 and, though he died young, was involved in his family's ship-owning business. His tomb is interesting, showing a marked foreign influence, perhaps Egyptian or Asian in origin. The carved faces are found on all four sides of the monument. They are identical and may be a likeness of Jones himself, nearly resembling a death mask.

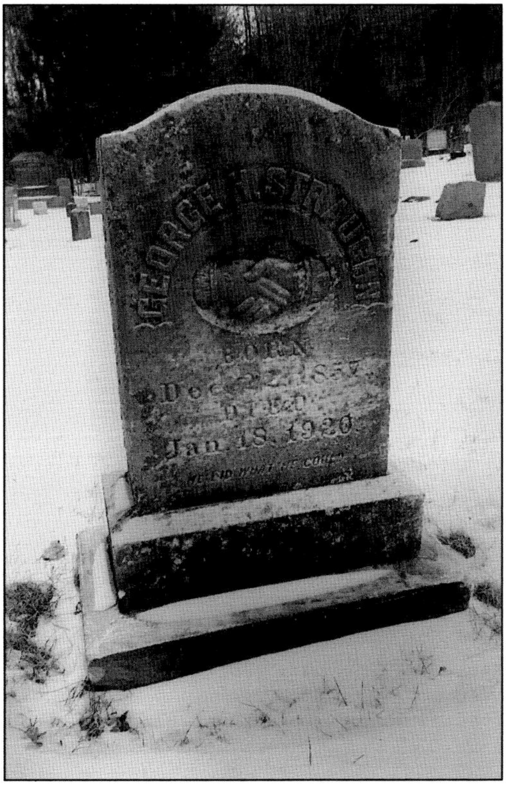

George Straughn, 1920, Sagamore Cemetery. A prominent African American citizen of Portsmouth, Straughn came from Petersburg, Virginia, and was a leading member in the People's Baptist Church for years. He also served as deacon and treasurer of the People's Mutual Benefit Society. The clasped hands shown here are a symbolic farewell and represent a hope of meeting in eternity. The epitaph reads, "He did what he could."

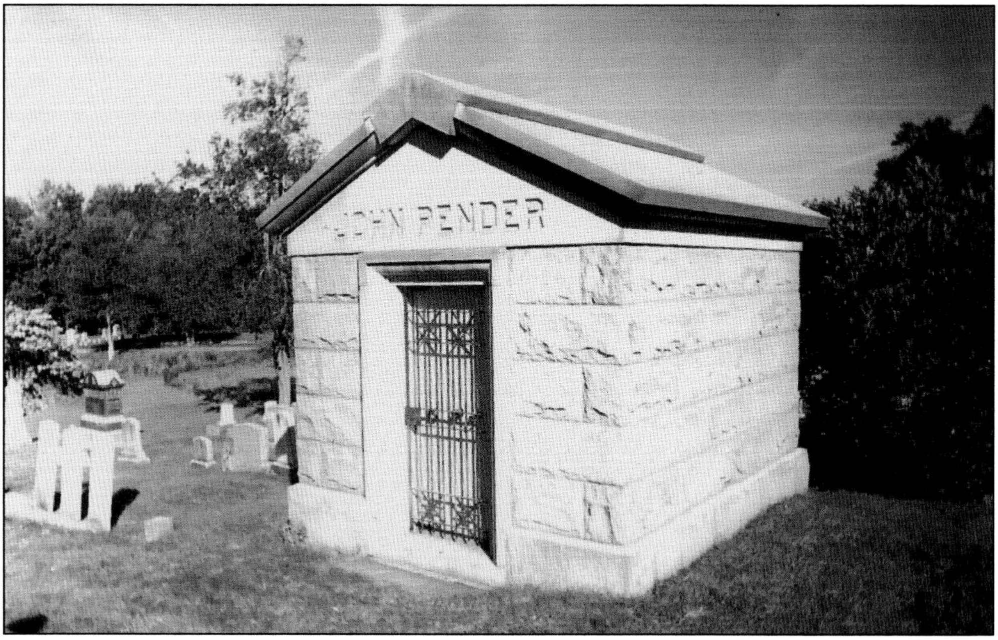

THE JOHN PENDER MAUSOLEUM, HARMONY GROVE CEMETERY. This simple mausoleum, made of marble and granite, measures about 10 square feet. Note the wrought-iron gate that adorns its entryway. The man interred here is likely the same Portsmouth man who served in the New Hampshire state senate during the 1911–1912 term.

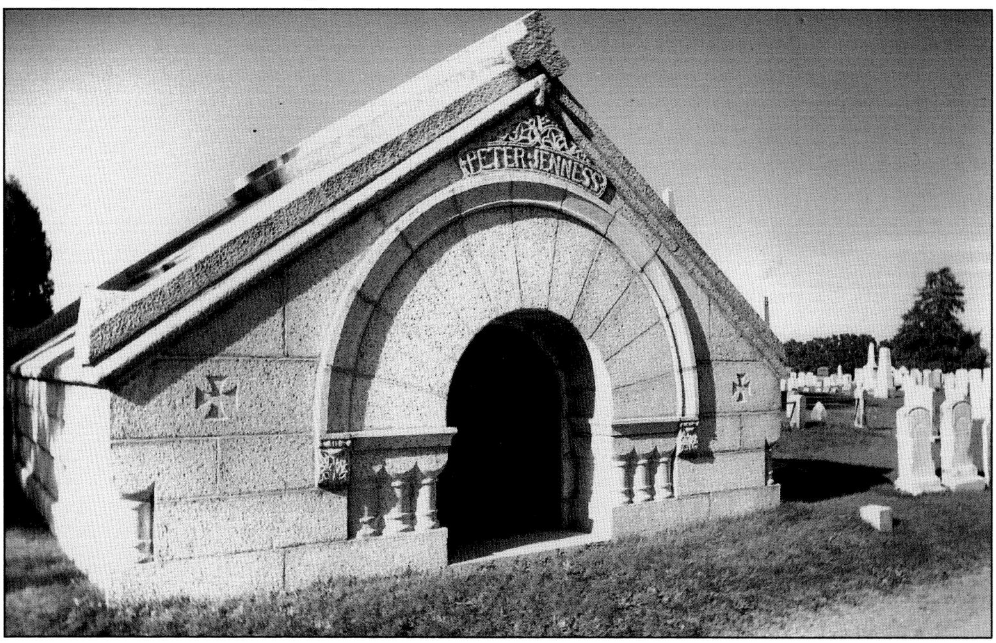

THE PETER JENNESS MAUSOLEUM, HARMONY GROVE CEMETERY. Resting in this elaborate and attractive mausoleum is a descendant of an old Portsmouth family that included Richard Jenness, an associate of New Hampshire royal governor Benning Wentworth. It is unknown whether the man interred here is the same Peter Jenness who was a part owner in the Piscataqua-built ships *Alice Ball* and *Sarah Pettigrew* in 1857, or his son.

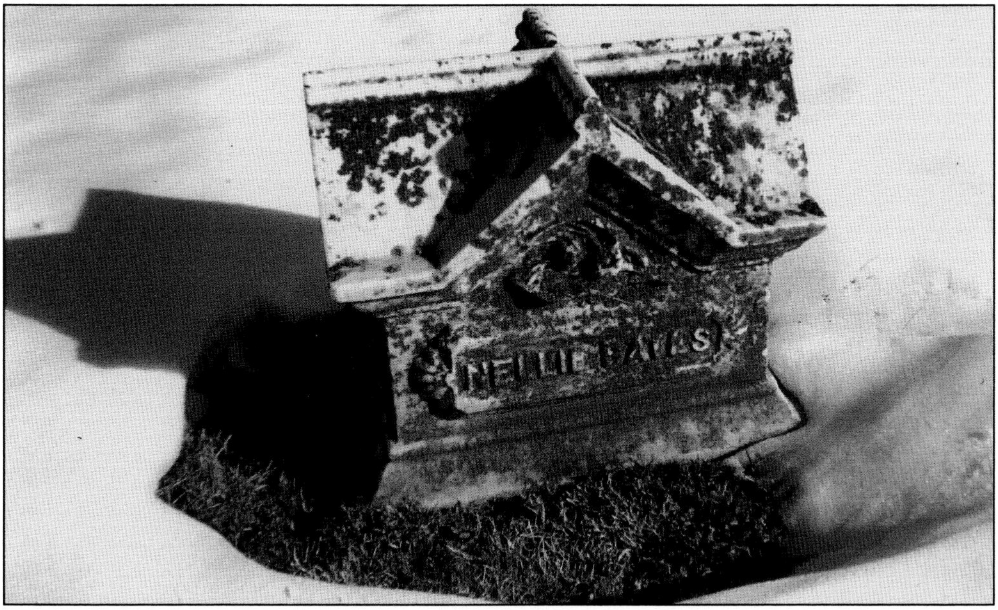

NELLIE BATES, PROPRIETOR'S CEMETERY. The date of this unusual gravestone, carved in the shape of a mausoleum, is unknown. It stands just one foot tall and is a rarity in Portsmouth. Interestingly, the peak of the roof is similar to that of the Jenness mausoleum, shown on the previous page. The size of the marker and its broken floral motif indicate that a child is buried here.

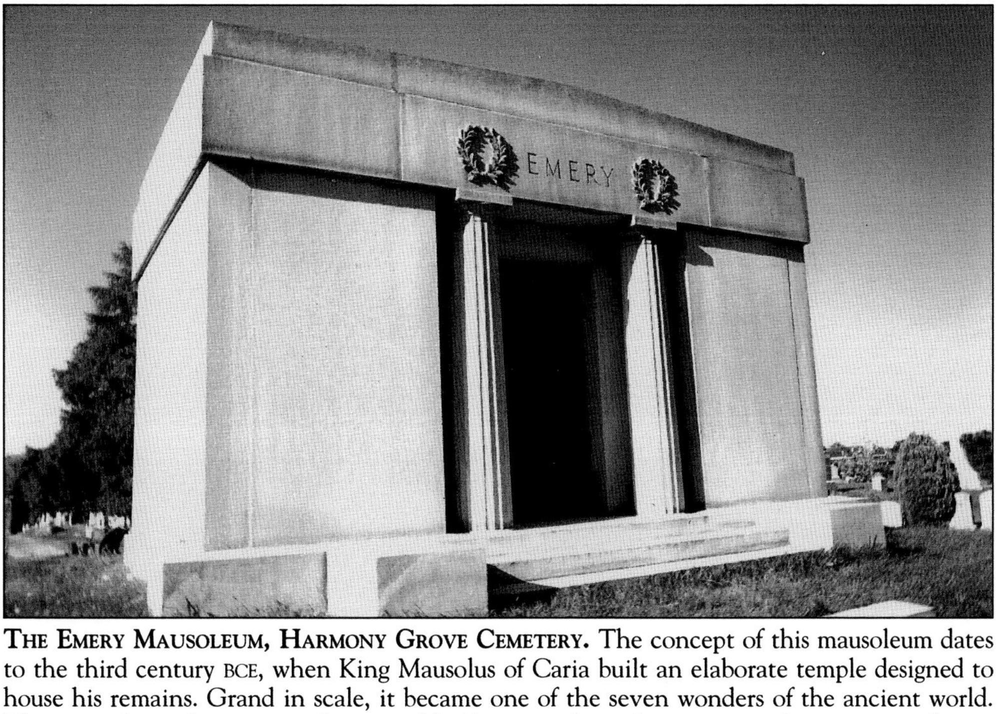

THE EMERY MAUSOLEUM, HARMONY GROVE CEMETERY. The concept of this mausoleum dates to the third century BCE, when King Mausolus of Caria built an elaborate temple designed to house his remains. Grand in scale, it became one of the seven wonders of the ancient world. This mausoleum, large in size for a city like Portsmouth, with imposing columns to match, is a modern-day descendant of that ancient wonder.

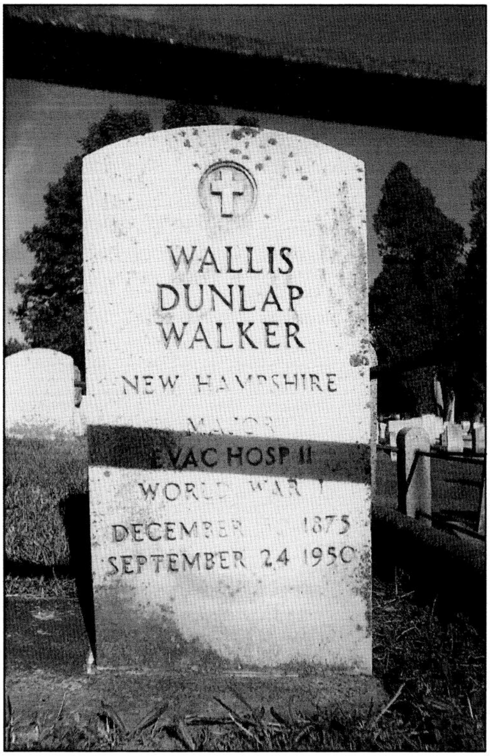

WALLIS WALKER, 1950, HARMONY GROVE CEMETERY. Veterans of nearly all of the country's wars, from the Revolution onward, have been buried at South Street. Many of their graves are marked by stones like the one shown here for a World War I veteran. Stones such as this are of a standard type provided by the government for deceased veterans and are still used today.

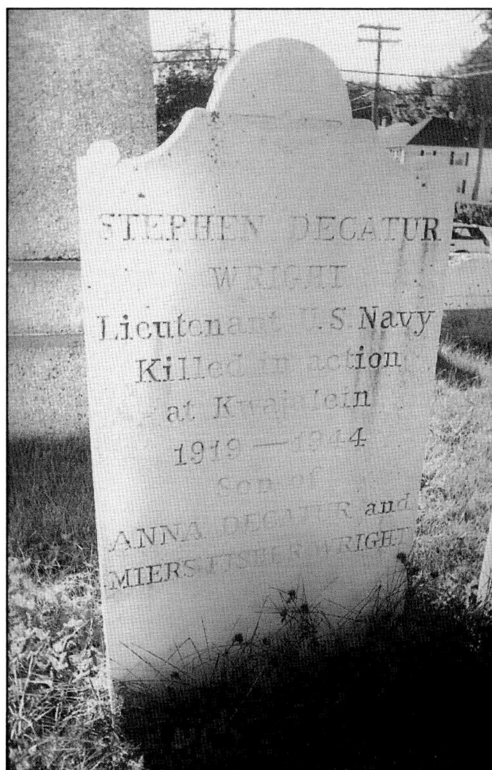

STEPHEN WRIGHT, 1944, PROPRIETOR'S CEMETERY. This marble stone, with a pair of naval aviator's wings carved at the top, marks the resting place of a young navy pilot killed during World War II. Wright died during the assault on Kwajalein in the Marshall Islands during January and February 1944, likely lost during one of the 96 sorties that were flown by carrier fighters just before army troops stormed ashore.

Five

African American Burial Sites, Family Cemeteries, St. Mary's, Temple Israel, and Calvary Cemeteries

In addition to the cemeteries discussed previously, Portsmouth has many other cemeteries located within its borders. Some are difficult to find and are often inaccessible. Nonetheless, all are important and provide an interesting view into the city's past.

The most unusual of these sites is the "Negro Burying Ground," located at what is now the corner of Court and Chestnut Streets near the downtown area. Identified on a 1705 town map, it may have even been used prior to this time. By 1800, the burial ground had been desecrated and built over as the city expanded. No surface remnants of this burial site remain, and roadwork over the years has often unearthed human bones and other artifacts. Still, no efforts at preservation were made. However, private initiatives by the Black Heritage Trail have resulted in the placement of a marker commemorating the location. The issue of this burial site and its preservation came to the fore once again in October 2003, when utility work at the site resulted in the discovery of 13 coffins. Eight of them were removed by archaeologists for study, with their remains later determined to be of African ancestry. The area where this burying ground is located may be closed to traffic and a suitable memorial erected. Public opinion supports this view, but it remains to be seen what course of action will be taken.

Private family cemeteries are another important but oft forgotten part of the city's past. Within the city limits, there are more than 30, some relatively large and some consisting of but a single grave, or none at all. Some are well maintained by private individuals and organizations, while others, such as the Hall Cemetery, have been effectively abandoned and are in danger of being lost.

St. Mary's Roman Catholic Church was the first Catholic parish in Portsmouth. In 1852, a wood structure was built for worship, serving until destroyed by fire in 1871. It was replaced in 1873 with a brick church that was used for many years. It is believed that St. Mary's Cemetery was established about this same time, around 1870. A beautiful cemetery, it is now maintained by the Immaculate Conception Parish.

Temple Israel Cemetery was established around 1905, when the first Jewish synagogue was built in Portsmouth. Prior to this time, the Jewish, whose presence dates back to the 1790s with Abraham Isaac, worshiped in private homes and buried their dead in public burial grounds and later in Jewish cemeteries in Dover and Somersworth. This cemetery offers a look at gravestones that are quite different from those found elsewhere.

Calvary Cemetery is the newest in Portsmouth, established around 1910. Still in active use, it is operated by the Immaculate Conception Parish.

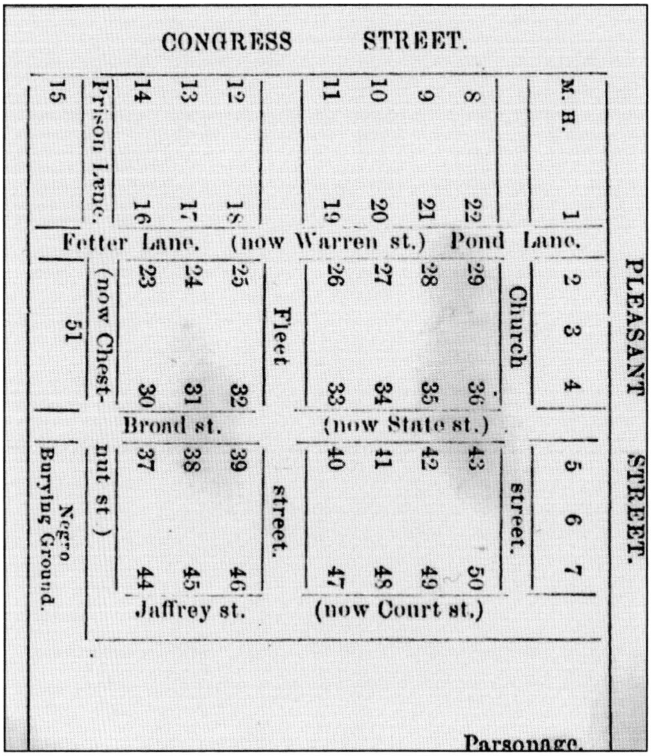

The Glebe Map of Portsmouth, 1705. This land, once owned by the church, was appropriated in 1705 and "laide out into house lotts for peopling the town." The town's "Negro Burial Ground" is shown at the lower left. Though its true size remains unknown, its existence, once thought by many to be uncertain, is no longer in doubt. (From *Rambles About Portsmouth, First Series*, by Charles Brewster, 1873 edition.)

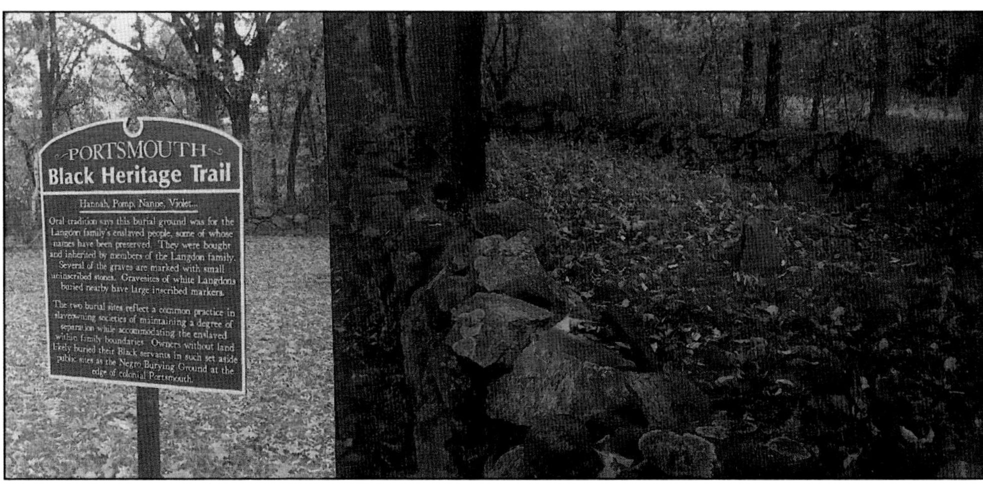

The Langdon Slave Burial Ground. This walled-in plot (right) lies behind the parsonage of Christ Church Episcopal on Lafayette Road. Measuring 44 feet long and 14 feet wide, it holds 15 graves with simple fieldstone markers. Nearly all slave gravestones in the area are unmarked, and the number of enslaved individuals really buried here is unknown. The site is now recognized with a sign erected by the Black Heritage Trail (left).

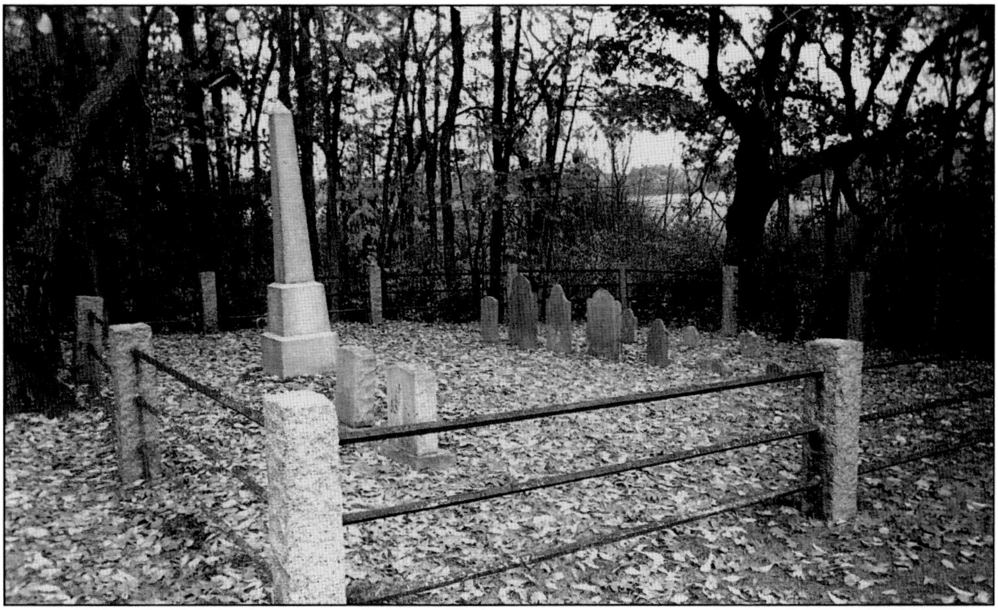

THE LANGDON FAMILY CEMETERY, URBAN FORESTRY CENTER. In contrast to the nearby Langdon Slave Burial Ground is this family plot for white members of the Langdon family. Professionally carved gravestones are the rule, not simple fieldstone markers. The earliest burials here may date as far back as 1664. This site lies on a tract of land farmed by generations of Langdons and Elwyns before it was willed to the state.

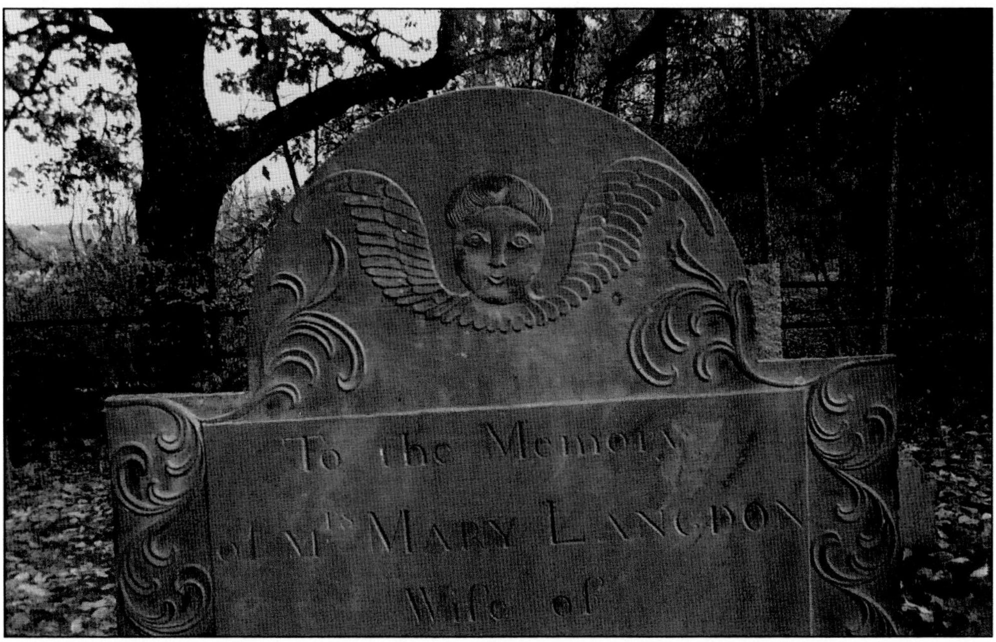

MARY LANGDON, 1789, LANGDON FAMILY CEMETERY. This attractive slate marker, with its wide-eyed angel and decorative scroll borders, was likely carved by the Lamson family. Mary Hall Langdon's stone proclaims her to be "a Lady of superior understanding, excellent accomplishments, and a most virtuous Character." She was the mother of patriot and future New Hampshire governor John Langdon Jr., as well as Judge Woodbury Langdon.

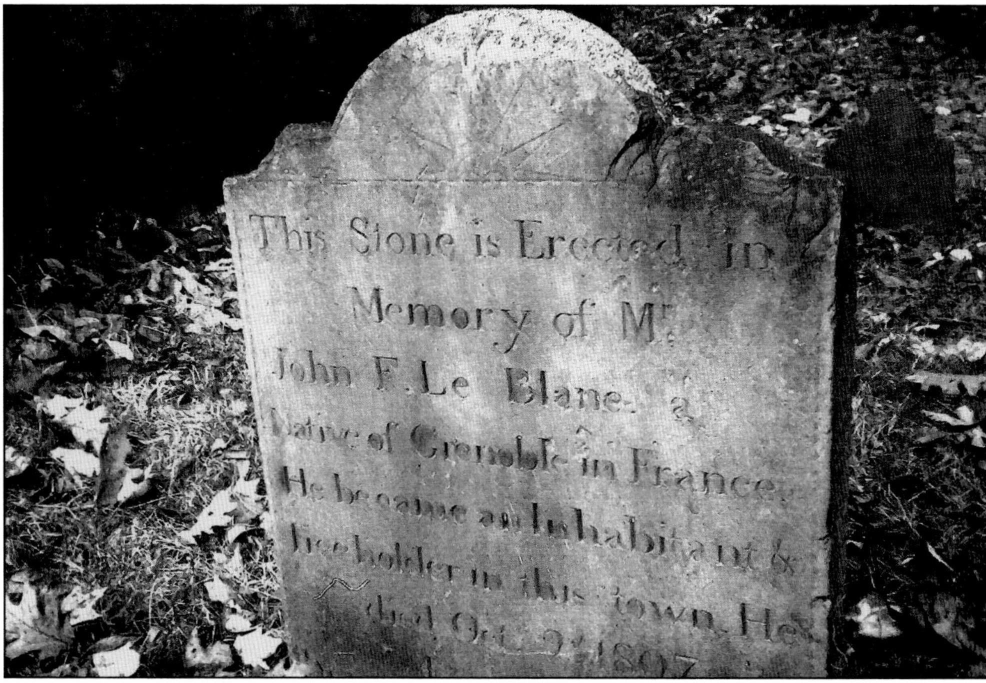

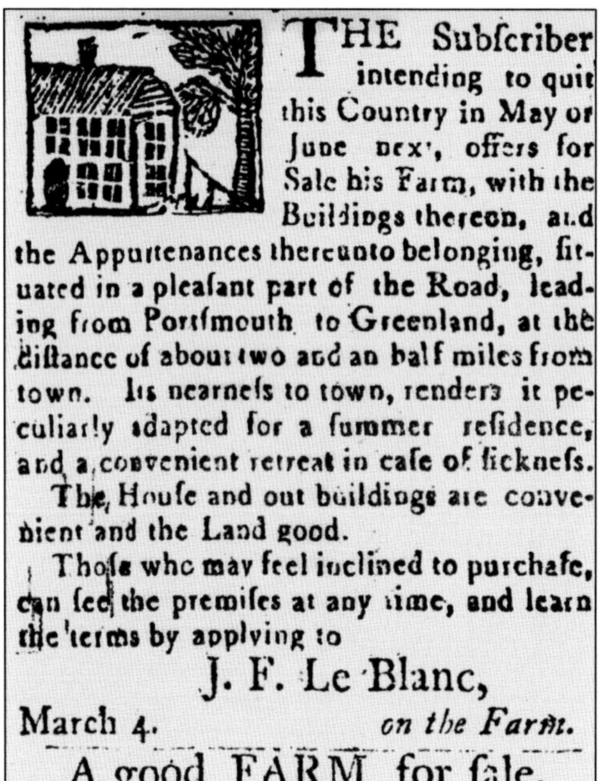
THE Subſcriber intending to quit this Country in May or June next, offers for Sale his Farm, with the Buildings thereon, and the Appurtenances thereunto belonging, ſituated in a pleaſant part of the Road, leading from Portſmouth to Greenland, at the diſtance of about two and an half miles from town. Its nearneſs to town, renders it peculiarly adapted for a ſummer reſidence, and a convenient retreat in caſe of ſickneſs.

The Houſe and out buildings are convenient and the Land good.

Thoſe who may feel inclined to purchaſe, can ſee the premiſes at any time, and learn the terms by applying to

J. F. Le Blanc,

March 4. *on the Farm.*

A good FARM for ſale.

JOHN LEBLANC, 1807, SHERBURNE GRAVEYARD. The family cemetery at Portsmouth Plains that includes this stone is unusual because it has remained in use by direct descendants of the original property since at least 1724. LeBlanc's gravestone, possibly carved by the Treat family or Noah Smith, notes that he was "a Native of Grenoble in France" and "an Inhabitant and Freeholder in this town." He was a neighbor of the Sherburnes and, as is evidenced by this advertisement (left) from the *New Hampshire Gazette* in 1806, intended "to quit this Country" and return to France. Sadly, LeBlanc never made his return, dying instead on October 2 at he age of 46.

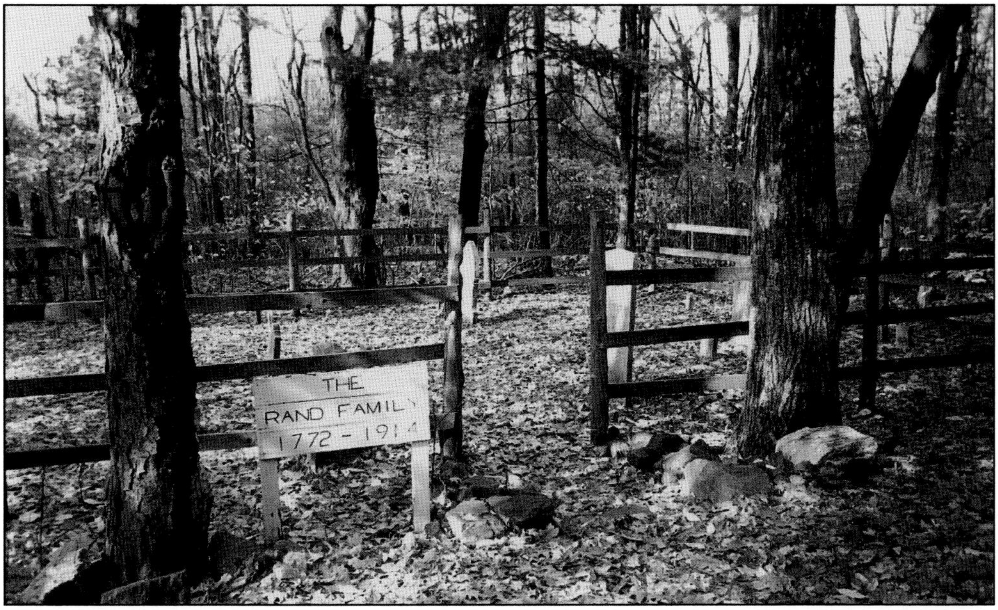

The Rand Family Cemetery, Lafayette Road. This cemetery contains burials for members of the Rand family, who once owned the surrounding land where the Colonial Pines Estates now stands. The earliest gravestone dates from 1827, while the latest is dated 1914. This site was restored in 1982 by Eagle Scout John Jacobsmeyer, with material assistance from several sponsors, and has remained in good shape.

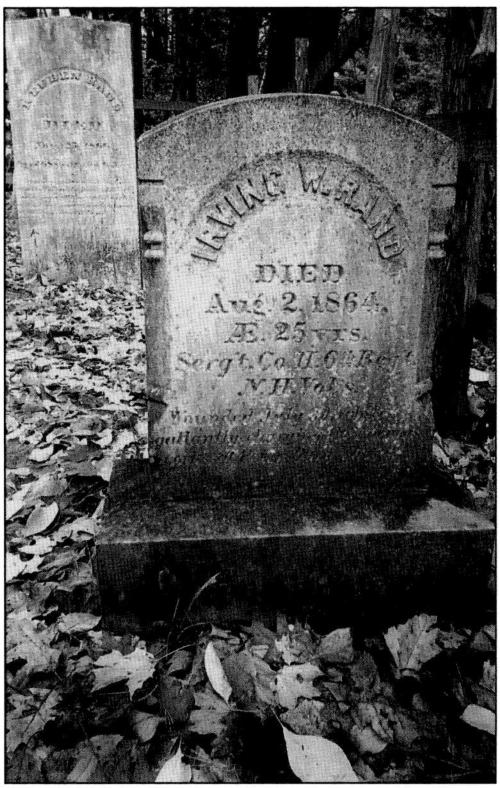

Irving Rand, 1864, Rand Family Cemetery. Irving Rand was the son of Reuben Rand. A sergeant in the 6th New Hampshire Regiment during the Civil War, he was wounded on July 30, 1864, "while gallantly charging the enemy works at Petersburg, Va." Like many soldiers on both sides during this bloody war, Rand died several days after the battle, on August 2, as a result of his wounds.

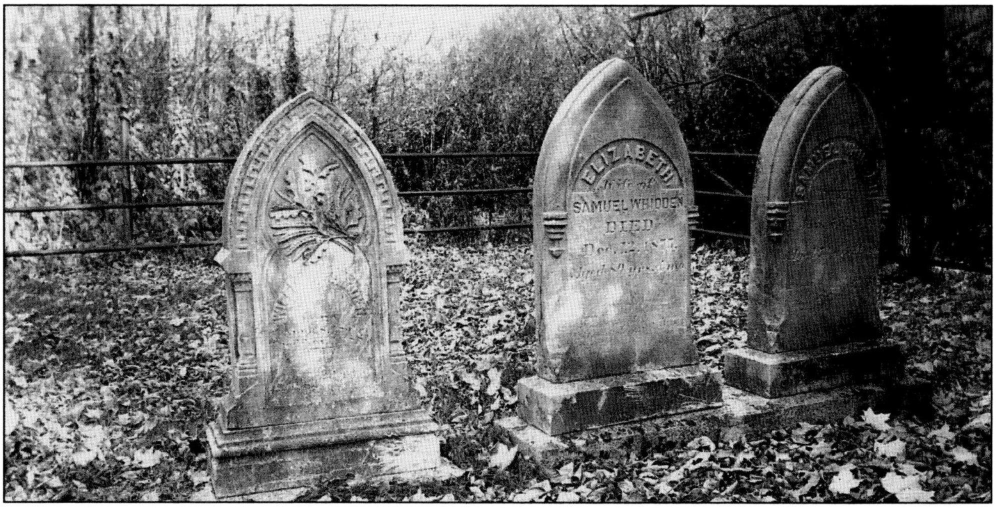

THE WHIDDEN FAMILY CEMETERY, EAST SIDE, LAFAYETTE ROAD. This site, one of two Whidden family plots on Route 1, highlights the Gothic-arch gravestones (from left to right) for William Whidden (1881) and parents Elizabeth Langdon Whidden (1875) and Samuel Whidden III (1875). Elizabeth Langdon Whidden was the daughter of Rev. Joseph Langdon, also buried in this plot. Like many young ladies of the day, she learned the art of needlework. Below is a sampler she stitched in 1805 at the age of 10. The verse states, "This work in hand My friends may have When I am dead And in my grave." Her friends had to wait a long time, as Elizabeth, who "smiled in death to meet her God," lived till a ripe old age. (Below, courtesy of the Newington Historical Society.)

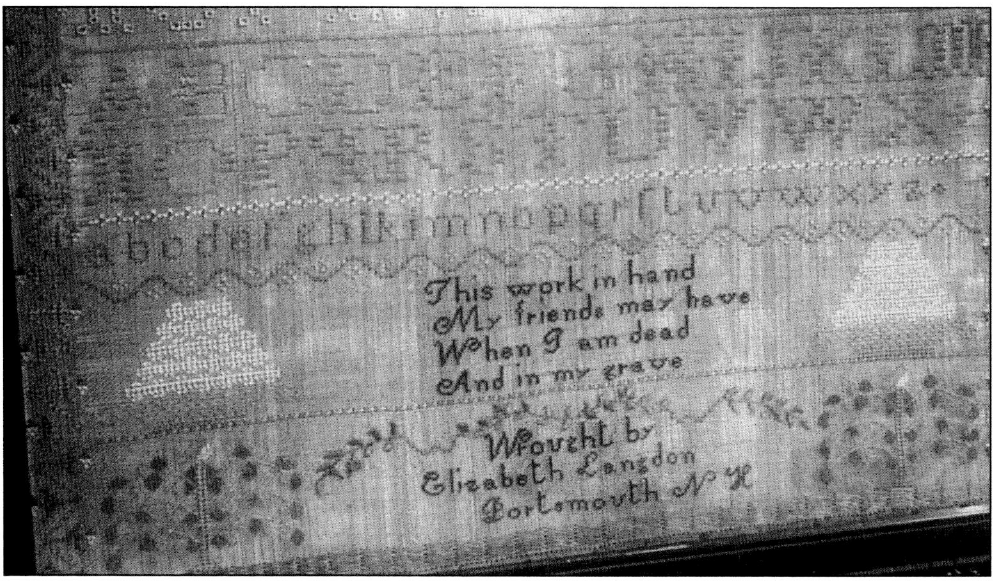

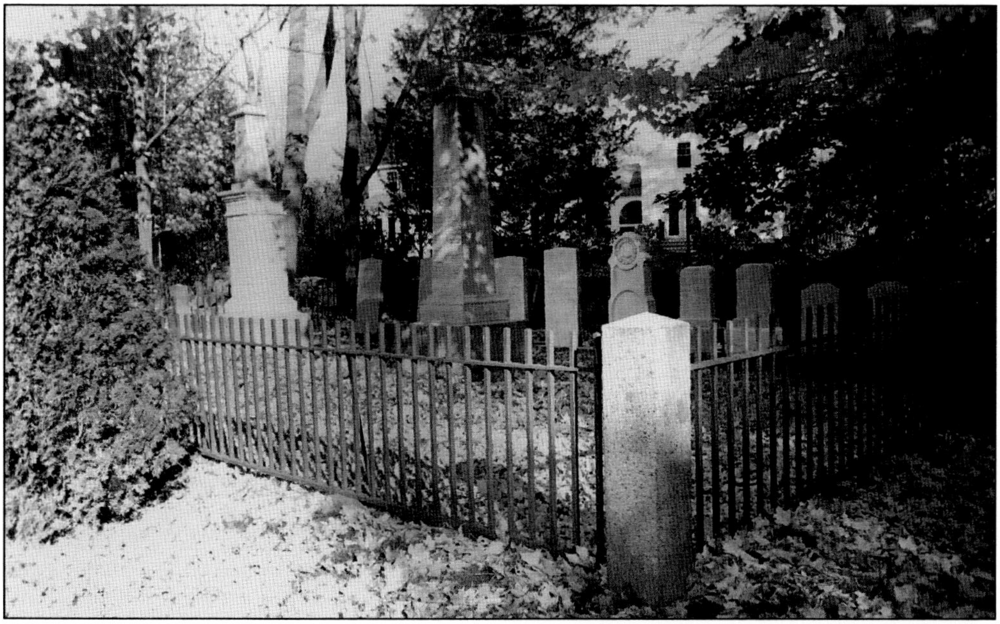

The Langdon Family Cemetery, Lafayette Road. Descendants of the Langdon family still care for this exquisite plot, and it remains in use today. Most of the markers here are made of marble, the earliest dated 1834 for Lt. Col. Samuel Langdon. He died at the age of 81, his epitaph stating that he gave the patriots of the Revolutionary War "his warm and constant support."

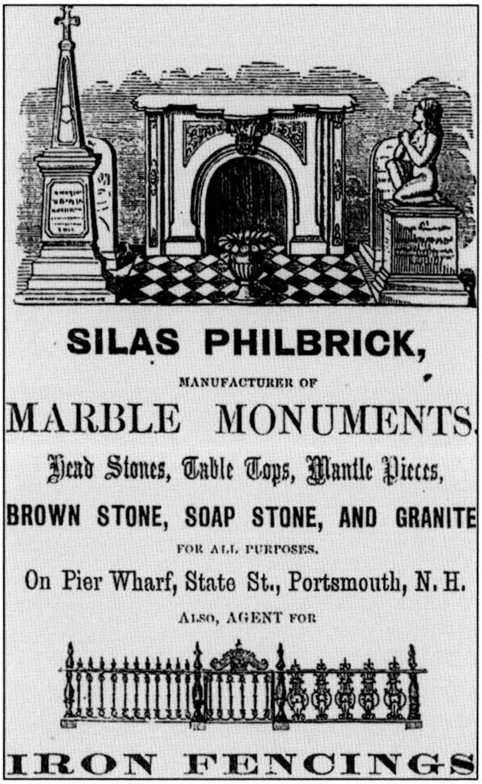

A Silas Philbrick Advertisement, 1864. Philbrick was a stonecutter in Portsmouth from around 1860 to 1895. This city directory advertisement shows his monument and fence work. The centerpiece monument of the Langdon Family Cemetery (see above, center) was provided by his firm. With lettering cut by a Mr. Borthwick (one of Philbrick's workers), it details the Langdon family genealogy from its first arrival in New Hampshire. (Courtesy of the Portsmouth Public Library.)

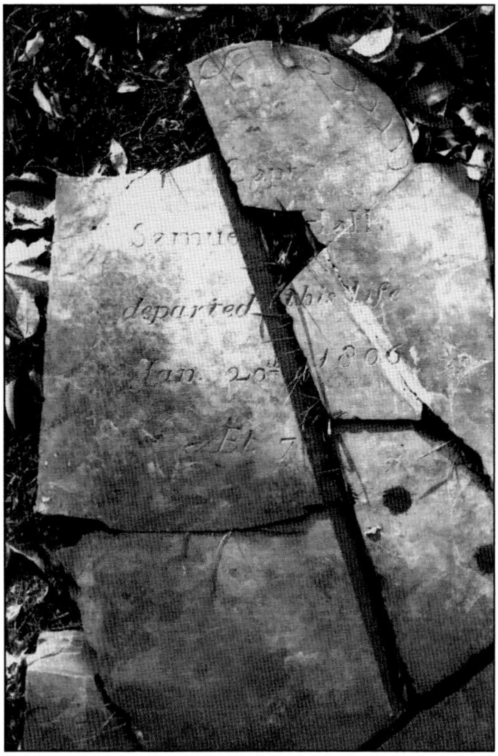

Samuel Hall, 1806, Hall Family Cemetery. Captain Hall is notable as the patriot entrusted to transport a large part of the gunpowder captured from the British at Fort William and Mary in December 1774 to Cambridge, Massachusetts, for use by militia groups. This photograph show his fragmented gravestone, carved by John Marble, in 1983. Recent attempts to find its remnants proved unsuccessful. (Courtesy of Louise Tallman.)

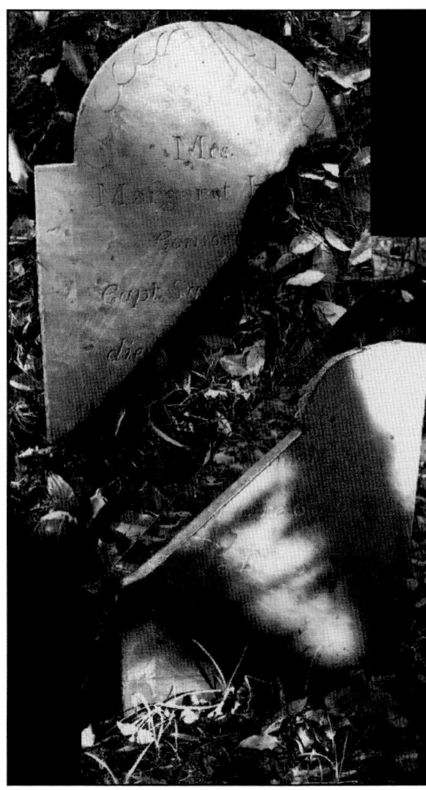

Margaret Hall, 1803, Hall Family Cemetery. The gravestone shown here demonstrates the terrible plight of this cemetery, called by historian Louise Tallman "the most complex as well as the most abused of all the family graveyards in Portsmouth." Margaret's stone was carved by stonecutter John Marble and is one of his more unusual works. (Courtesy of Louise Tallman.)

JOB TABOR, 1833, BECK-TABOR FAMILY CEMETERY. Tabor's gravestone was carved by the Treat family, likely Allen, of Portsmouth and shows the common urn and willow motif. Tabor, who died at the age of 26, has an epitaph reading, "Blooming youth as you pass by, As you are now so once was I, As I am now so you must be, Prepare to die and follow me."

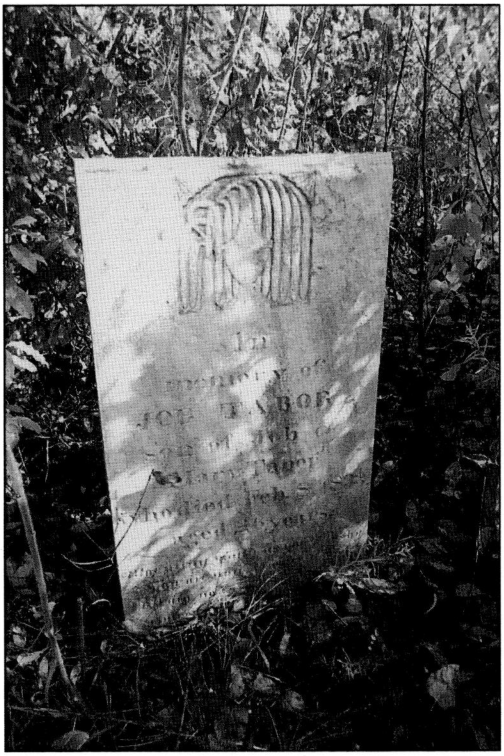

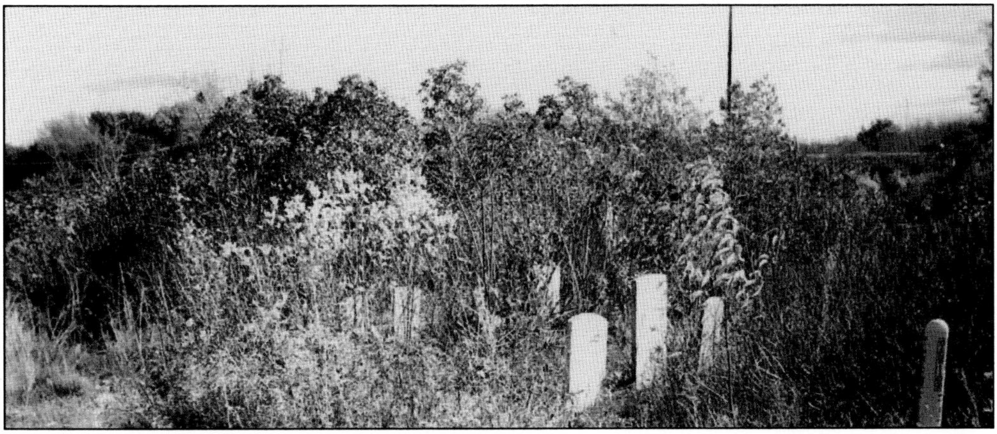

THE BECK-TABOR FAMILY CEMETERY, GRAFTON DRIVE. This family cemetery is yet another that hovers on the brink of extinction. Located in a wooded area behind the bus terminal, just beyond the parking lot, it is extremely overgrown and receives little care. The site contains 20 marked burials, and at least two others whose markers have gone missing.

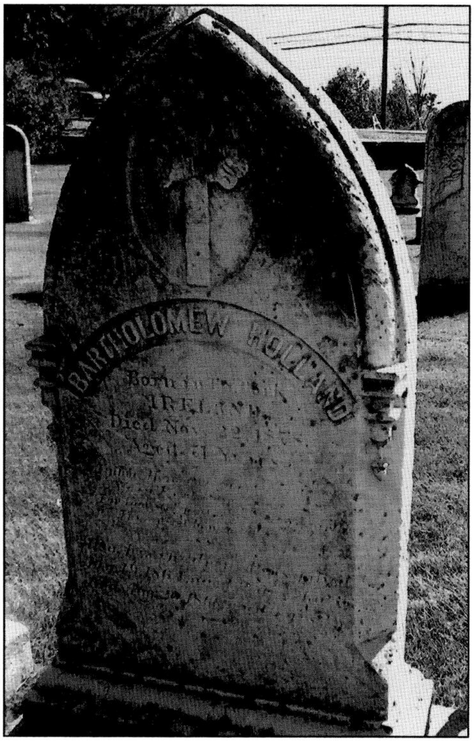

BARTHOLOMEW HOLLAND, 1878, ST. MARY'S CEMETERY. Many of the earliest burials in this Catholic cemetery were for Irish immigrants. As his gravestone states, Holland was a native of County Cork, Ireland, and died at the age of 71. Whether he immigrated here during the great Potato Famine of the 1840s is unknown. Also memorialized on this stone are several of his children who died between 1864 and 1866.

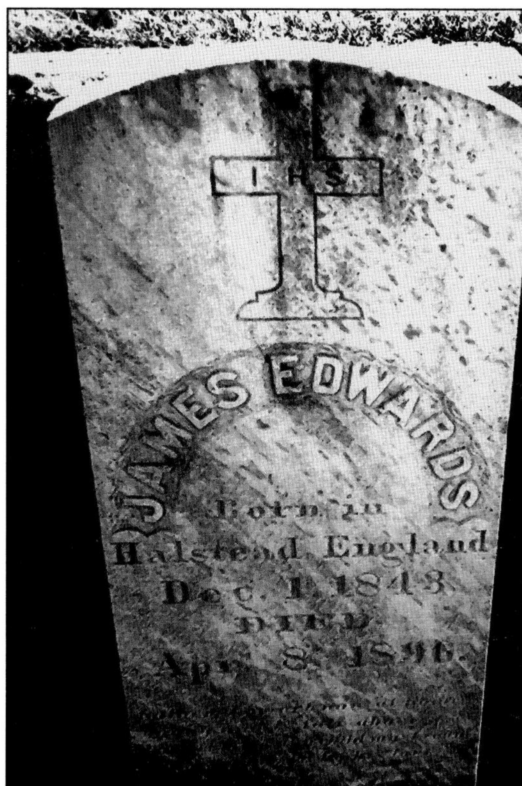

JAMES EDWARDS, 1896, ST. MARY'S CEMETERY. The cross adorning this gravestone of an English native is typical of those found in this cemetery. The letters "IHS" on the cross have a dual meaning, one being an acronym for the Christian phrase "In His Service." These letters also spell the name of Jesus in ancient Greek and, depicted in this fashion, symbolize Jesus on the cross.

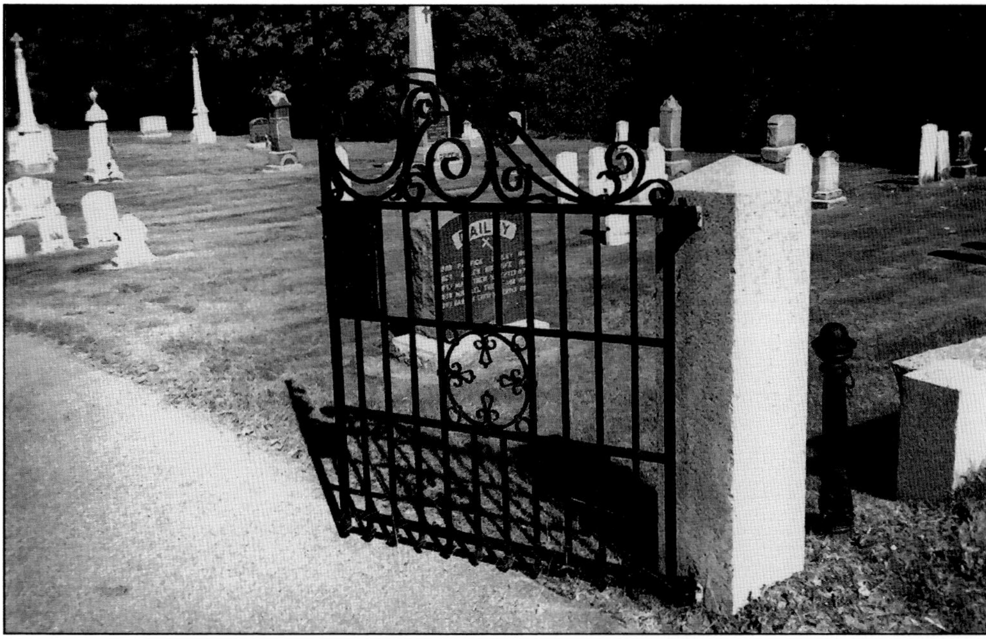

St. Mary's Cemetery. The wrought-iron gate at the cemetery's entrance is an attractive feature. Most of the markers within St. Mary's are made of marble and, in later years, granite. Burials still occur here in established family plots from time to time but have lessened as the years have passed.

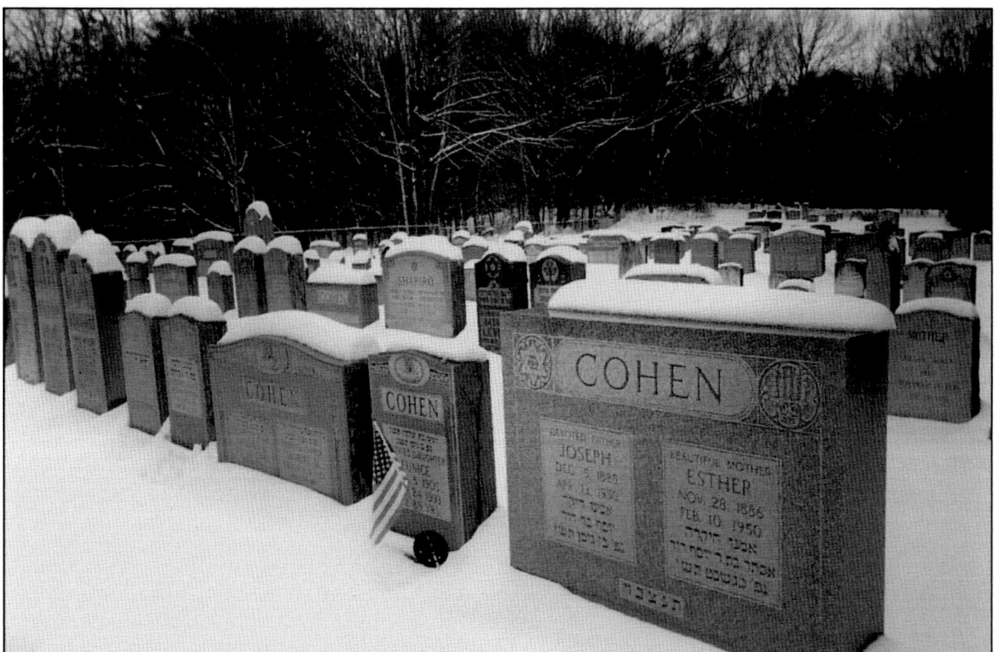

Temple Israel Cemetery. This Jewish cemetery on Banfield Road, established around 1907, offers a distinctly different style of gravestone carving and tradition. One such tradition in Jewish cemeteries is the use of "visiting stones," small stones and sometimes shells that are placed on the tops of gravestones to signify their visitation by family and friends.

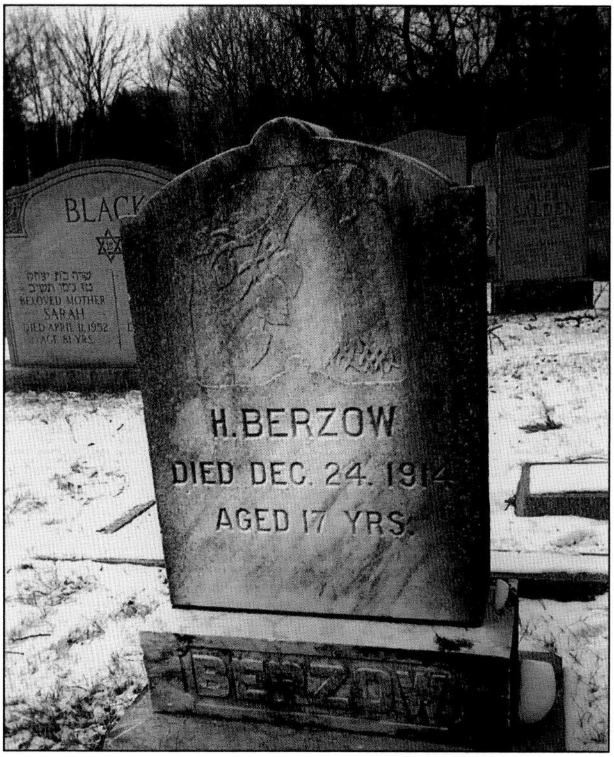

H. Berzow, 1914, Temple Israel Cemetery. The motif on this gravestone, one of the oldest in Temple Israel, is similar to those found in most Portsmouth cemeteries. The broken tree signifies death at a young age, fitting for this 17-year-old youth. The carving details on this stone, whose origin is unknown, are notable, especially the roots and leaves of the tree.

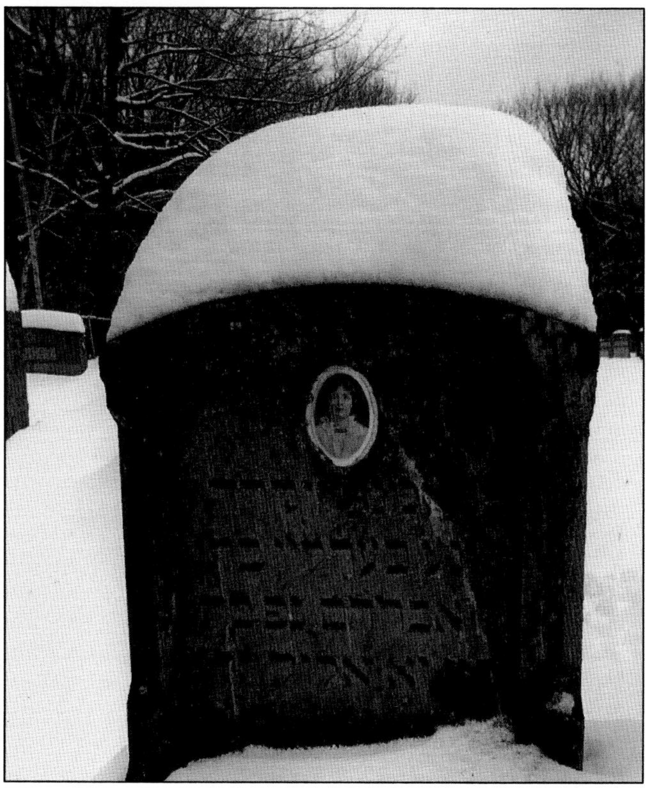

Paula Berlin, 1920, Temple Israel Cemetery. Hebrew script on the front of this stone records the name of the deceased, date of death, and her parents, while similar information is recorded on the reverse side in English. This marker's most unusual feature is the cameo portrait of the deceased, made of porcelain. Portraits of this nature were popular on gravestones early in the 20th century in urban areas but are uncommon in Portsmouth.

MAURICE LICHTUNG, 1922, TEMPLE ISRAEL CEMETERY. Portsmouth has had many scholars in its past, but none probably came from as far away as Lichtung. His worn gravestone, with its Star of David motif, states that he was "born in Palestine" and was an "educator" and "Hebrew scholar." Lichtung likely taught at a local yeshiva, possibly at the same time pursuing Talmudic studies, perhaps with the intent of someday becoming a rabbi.

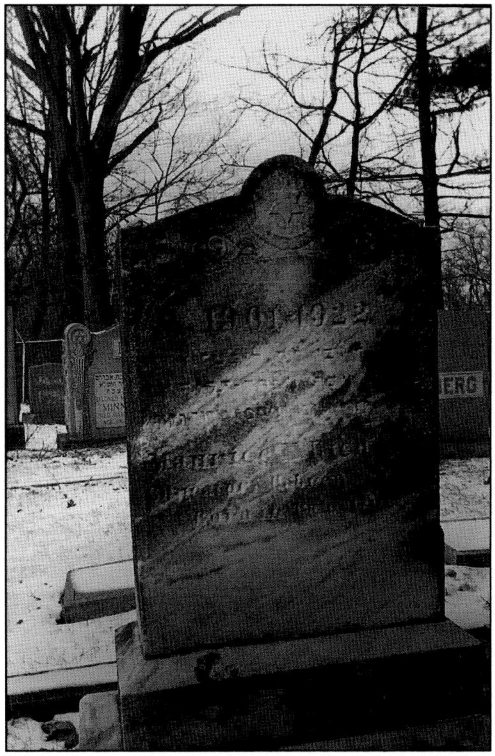

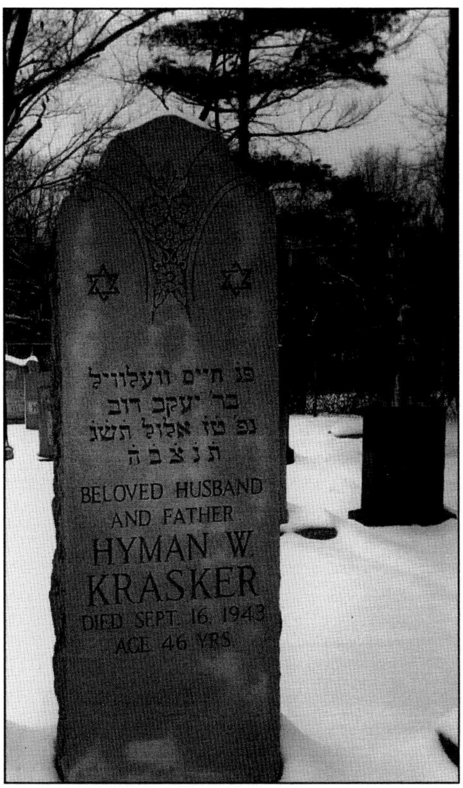

HYMAN KRASKER, 1943, TEMPLE ISRAEL CEMETERY. This late version of a Jewish gravestone stands nearly six feet tall. In addition to its Star of David and Hebrew script, it also depicts a grouping of morning glory flowers, a motif that has also been used on Christian gravestones for more than 100 years.

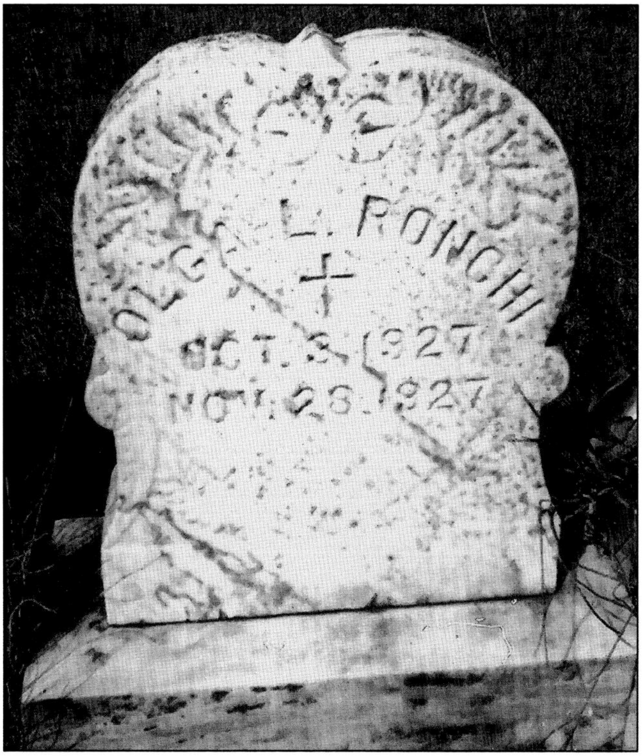

OLGA RONCHI, 1927, CALVARY CEMETERY. One of the older gravestones found in Calvary Cemetery, this marble marker for an infant bears an attractive heart-shaped design and floral motif.

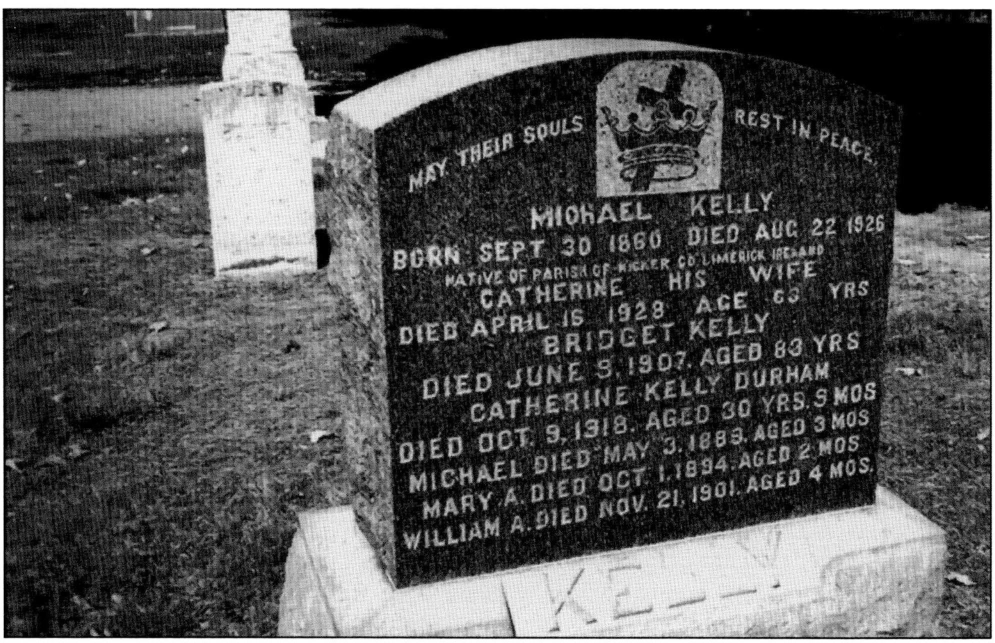

THE KELLY MONUMENT, CALVARY CEMETERY. Monuments such as this one, erected after 1900 for an Irish family from Wicker Parish, County Limerick, often have an additional purpose: to memorialize family members whose original burial site is elsewhere. Michael and Catherine are certainly buried here, but perhaps not their children, whose deaths predate the establishment of Calvary Cemetery.

Six

Early Gravestone Carvers of Portsmouth

Since early Colonial times, professionally carved gravestones have made their way into Portsmouth cemeteries. From about 1660 to 1700, they came almost exclusively from the Boston area, where America's first carvers operated. From around 1714 onward, stones carved in the Merrimack Valley from Haverhill, Massachusetts, and the surrounding area also made their appearance. With Portsmouth's maritime ties to Boston and other points in Massachusetts, the "importation" of gravestones was a common occurrence, and there was no need for a resident stonecutter. However, as the business of carving grew in the Boston area, competition grew fierce, and young men practicing the trade, such as Bartlett Adams, had to seek opportunity further afield. This competition, combined with the town's growth and maritime prominence, resulted in Portsmouth getting its first stonecutter, John Marble, in 1801.

Marble came to town from Quincy and was an experienced carver upon his arrival. Born in 1764, he learned the trade from his father, Joseph Marble, and worked in the Merrimack Valley from about 1780 until 1798, when he moved southward. When John Marble moved to Portsmouth, he soon had all the work he could handle. He practiced his trade here for six years. In 1807, however, he suddenly sold his carving business and moved back to his old home, Bradford, Massachusetts. Married late that same year, he continued his own carving shop in Massachusetts until his death in 1844.

Marble's successor in Portsmouth was the firm of Noah Smith and Company, which soon went by the name of Smith and Treat. Little is known of Noah Smith, his origin, or his gravestone-carving background. His partner was Shubael Treat, who had previously come to the area from Middleton, Connecticut, and learned the stonecutter's trade. Samuel Treat, Shubael's cousin, had arrived in Portsmouth from Connecticut by 1807 and apprenticed with him. The Smith and Treat partnership, which consisted of shops in Portsmouth and Newburyport, was formally dissolved in 1810. The following year, Samuel Treat purchased land on Deer Street in Portsmouth and was a tenant in common with Noah Smith. From 1811 to 1815, the two may have worked together in a loose partnership in the gravestone business until Samuel opened his own shop. From that time on, Samuel Treat was Portsmouth's premier carver, even though Smith continued as a friendly competitor until about 1821. Because of the several men involved in these shops, Smith, the Treats, and an apprentice named Moses Warren, the attribution of a carver for gravestones dating from 1807 to 1821 is often uncertain. However, Samuel Treat's individual style and characteristic lettering and phrasing can often be identified. What role his cousin Shubael, who operated his own stonecutting shop in Newburyport and died at sea in 1823, further played in the Portsmouth scene, if any, is not fully understood. In any case, the Treat family became the leading carvers in Portsmouth for nearly 100 years. Their stones are found all along the northern New England coast from Maine to Cape Cod.

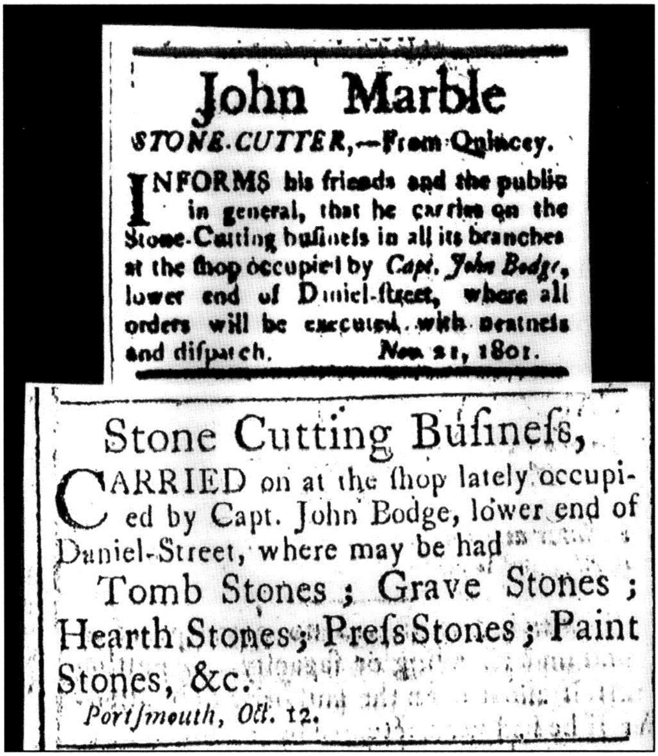

John Marble

STONE-CUTTER,—From Quincey.

INFORMS his friends and the public in general, that he carries on the Stone-Cutting buſineſs in all its branches at the ſhop occupied by Capt. John Bodge, lower end of Daniel-ſtreet, where all orders will be executed with neatneſs and diſpatch. Nov. 21, 1801.

Stone Cutting Buſineſs,

CARRIED on at the ſhop lately occupied by Capt. John Bodge, lower end of Daniel-Street, where may be had

Tomb Stones ; Grave Stones ; Hearth Stones ; Preſs Stones ; Paint Stones, &c.

Portſmouth, Oct. 12.

JOHN MARBLE ADVERTISEMENTS, 1801–1802. Appearing in the *Oracle of the Day*, the advertisement at the top announced John Marble's arrival. The other, dated 1802, appeared in the *Republican Ledger*. Though Marble's name is not mentioned, the location of the shop is identical to that in the other advertisement. Note that the first type of stonecutting Marble mentions is that of "Tomb Stones."

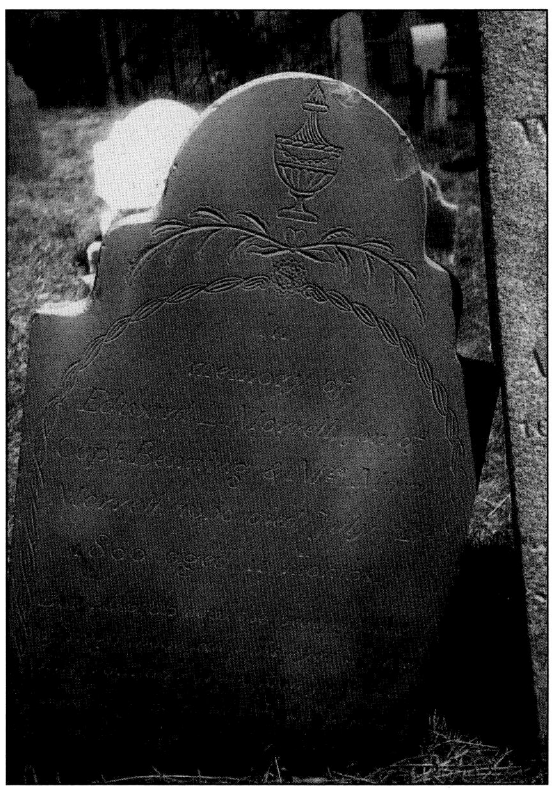

EDWARD MORRELL, 1800, COTTON CEMETERY, SOUTH STREET. The elegant lettering on this back-dated stone demonstrates a hallmark of Marble's work. He sometimes collaborated with local poet Jonathan Mitchell Sewall (see page 56) when providing an epitaph, and might have done so here. The epitaph for this infant reads in part, "The heavy shades of night have seal'd his eyes. . . . His breath & all his bosom wears the dews of death."

ABIGAIL AUSTIN, 1801, NORTH CEMETERY. This gravestone is one of the many carved by John Marble found in North Cemetery. Several distinguishing features that identify this as Marble's handiwork include the capital letter "A" in the name of the deceased, which uses a small "v" for a crossbar, the sweeping lines used on the left side of the cursive letters "M" and "A," and the circular pattern on the side borders.

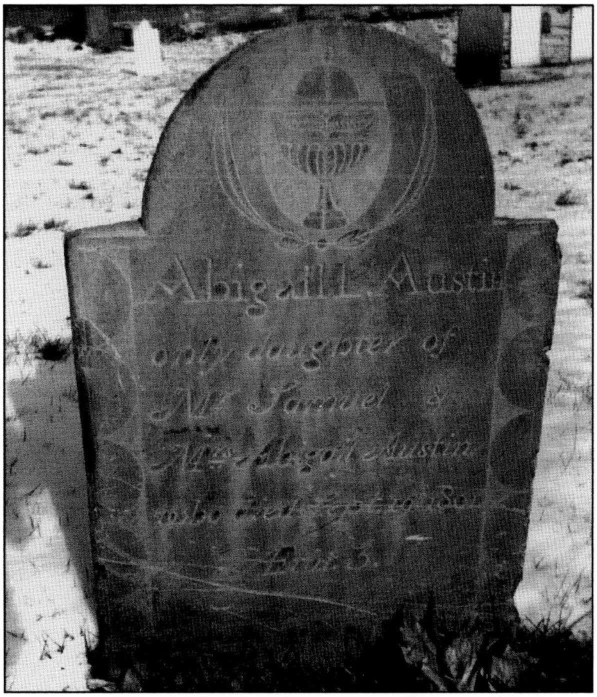

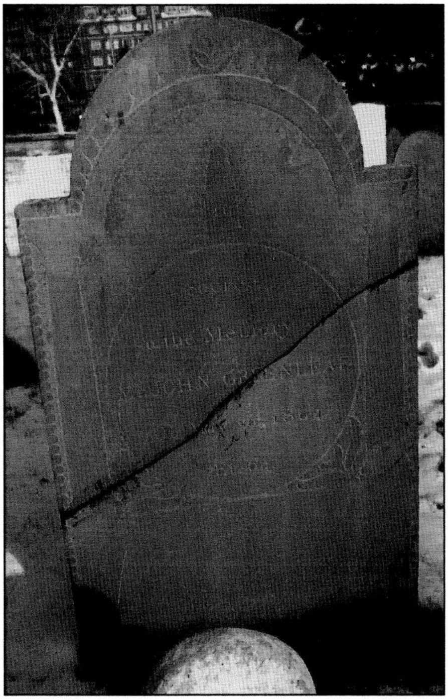

JOHN GREENLEAF, 1804, NORTH CEMETERY. Greenleaf was well known in town as the keeper of the famous Bell Tavern. Distinguished by a blue sign in the shape of a bell, it was a popular gathering place for patriots during the Revolutionary War. The acanthus leaf and ropelike design is typical of John Marble's carving style, though the rest of this design is unique.

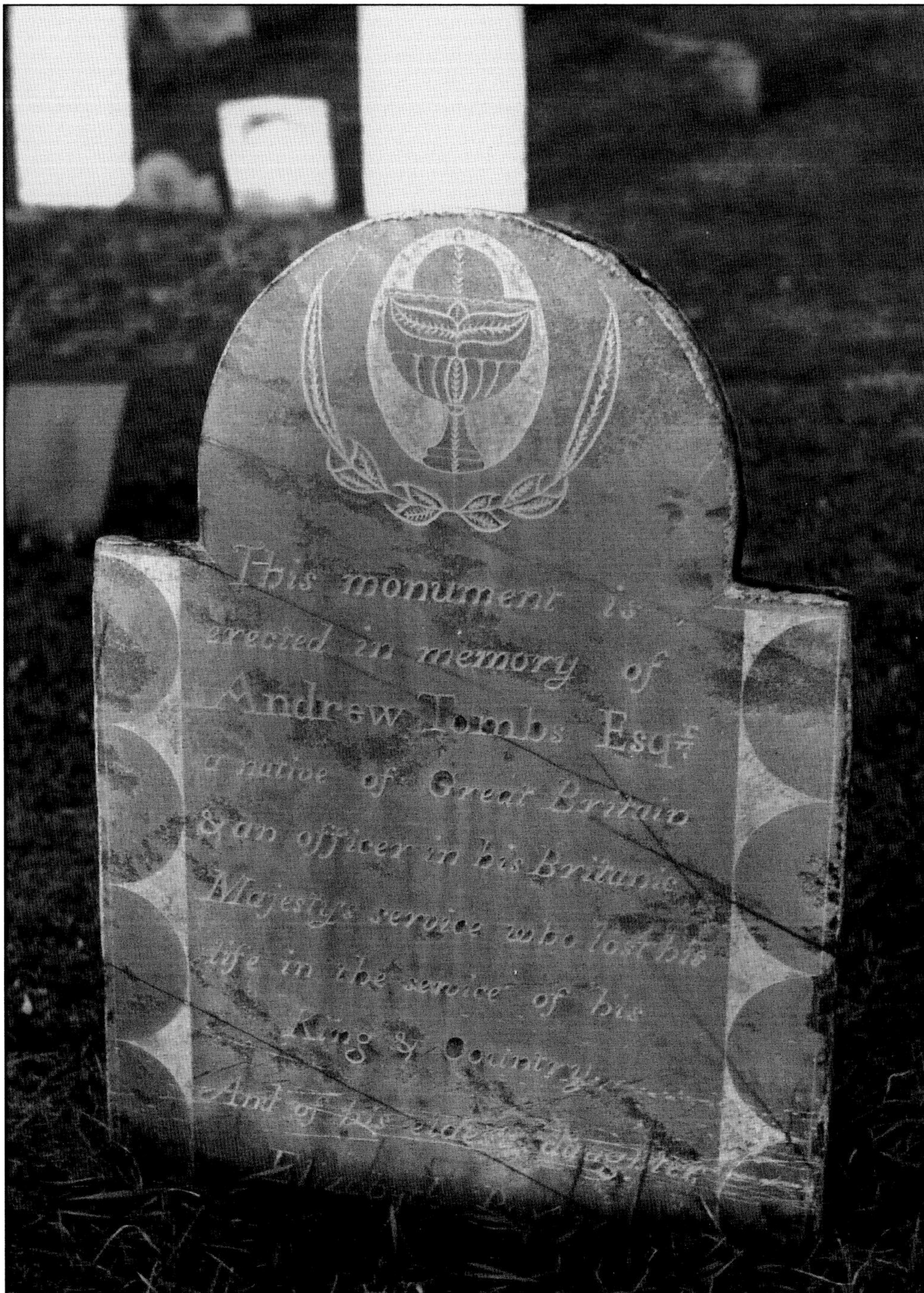

Andrew Tombs and Elizabeth Baxter, 1805, North Cemetery. Unfortunately, little is known about the individuals memorialized here other than what was carved on their gravestone. This stone, made for a British naval officer and his daughter, is one of the best-preserved examples of John Marble's work found in Portsmouth. It depicts his cursive lettering style, half-circle border design, and acanthus leaf and urn motif at its best.

Sarah Ann Neal, 1806, North Cemetery. This gravestone is typical of the size John Marble used for children, though the amount of wording shown here is rather sparse compared to his other works. Sarah's father, Capt. Joshua Neal, was a well-known shipmaster and merchant in town, dealing in rum, sugar, coffee, and molasses. Among the ships he commanded were the *Cato* (1799), *Watson* (1805), and the *Trajan* (1818).

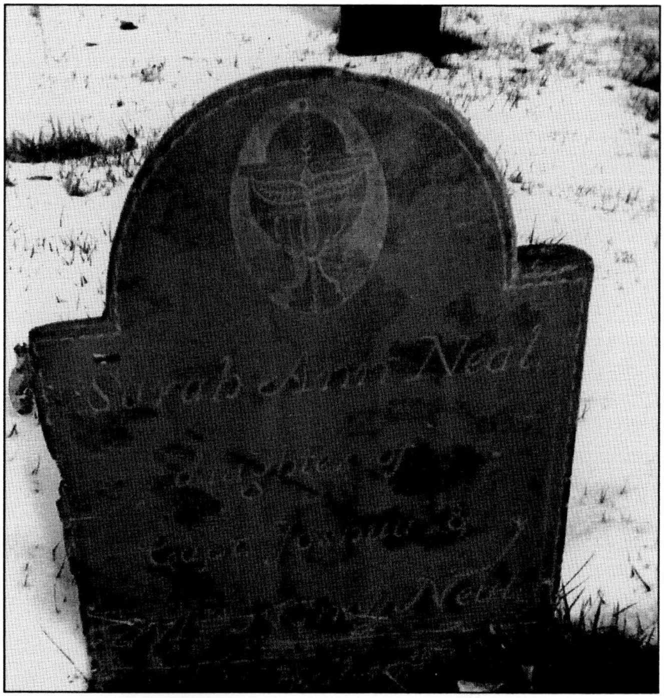

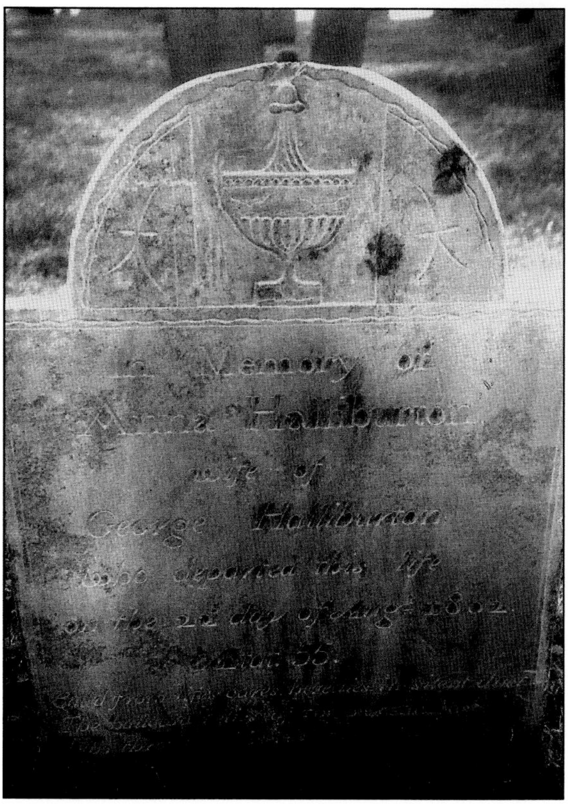

Anna Halliburton, 1802, North Cemetery. Though this stone bears many typical elements of Marble's lettering style, especially his distinctive capital letter "A," its design motif is more unusual. Note the urn at center, flanked by two simple starred lines, while the top has a scalloped border. The epitaph below reads in part, "Call'd from life's cares, here lies in silent dust The hallow'd relics of the peaceful just."

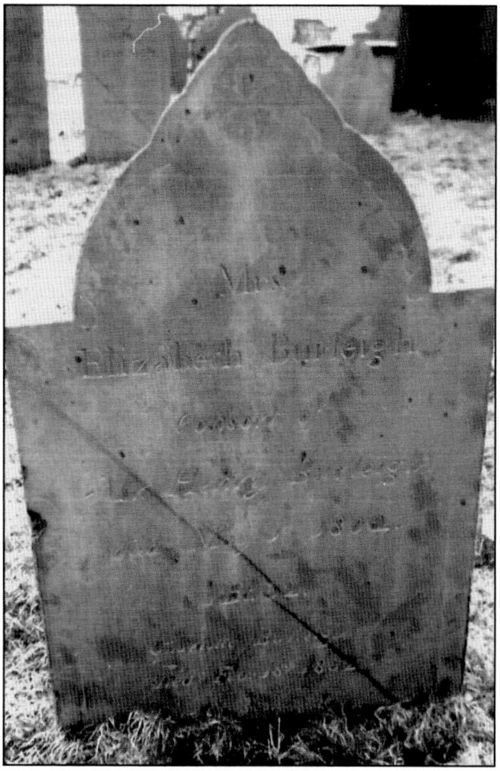

ELIZABETH AND CHARLOTTE BURLEIGH, 1802, NORTH CEMETERY. This gravestone for a mother and her eight-month-old daughter is interesting for several reasons. Though the acanthus leaf disk and roped border at the top and the half-circle side borders are common elements in John Marble's work, the pointed shape is unusual. So, too, is the small inscription at bottom for Charlotte, who died in February, over two months before her mother.

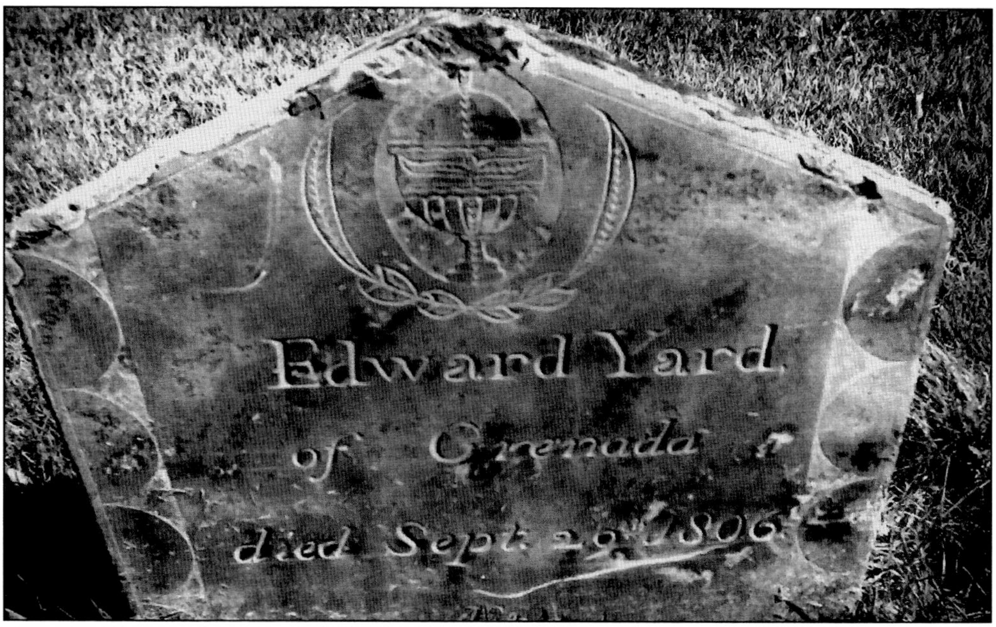

EDWARD YARD, 1806, NORTH CEMETERY. Yard was a merchant from the island of Grenada who died suddenly while on a trading voyage. Because he died intestate, his burial and affairs in Portsmouth were handled by those he knew here. This may explain the simplicity and size of this Marble-carved gravestone. While the motif and design are typical of his work, the angled top is more unusual.

MARY HILL, 1806, NORTH CEMETERY. John and Eunice Hill were communicants of North Church and buried several children in this cemetery. All of their gravestones were carved by John Marble and use a variegated color slate that probably came from quarries near Quincy, Massachusetts.

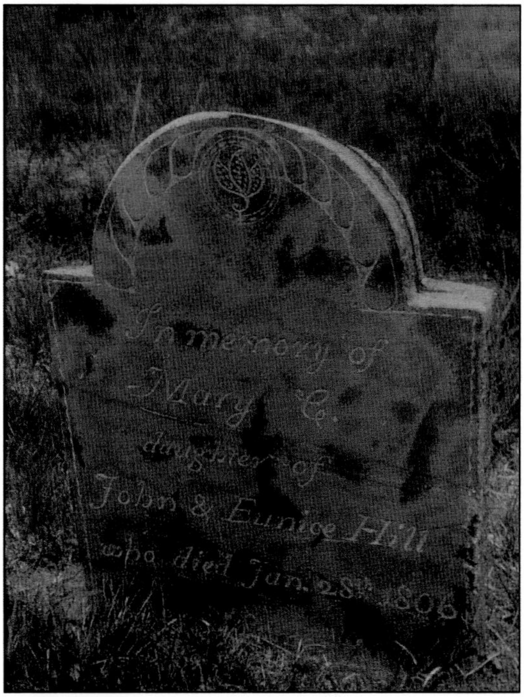

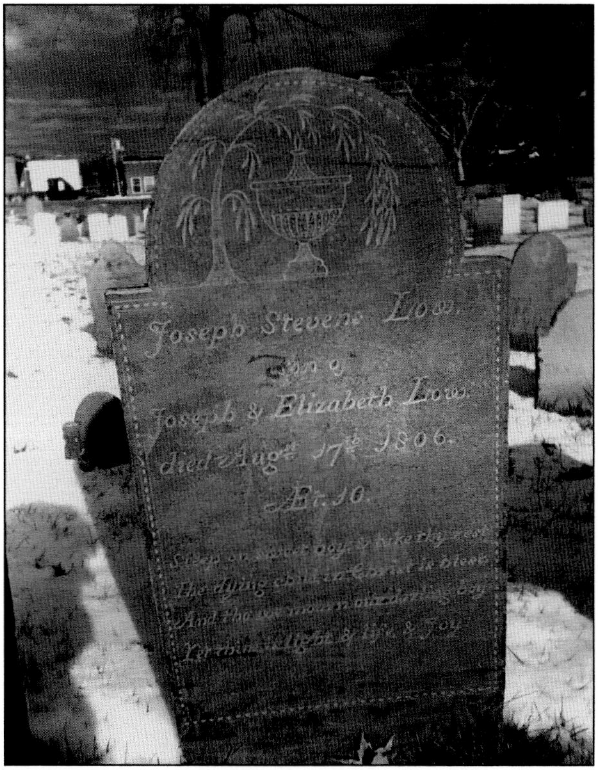

JOSEPH LOW, 1806, NORTH CEMETERY. This stone, for a 10-year-old boy, was carved by John Marble before his move back to Bradford, Massachusetts, in 1807. Its classic epitaph reads as follows: "Sleep on sweet boy & take thy rest. The dying child in Christ is blest. And tho' we mourn our darling boy. Yet thine is light & life & Joy!"

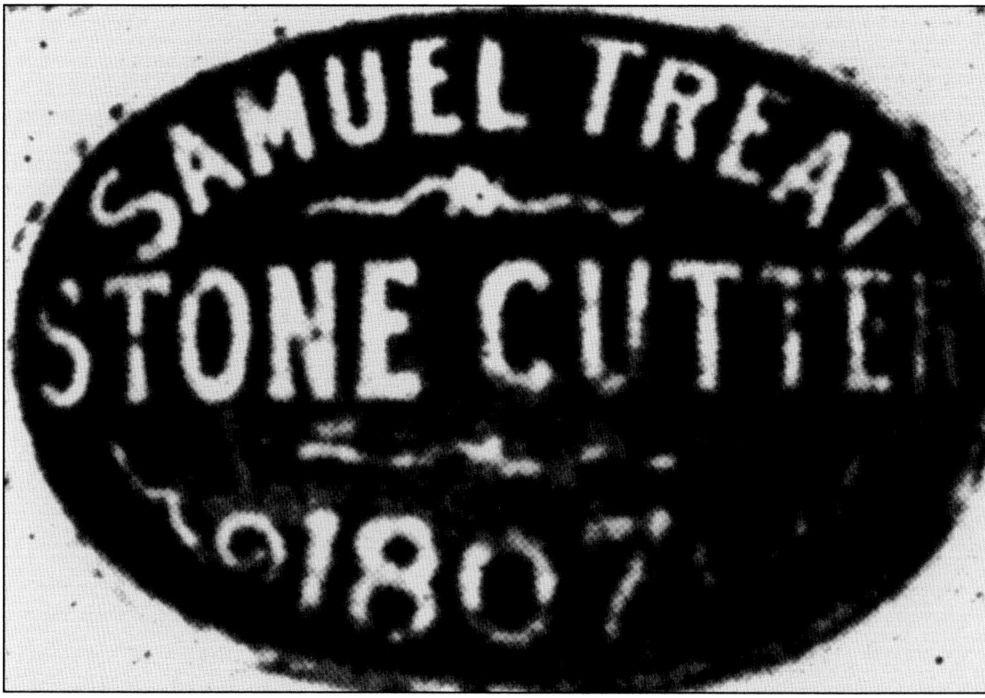

A SAMUEL TREAT SIGN, 1807. This sign, though its origin is unknown, is a sure indicator of when Treat began his stonecutting business in Portsmouth. It was likely about this time that the 19-year-old Treat arrived in town. He learned the gravestone-carving trade from his cousin Shubael Treat. (From *Praises on Tombs in the Old North Burial Ground* [1932], by A. I. Harriman.)

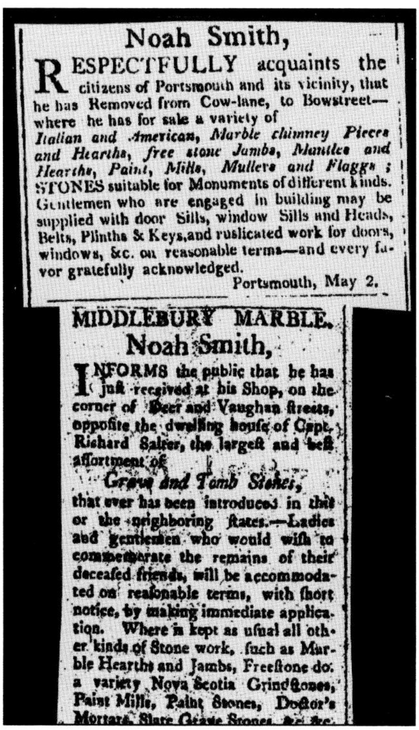

Noah Smith,

RESPECTFULLY acquaints the citizens of Portsmouth and its vicinity, that he has Removed from Cow-lane, to Bowstreet—where he has for sale a variety of *Italian and American, Marble chimney Pieces and Hearths, free stone Jambs, Mantles and Hearths, Paint, Mills, Mullers and Flaggs*; STONES suitable for Monuments of different kinds. Gentlemen who are engaged in building may be supplied with door Sills, window Sills and Heads, Belts, Plinths & Keys, and rusticated work for doors, windows, &c. on reasonable terms—and every favor gratefully acknowledged.

Portsmouth, May 2.

MIDDLEBURY MARBLE.

Noah Smith,

INFORMS the public that he has just received at his Shop, on the corner of Deer and Vaughan streets, opposite the dwelling house of Capt. Richard Salter, the largest and best assortment of

Grave and Tomb Stones,

that ever has been introduced in this or the neighboring states.—Ladies and gentlemen who would wish to commemorate the remains of their deceased friends, will be accommodated on reasonable terms, with short notice, by making immediate application. Where is kept as usual all other kinds of Stone work, such as Marble Hearths and Jambs, Freestone do. a variety Nova Scotia Grindstones, Paint Mills, Paint Stones, Doctor's Mortars, Slate Grave Stones, &c. &c.

NOAH SMITH ADVERTISEMENTS, 1807–1811. Smith is the mystery man regarding the gravestone business in Portsmouth. The smaller of these advertisements (top) ran in the *Oracle of the Day* in 1807 and records that Smith supplied stones "suitable for monuments," but makes no mention of carving gravestones. In 1811, as shown by the large *New Hampshire Gazette* advertisement (bottom), Smith mentions receiving gravestones, but they were possibly carved by Samuel Treat.

SAMUEL HALE, 1807, NORTH CEMETERY. Hale was long a distinguished teacher in Portsmouth, starting at the grammar school in 1748 for a starting salary of £45 and retiring in 1789. It was said by Charles Brewster that he "gave the right bend to the twigs of those days." Hale's stone was likely carved, at least in part, by Samuel Treat and may have been executed under the guidance of John Marble.

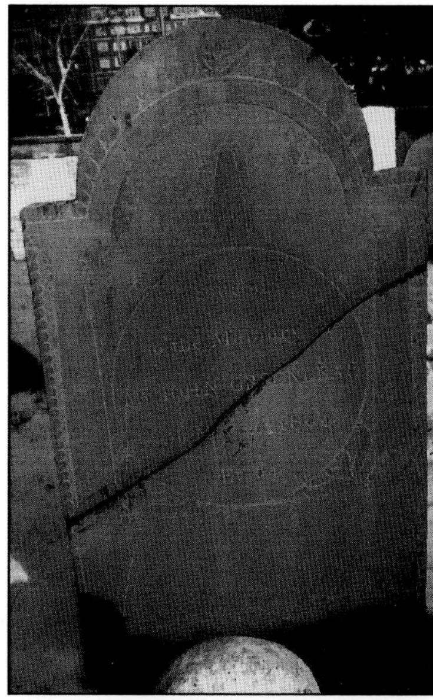

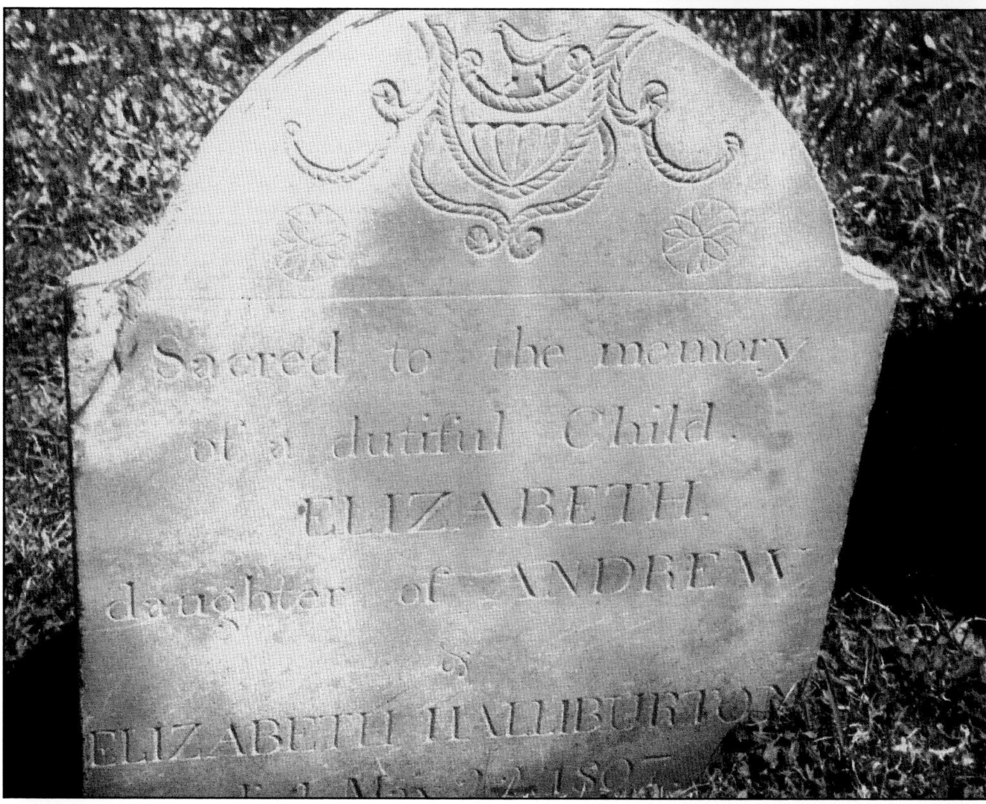

ELIZABETH HALLIBURTON, 1807, NORTH CEMETERY. This back-dated stone for a "dutiful Child" may be one of Samuel Treat's most unusual works. His characteristic lettering includes a rounded lowercase letter "a," the sweeping tail of the lowercase letter "y," and the heavily etched right leg of the capital "A." By examining such distinguishing features, a specific carver's work can be identified, much like a personal signature.

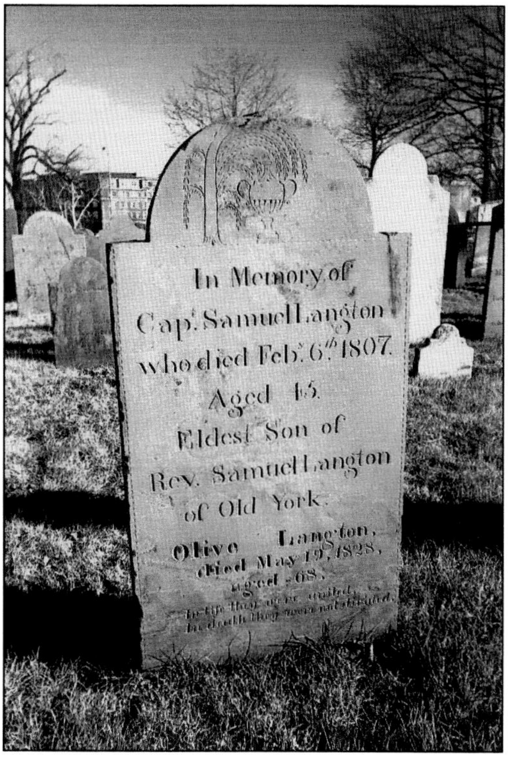

SAMUEL LANGTON, 1807, AND OLIVE LANGTON, 1828, NORTH CEMETERY. On this work by Samuel Treat, the lower portion was added for Olive Langton in 1828, a common practice of his. The Langtons were relatives of treat on his mother's side and were likely the reason he came to the Portsmouth area. Fittingly, the epitaph at the bottom reads, "In life they were united, In death they were not divided."

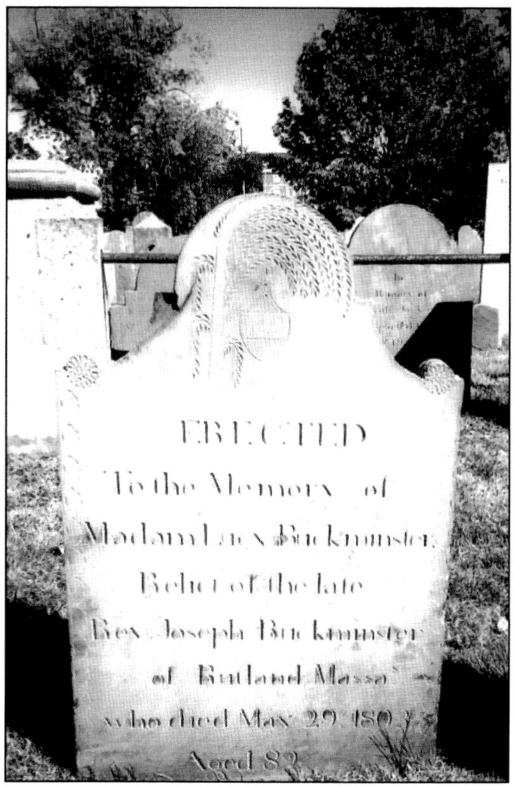

LUCY BUCKMINSTER, 1803, NORTH CEMETERY. This back-dated gravestone was probably carved around 1812 by Samuel Treat and bears his signature characteristics. "Madame Lucy" was formerly the widow of Eliphalet Ladd before she married the popular minister of North Church, Rev. Joseph Buckminster. Presiding over the pulpit in Old North from 1779 until his death in 1812, Buckminster was an ardent patriot and was highly esteemed by his fellow citizens.

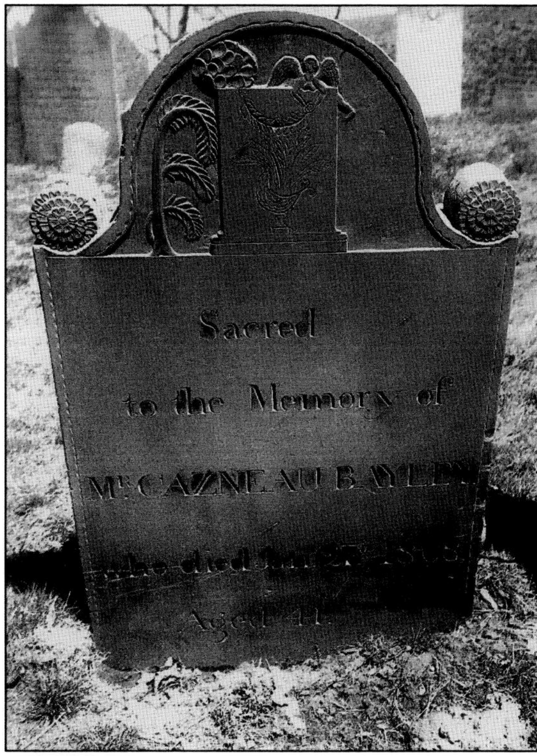

CAZNEAU BAYLEY, 1808, NORTH CEMETERY. Bayley was a well-known merchant and, as is shown by this advertisement (below) in the *Oracle of the Day* in 1793, operated his store at the sign of the spinning wheel on Daniel Street. His unique gravestone (right) was likely carved by young Samuel Treat. While the lettering on this stone is well done and typical of Treat's style throughout his carving career, the motif is unusual and shows a bit of experimentation by an inexperienced carver. Though charming, the small angel is awkward in execution and appearance, as is the willow tree. Equally interesting is the contrast in carving methods displayed by Treat. The bird and floral motif on the tablet at center were lightly etched, while the angel, tree, and floral finials were accomplished in a heavier style.

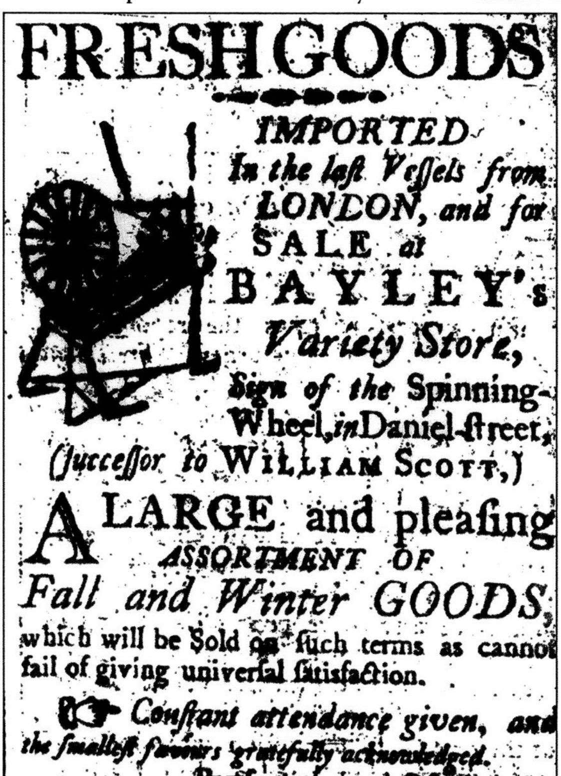

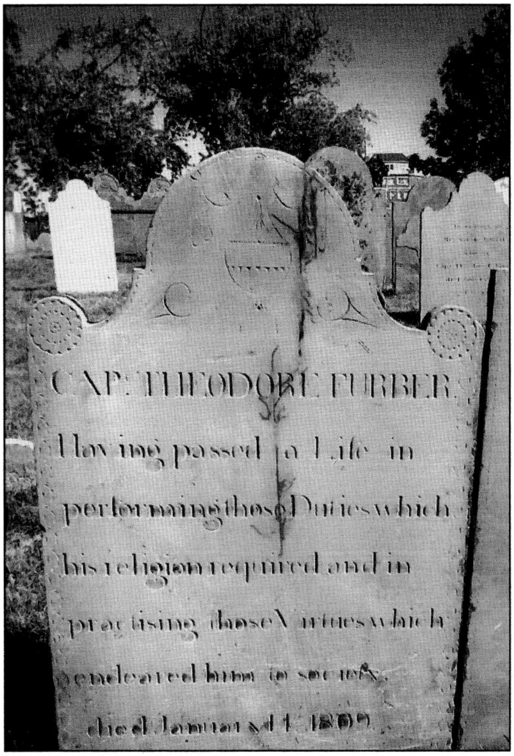

Theodore Furber, 1809, North Cemetery. Captain Furber's stone is important as the earliest documented stone identifying the work of the Treat family. On December 6, 1809, five months and 22 days after the stone was erected, Smith and Treat were paid $17 for the gravestones (Rockingham County Probate records, Roll 19, No. 8057). The lettering is typical of Samuel Treat's style, while the lightly etched heart-and-urn motif is more unusual.

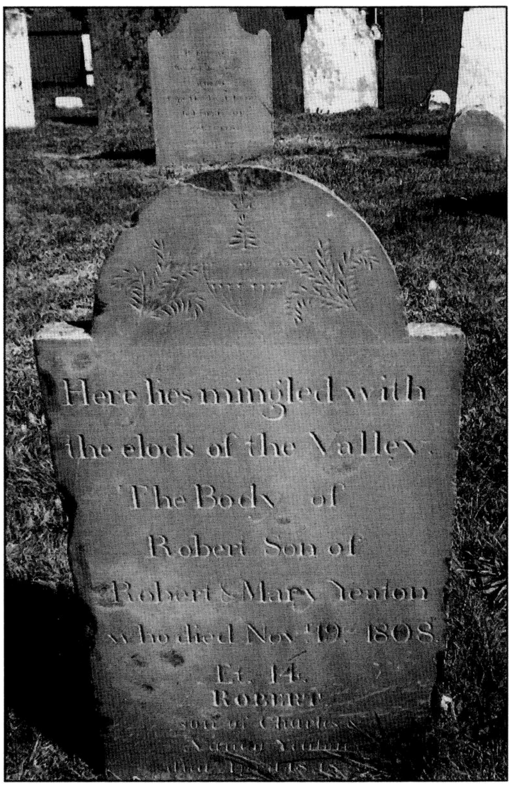

Robert Yeaton, 1808, and Robert Yeaton, 1826, North Cemetery. This stone by Samuel Treat exhibits one of the most unusual, if not intangible, traits found in his work. The eloquent and descriptive epitaph for this young man gives one the sense that Treat knew his clients well and really strove to offer them hope and comfort through his carvings. Interestingly, both Roberts were cousins, separated in death by 16 years but remembered on the same gravestone.

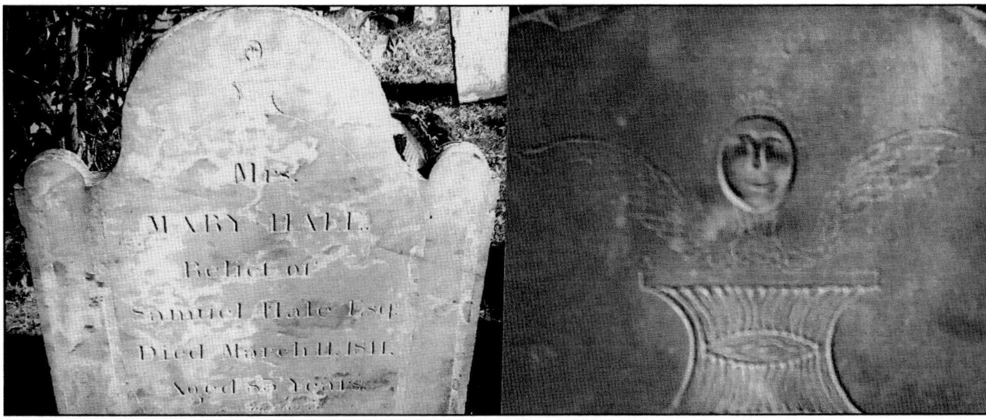

Mary Hale, 1811, North Cemetery. Mary Hale was the "relict," or widow, of schoolteacher Samuel Hale, and her gravestone is most unusual. The lettering of the stone is distinctly that of Samuel Treat, while the angel-face motif (see detail), both odd and appealing, is a one-of-a-kind carving in Portsmouth and may have been executed by Noah Smith.

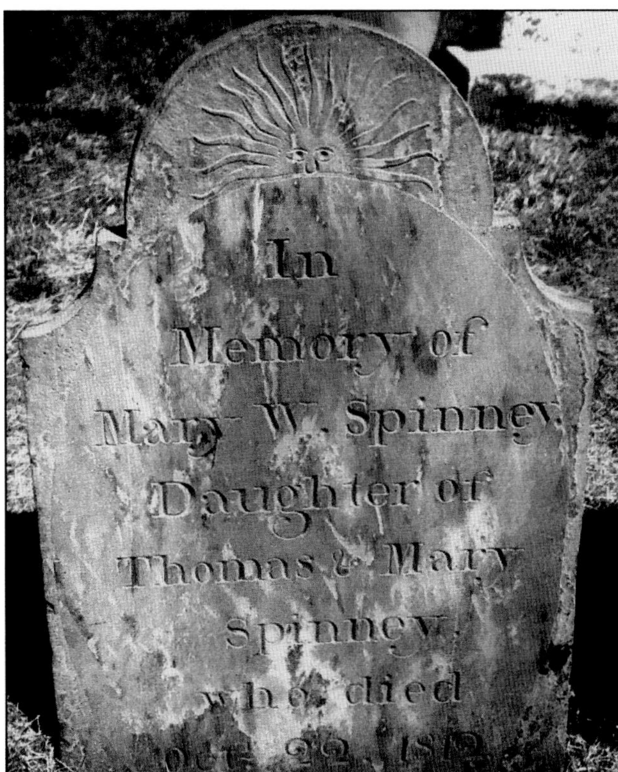

Mary Spinney, 1812, North Cemetery. The sun motif on this attractive gravestone was used several times in Portsmouth by Samuel Treat from 1806 to 1812 (see page 96). The lettering is characteristic, too, of Treat's work, especially his unusually curved number "2," as seen at the bottom of the stone. Young Mary was the daughter of Thomas Spinney, a ship carpenter, and one of four Spinney children to die young.

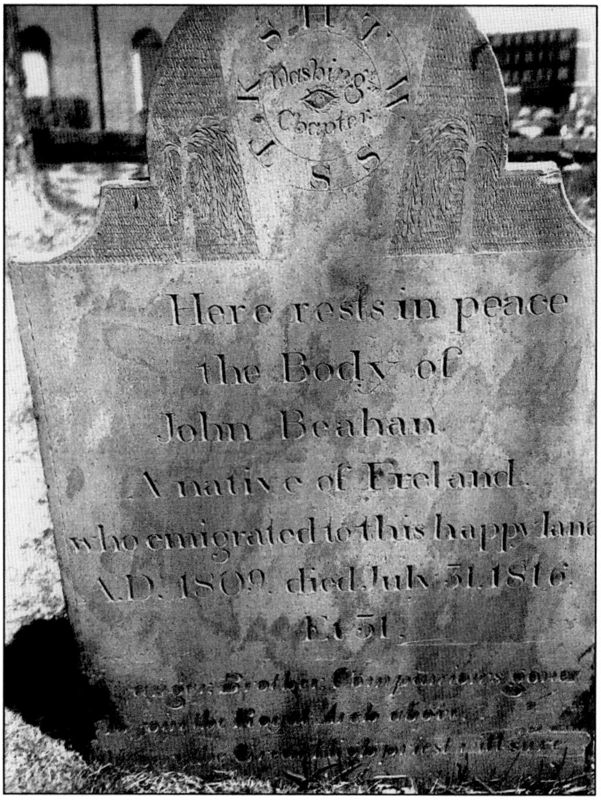

JOHN BEAHAN, 1816, NORTH CEMETERY. Little is known about this Irish native, a hatter who lived seven years in "this happy land." However, the motif on his gravestone, carved by Samuel Treat, shows he was a member of the Washington Chapter of Royal Arch Masons in Portsmouth. The name of Beahan's temple is cleverly included in his epitaph, which reads, "Stranger; Brother; Companions gone. To join the Royal Arch above."

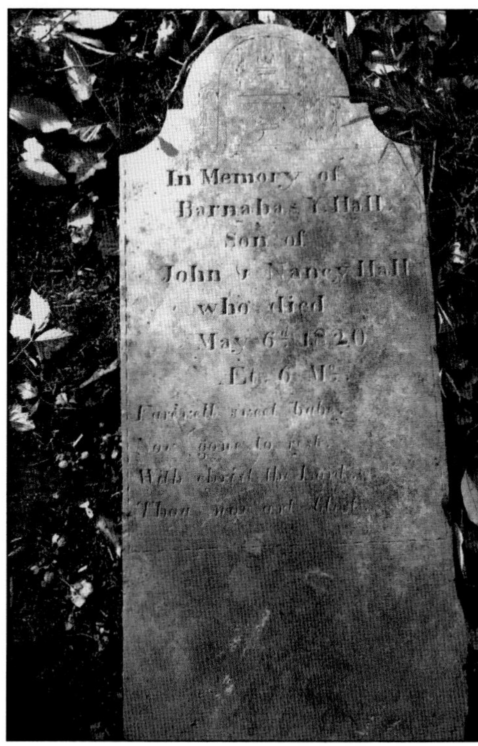

BARNABAS HALL, 1820, HALL CEMETERY. The urn-and-willow motif shown here is typical of the work of Samuel Treat. The epitaph for the infant son of John and Nancy Hall reads, "Farewell sweet babe. Now gone to rest. With Christ the Lord. Thou now art blest." Like many others in this neglected cemetery, Barnabas's stone is in danger of being lost. (Courtesy of Louise Tallman.)

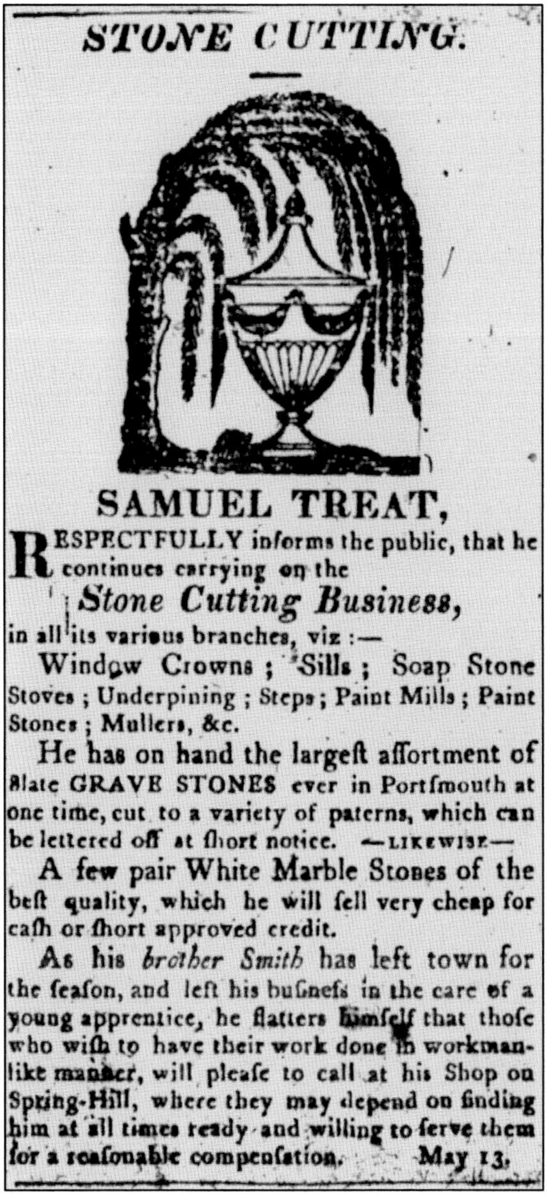

A Samuel Treat Advertisement, 1817. By 1815, less than 10 years after arriving in Portsmouth, Samuel Treat was well entrenched not only as a businessman but as an active community member. In 1811, he married Lydia, the daughter of well-known tailor John Shelden. He was also active during the War of 1812, helping to build the forts in Portsmouth Harbor. This is the earliest known advertisement for his business, which appeared in the *New Hampshire Gazette* on May 13, 1817. Note that in the last paragraph, he wittily refers to his "brother Smith," former partner Noah Smith. During the summer of 1817, Smith went to Washington, D.C., for unknown reasons, leaving his stonecutting business in the hands of a mere apprentice named Moses Warren. No doubt, Treat saw an opportunity to increase his business, counting on his greater experience to gain extra customers. Interestingly, Warren was a cousin to Shubael Treat's wife, Mary Warren, and within a few years owned his own stonecutting shop in Newburyport. (Courtesy of the Portsmouth Public Library.)

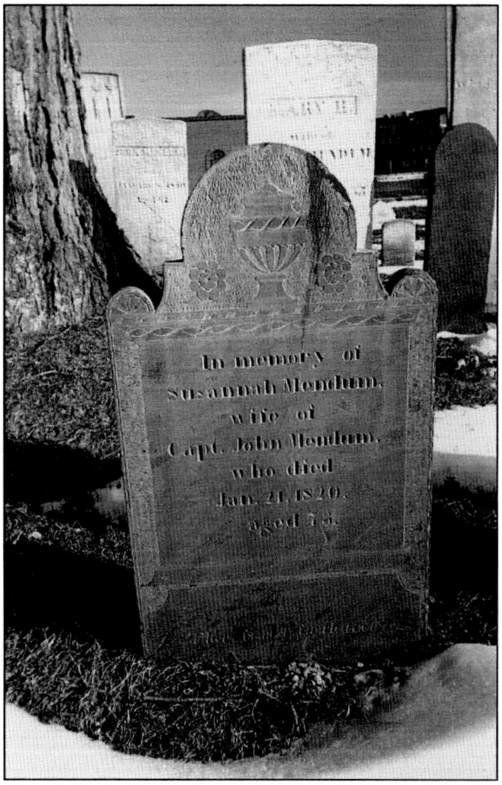

SUSANNAH MENDUM, 1820, NORTH CEMETERY. That Samuel Treat, by 1820, was an experienced carver is evidenced by his many unusual variations of the urn-and-willow motif. The floral devices seen on this stone are repeated in several others of his. Susannah was the wife of a shipmaster who commanded the brig *Catharine* on a voyage to Martinique in 1783, and the ship *Charlotte* to Ireland in 1790.

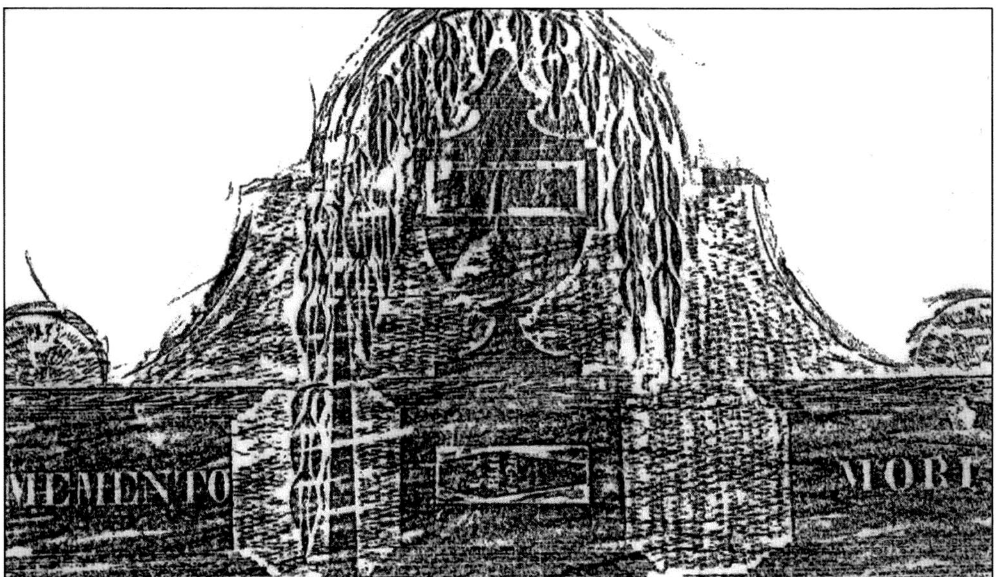

FIDELIA SHELDEN, 1820, NORTH CEMETERY. This rubbing shows the gravestone for Samuel Treat's sister-in-law, who died at age 16. The coffin at center, with her initials and death date, is flanked by the Latin phrase meaning "Remember Death." The design was personal for Treat. Having known Fidelia since 1811, he was clearly moved by her death, as is evidenced by her epitaph, which includes his signature phrase, "Friendship Erected this stone."

SARAH DENNETT, 1825, NORTH CEMETERY. This Treat stone displays his typical lettering style and the corner sunburst pattern he used on occasion. This urn-and-willow motif, however, is less elaborate than his other versions, and the use of black slate stone is atypical. Sarah Dennett is probably a descendant of the Ephraim Dennett who lived nearby on Christian Shore.

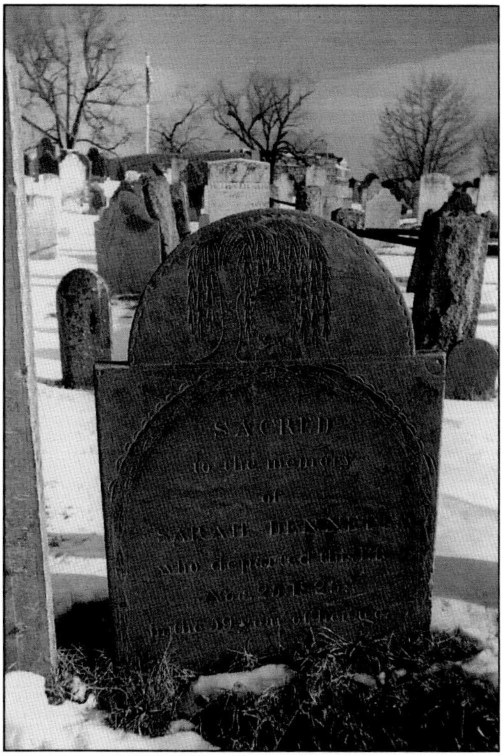

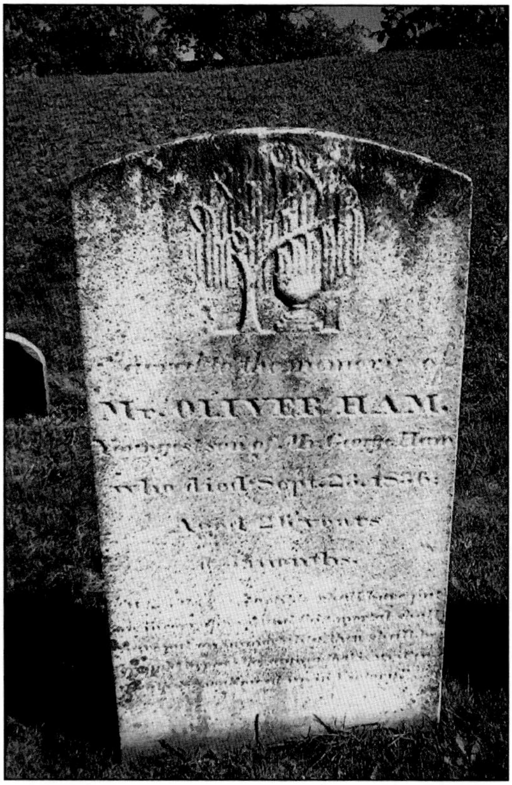

OLIVER HAM, 1836, NORTH CEMETERY. After 1830, it is not always possible to tell who carved a Treat-style gravestone. Samuel Treat married Lydia Shelden in 1811, and their first son, Allen, was born in 1812. Trained by his father, he too became a stone carver. This marble gravestone was likely carved by Allen Treat, as it retains some, but not all, of his father's lettering characteristics.

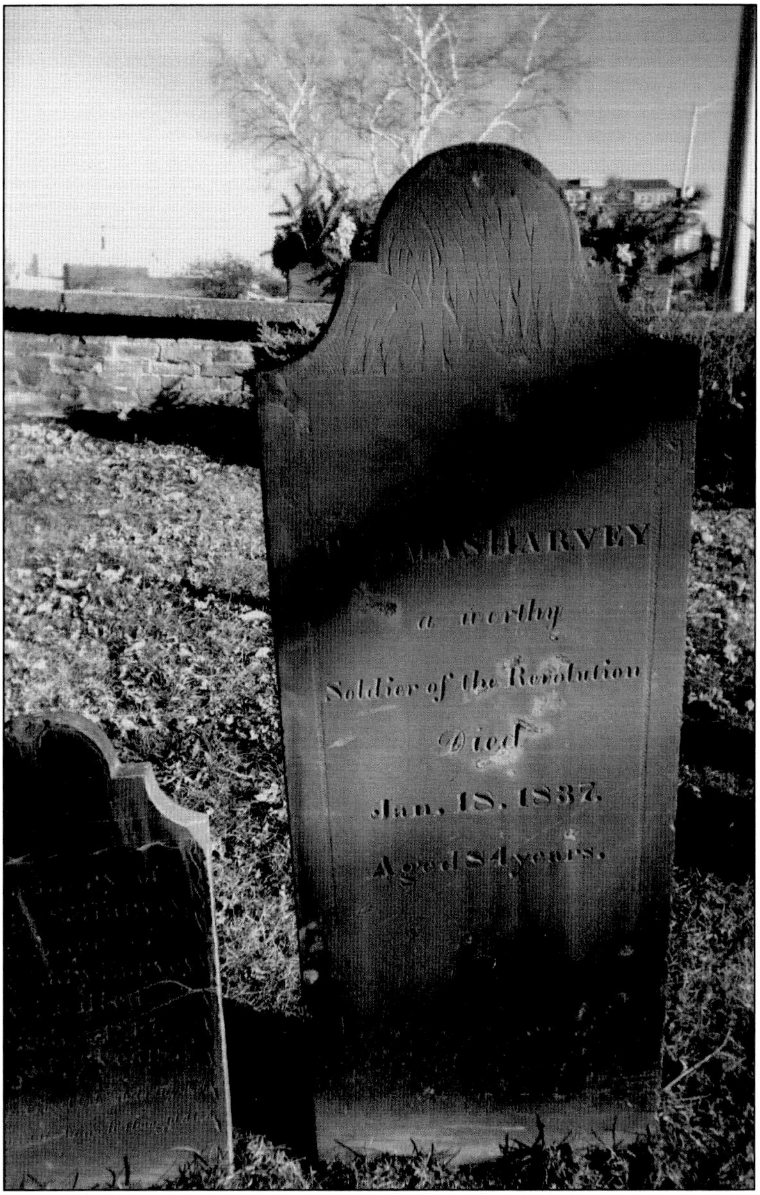

THOMAS HARVEY, 1837, NORTH CEMETERY. The esteem in which Samuel Treat held his fellow townsmen is evident in this stone. Thomas Harvey joined the Continental army from Kittery in early 1777, serving in the 12th Massachusetts Regiment. He took part in the Battle at Brandywine in September 1777 and, during the action, saved a wounded French volunteer who was fighting for the Americans. This man was none other than the Marquis de Lafayette. Washington was so impressed by Lafayette's service that afterward, he gave him his own command. Thus, Harvey's action to save Lafayette indeed made him "a worthy Soldier of the Revolution." Years afterward, Harvey met Lafayette when he visited Portsmouth. In his later years, Harvey lived in Portsmouth and frequently regaled Treat with stories of his war service while visiting his stonecutting shop. He also bemoaned the fact that he would not have a proper gravestone to mark his burial place, but Treat assured him that he would, and held true to his word.

"By art and Industry we thrive and make the most untoward substance yield to our perfection."

SAMUEL TREAT & SON,

STONE CUTTERS,

No. 17 Deer street.

KEEP constantly on hand a handsome assortment of GRAVE STONES, MARBLE and SLATE, which they offer as cheap as can be purchased elsewhere, and warrant them inferior to none

Connecticut FREE STONE, MARBLE and GRANITE cut to any pattern at short notice.

They also intend keeping on hand EDGE STONE ready hammered, 8 inches thick and 1 foot wide; at the

A SAMUEL TREAT & SON ADVERTISEMENT, 1839. By the time this advertisement appeared in a city directory, the Treat family was operating what was still Portsmouth's only resident stonecutting firm. With both father and son working in the trade at their original stone yard on Deer Street, their business was considerable. (Courtesy of the Portsmouth Public Library.)

CITY STONE YARD,

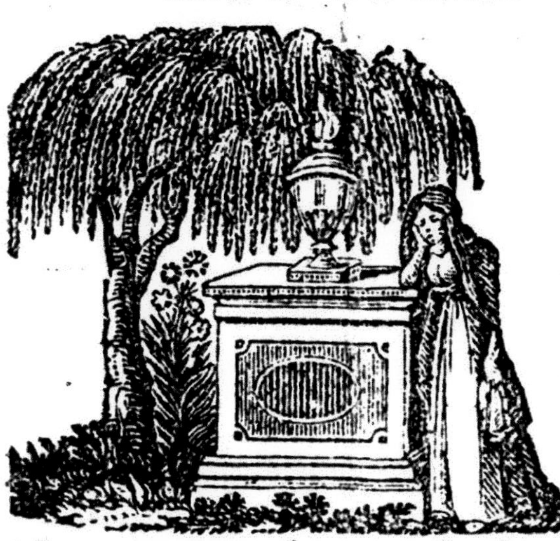

No. 4
GREEN STREET,
PORTSMOUTH,
May be found all kinds
— of —
STONE
WORK
usually kept in the largest cities, and warranted as cheap—such as
MONUMENTS,
GRAVE STONES,
FLAGGS, GRANITE, SLATE,
BROWN
and
SOAP STONES.

A large assortment always on hand, and the oldest Establishment of this kind in the New England States.

ALLEN TREAT.

AN ALLEN TREAT ADVERTISEMENT, 1856. Samuel Treat had pretty much turned over the family business to his son by the 1850s, despite the fact that census records still listed his occupation as that of a mason. Allen Treat moved the business to Green Street around 1850, though it was later moved back to Deer Street. (Courtesy of the Dover Public Library.)

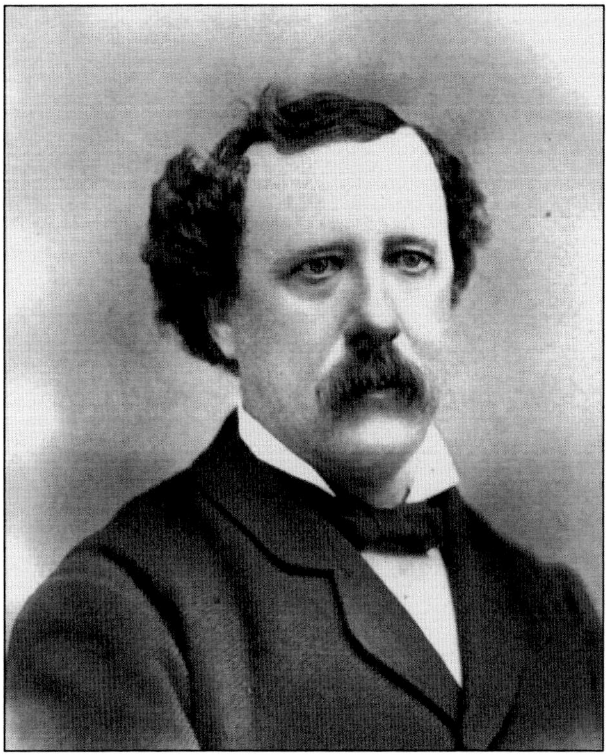

John Shelden Treat, c. 1890. Born in 1837, John was the son of Allen Treat. Educated at Phillips Exeter Academy, he learned stonecutting from his father and, in 1855, moved to Richmond, Virginia. He subsequently moved to Mobile, Alabama, and operated his own marble yard. During the Civil War, he enlisted with the Confederacy, serving in the 2nd Alabama Light Artillery. Soon after war's end, Captain Treat returned to Portsmouth. (From *Geneological and Family History of the State of New Hampshire* [1908], by Ezra Stearn; courtesy of the Portsmouth Public Library.)

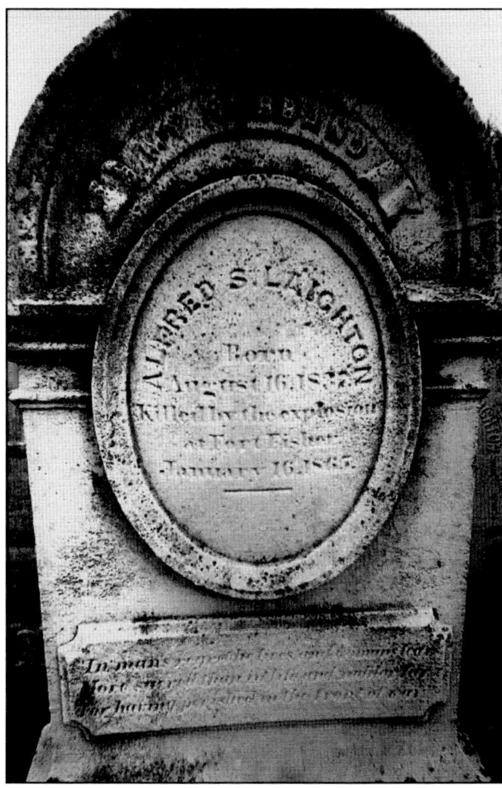

Alfred Laighton, 1865, Harmony Grove Cemetery. Laighton, an acting ensign on the Union warship *Gettysburg*, was born just two days after John Treat. He took part in the storming and capture of Fort Fisher on January 15, behaving "gallantly," but died the next day when the fort's powder magazine was accidentally ignited. Ironically, this stone was carved by Allen Treat, while his own son was serving in the Confederate army.

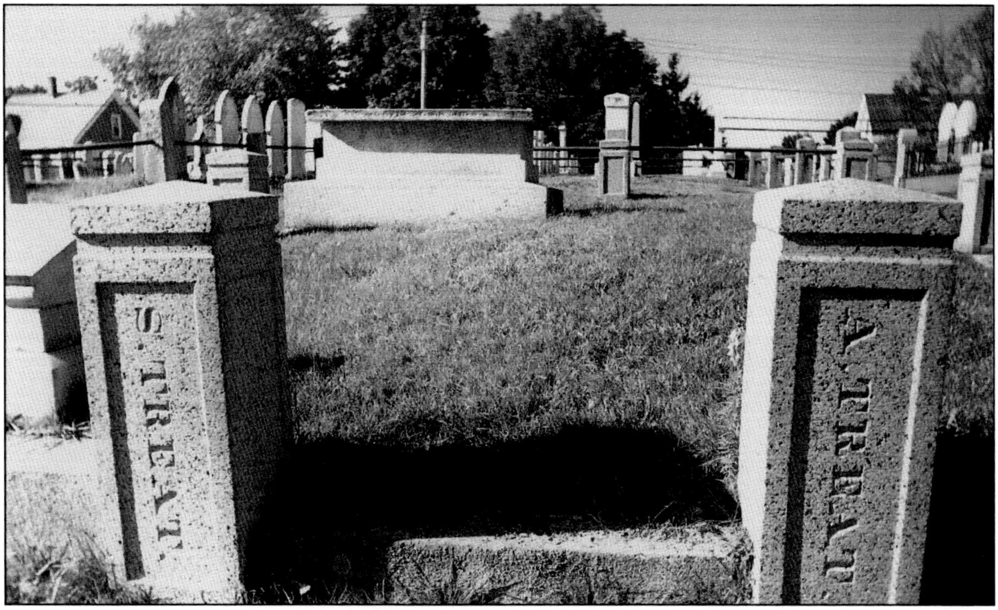

THE TREAT FAMILY PLOT, PROPRIETOR'S CEMETERY, SOUTH STREET. Buried here are several generations of the Treat family, including Samuel (d. 1862) and his son Allen (d. 1875). After the Civil War ended, John Treat returned to Portsmouth and acquired the family stonecutting business. A Treat family member—Allen or John—made the posts for this plot, as evidenced by the capital letter "A," with its deeply carved right leg.

A JOHN TREAT ADVERTISEMENT, 1875. John Treat continued the family business in gravestone carving, noted as the oldest of its kind in New England. For years, he advertised his yard at the "Sign of Old Father Time" and, despite his Confederate service, served as mayor of Portsmouth. His death in 1897 brought an end to the Treat tradition of stonecutting, though their yard was operated into the 20th century by others.

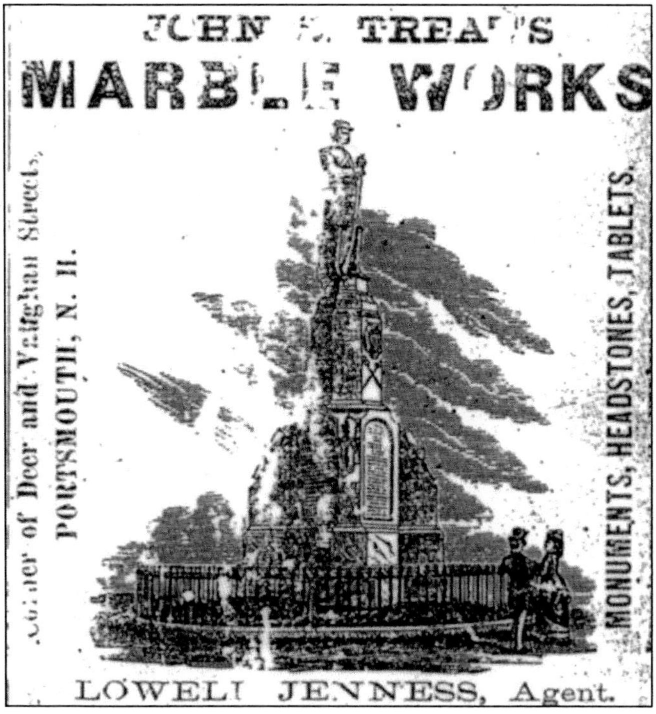

List of Portsmouth Cemeteries

Numbers 1–12 are public cemeteries. The remainder are private family sites. Dates given indicate establishment time or range of burials.

1. Calvary Cemetery, *c.* 1910, Greenland Road
2. Cotton Cemetery, 1671, South Street
3. Elmwood Cemetery, South Street
4. Harmony Grove Cemetery, 1847, South Street
5. North Burial Ground, 1753, Maplewood Avenue
6. Pleasant Street Cemetery, 1754
7. Point of Graves, *c.* 1669, Mechanic Street
8. Proprietor's Cemetery, 1831, South Street
9. Sagamore Cemetery, 1871, South Street
10. St. John's Churchyard, *c.* 1732, Bow Street
11. St. Mary's Cemetery, *c.* 1870, Greenland Road
12. Temple Israel Cemetery, *c.* 1907, Banfield Road
13. Balch Cemetery, 1876–1889, Lafayette Road
14. Beck-Tabor Cemetery, 1820–1882, Grafton Drive
15. Fieldstone Cemetery, Ocean Road
16. Green Street Cemetery, *c.* 1674–1740, South Street (relocated 1875)
17. Hall Cemetery, 1789–1883, South Street
18. Huntress-Shannon Cemetery, 1829–1900, Echo Avenue
19. Lang Cemetery, 1833–1888, Lang Road
20. Langdon Cemetery, 1724–1974, Urban Forestry Center, Elwyn Road
21. Langdon Cemetery, 1834–1978, Lafayette Road
22. Langdon Slave Cemetery, *c.* 1730, Lafayette Road, Christ Church
23. Marden Cemetery, 1760–1843, Lafayette Road
24. Marden Cemetery, 1866–1892, Lafayette Road
25. Marden-Dorr Cemetery, 1855–1944, Wallis Road
26. Marden-Rand Cemetery, 1856, Wallis Road
27. Marston Cemetery, 1825–1839, Cutts Avenue
28. Marston-Rand Cemetery, 1867–1930, Suzanne Drive
29. Moses-Odiorne Cemetery, 1857–1899, Elwyn Road
30. Norton Cemetery, 1835–1898, Lafayette Road
31. Otis Cemetery, 1816–1906, Banfield Road
32. Perkins Cemetery, 1859–1888, Lang Road
33. Sherburne Cemetery, 1724–1980, Islington Street, Portsmouth Plains
34. Whidden Cemetery, 1794–1912, Lafayette Road (West)
35. Whidden Cemetery, 1810–1884, Lafayette Road (East)
36. Joseph White, 1829, single gravestone, Spinney Road